School Law fo
The Essential Guide

With Practical Skills and Practice Tips

John Dayton, J.D., Ed. D.

Wisdom Builders Press ™

www.wisdombuilderspress.com

ISBN: ISBN-13: 978-1717103888
ISBN-10: 171710388X

About the Author

John Dayton, J.D., Ed. D.

John Dayton is a Professor of Education Law and Policy, Adjunct Professor of Higher Education, Editor-in-Chief of the *Education Law & Policy Review*, and the Director of the Education Law Consortium (*see*, www.edlawcon.org), a non-partisan pro bono research group dedicated to advancing knowledge and practice in education law. Professor Dayton is an internationally recognized expert on law and policy. He is a lawyer with experience in public and private legal practice. He has also served as a judicial clerk, and as a public school educator and program director. In recognition of his academic achievements he was offered academic scholarships from many outstanding law schools including the Indiana University-Bloomington School of Law in his home state. Professor Dayton holds both a law degree and a doctoral degree in educational administration and policy from Indiana University. Dr. Dayton has taught law and policy courses for three decades including education law; higher education law; special education law; medical law; and professional ethics. Dr. Dayton is currently a professor at the University of Georgia where he was the first recipient of the Glickman Award for excellence in research and teaching. He is a member of the prestigious University Teaching Academy and serves on the editorial boards of the leading scholarly journals in education law, policy, and finance. Dr. Dayton is the author of over a 100 law review articles, books, and other publications on law and policy. He is an internationally recognized author and speaker on law and policy issues.

Summary of Contents

Table of Contents

Preface

School Law for Everyone is the essential textbook and legal guide for teachers, administrators, parents, students, and everyone working with schools. After decades of teaching law to thousands of students, I can tell you with great certainty that if you want to acquire a powerful working knowledge of school law in practice, this is the book you need. From cover to cover this book is designed to actively engage you in building a strong working knowledge of the law in practice. This book is unique in that it:

- Clearly explains even the most complex principles of law in a concise and understandable manner;
- Connects essential principles of law to current policies and practices;
- Harmonizes complex and contradictory case law into a clear and concise statement of current law;
- Provides helpful flowcharts, visual aids, and summaries; and
- Teaches useful practice skills and practice tips for effectively putting legal knowledge into practice in schools.

Ten chapters cover the essential areas of school law. Each chapter includes a legal overview; essential questions and answers; practice skills; practice tips; essential points, terms, and cases; a closer look at key aspects of the law; questions for further exploration and discussion; and suggested activities for further learning. The focus throughout this book is on helping the reader to master essential principles of school law and their application in practice, along with useful practice skills, in an engaging and succinct format. Specifically, each chapter provides:

A legal overview: Concisely introducing the legal topic in its illuminating historical and social context.

Essential questions & answers: Answering key legal questions of greatest interest and value to readers.

Essential practice skills: Teaching useful practice skills related to each chapter's legal topic including conducting effective meetings; preventing abuse and neglect; respecting church-state boundaries; improving communication and presentation skills; managing administrative searches; conducting investigations and hearings; preventing sexual harassment; developing cultural competence;

building positive school-parent relationships; helping children receive needed services; navigating employment issues; avoiding tort liability; promoting school safety and security; and understanding and applying principles of professional ethics in practice.

Essential practice tips: Common sense suggestions rooted in the law and providing the practical knowledge needed to safely steer away from common but avoidable legal problems.

Essential points: Concise summaries of the most important points of law related to the chapter's legal issues.

Essential terms: A selection of essential terms necessary to understanding the area of law.

Essential cases: Brief summaries of key cases distilled to their essence providing useful guidance to non-lawyers with legal citations to access the complete case opinions online for further learning.

A closer look at the law: A more detailed examination of a selected legal issue to explore the broader implications of the law in practice.

Law and professional ethics in practice: Addressing important legal/ethical issues to help readers to better navigate legal/ethical challenges in practice.

Questions for further exploration: Provides thought provoking questions to stimulate further thought, broader consideration, exploration, and discussion of important legal issues in practice.

Suggested activities for further learning: Activities to encourage readers to continue their learning in the area and to better connect legal learning to daily events in their schools and communities.

In discussing school law cases there is the perspective of the institution (generally the defendant) and the perspective of the person challenging the institution (generally the plaintiff). This book is written for all persons, potential plaintiffs and defendants. But it quickly becomes too laborious reading both perspectives on every potential legal issue. For this reason, the book generally discusses the perspective of the institutional administrator, as a potential defendant. But from this, it is also obvious what the perspective of the plaintiff would be as well, making this book useful for all parties.

In this book every effort was made to present you with an accurate academic presentation of the law. Perfect objectivity is impossible. But this book has no agenda other than to explain the essential principles of school law in practice. It is important to note, however, that no book can give you legal advice. Legal advice can only be obtained from an attorney licensed to practice law in your jurisdiction and familiar with the unique facts in your case. If you need to seek legal counsel, however, having a solid working knowledge of the relevant law will help you to work more effectively, efficiently, and successfully with your attorney.

I hope that you will enjoy your journey through the unique and fascinating realm of the law. By studying the law it is guaranteed that you will gain both knowledge and wisdom. You will understand the world around you much better and you can become a more able participant in the promotion of justice, democracy, and the shaping of a better future for yourself and others in your schools and communities.

Over the years your understanding of this important knowledge and useful skills will continue to grow. This is only the beginning of your journey, and it is a voyage that will change and improve your life and the lives of others around you. I want to give you my very best personal wishes for an enjoyable adventure in learning. It is my great hope that you will find your studies engaging, enlightening, and highly useful in your future.

Very best wishes.

John Dayton

How Much Do You Already Know About School Law?
Test Your Current Legal Knowledge

For all of the following questions please answer True (T) or False (F) according to which of these answers is the *best choice* for each question:

1) ____ The state can legally require that children attend public schools.

2) ____ Schools must prohibit children from praying during school hours because of church-state separation.

3) ____ If your high school has established a "limited open forum" this allows you to exclude student hate groups such as the American Nazi Party, the Ku Klux Klan, and Satanists from meeting after school.

4) ____ Although students cannot be required to recite the Pledge of Allegiance, they must stand for the Pledge.

5) ____ The U.S. Supreme Court has ruled that public schools cannot require that male students cut their hair unless a similar rule is applied to female students.

6) ____ Students cannot be punished by school officials for any offense that occurs off of public school property.

7) ____ Education is a fundamental right under the U.S. Constitution.

8) ____ To avoid potential legal liability, including suits by parents and others, you should only report incidents where you have solid evidence of child abuse.

9) ____ Where de facto racial segregation exists federal courts can order a judicially supervised desegregation plan.

10) ____ As the school principal, if you do not renew the contract of a nontenured teacher, you must be certain that you give the teacher a legally and educationally sound reason for the nonrenewal.

Answers: Test Your Current Legal Knowledge

1) _____ The state can legally require that children attend public schools.

False. While state officials can require school attendance, they cannot limit that attendance to only public schools. As long as parents are in compliance with applicable state laws and standards, parents may instead choose for their children to attend a private school or a home study program. See, *Pierce v. Society of Sisters*, 268 U.S. 510 (1925).

2) _____ Schools may prohibit children from praying during school hours because of church-state separation.

False. Requirements of "church-state" separation created by the First Amendment's Establishment Clause only apply to government agents and institutions. In public schools, students are private citizens, not government agents. Accordingly, it is the Free Exercise clause of the First Amendment that applies to students in schools, and the Free Exercise protects students' rights to, for example, engage in private student initiated prayer, subject only to reasonable time, place, and manner restrictions. Students cannot, for example, pray loudly at a time when this prayer would interfere with instruction, but anytime students can engage in free speech, they may also engage in prayer, prayer protected by both the free speech and free exercise provisions of the First Amendment.

3) _____ If your high school has established a "limited open forum" this allows you to exclude student hate groups such as the American Nazi Party, the Ku Klux Klan, and Satanists from meeting after school.

False. Under the Federal Equal Access Act, 20 U.S.C. § 4071, if a school has established a "limited open forum" by allowing any non-curriculum related groups to meet, the school must then allow all interested groups of students to meet, regardless of the "religious, political, philosophical, or other content of the speech at such meetings." All groups must comply with school rules, applicable laws, and reasonable time, place, and manner restrictions, but otherwise, even "hate" speech becomes protected speech under this Act, if participants otherwise comply with legitimate regulations.

4) _____ Although students cannot be required to recite the Pledge of Allegiance, they must stand for the Pledge.

False. Students cannot be required to either say the pledge or stand. In *West Virginia v. Barnette*, 319 U.S. 624 (1943), the U.S. Supreme Court declared that: "[N]o official, high or petty, can prescribe what shall be orthodox in politics, nationalism, religion, or other matters of opinion or force citizens to confess by word or act their faith therein."

5) _____ The U.S. Supreme Court has ruled that public schools cannot require that male students cut their hair unless a similar rule is applied to female students.

False. The U.S. Supreme Court has not ruled on student dress and grooming issues directly. By default, these issues are governed by varying decisions from U.S. Courts of Appeals and differing state and local policies on student dress and grooming, resulting in notable diversity across the nation in legal standards on student dress and grooming regulation.

6) _____ Students cannot be punished by school officials for any offense that occurs off of public school property.

False. If school officials can establish a "logical nexus" between the off campus misconduct and a sufficient negative impact on discipline in the school, school officials can acquire legitimate jurisdiction over issues that occurred off of school property and outside of school hours, such as a student's cursing at a teacher or principal in a grocery store in retaliation for being disciplined in school.

7) _____ Education is a fundamental right under the U.S. Constitution.

False. In *San Antonio v. Rodriguez*, 411 U.S. 1 (1973), the U.S. Supreme Court held that under the U.S. Constitution fundamental rights are those rights expressly included in the Constitution. Education is not included in the U.S. Constitution and is therefore not a fundamental right under the U.S. Constitution. Many state courts have, however, found that education is a fundamental right under the education provisions of their state constitution.

8) ____ To avoid potential legal liability, including suits by parents and others, you should only report incidents where you have solid evidence of child abuse.

False. All 50 states have statutes requiring child care professionals, including public school educators, to report all *suspected* child abuse. These statutes intentionally cast an over broad net, seeking too many reports rather than two few. These statutes also provide immunity from prosecution for all good faith reports, whether than are ultimately proven or not.

9) ____ Where de facto racial segregation exists federal courts can order a judicially supervised desegregation plan.

False. Courts only have jurisdiction over *de jure* (caused by government actions) not *de facto* (caused by private choices) segregation.

10) ____ As the school principal, if you do not renew the contract of a nontenured teacher, you must be certain that you give the teacher a legally and educationally sound reason for the nonrenewal.

False. Due process of law is triggered when government officials make statements that negatively impact an individual's good name, reputation, honor, or integrity. School administrators are commonly advised not to provide any reason for nonrenewals to avoid negative statements that could result in unnecessary, burdensome, and expensive due process proceedings.

Chapter 1: Introduction to Law and Governance

Before beginning the study of any area of law, including school law, it is essential to first understand the foundational framework on which that law functions. An understanding of the framework of U.S. law and governance will prove invaluable to your understanding of school law and its application in practice.

Much of the success of the United States is due to its early commitment to the rule of law and the establishment of a constitutional system of democratic governance. Rooted in the principles of the U.S. Declaration of Independence, the Constitution, and the Bill of Rights, our laws and system of governance are intended to support individual liberty and democracy.

Liberty and democracy are not guaranteed. The lessons of liberty and democracy must be learned and practiced. Liberty and democracy can be lost in a single generation if we do need teach their essential lessons to the next generation of citizens.

Schools are the essential nurseries of our democracy, preparing children for future citizenship. For this reason all persons associated with schools should know and understand our system of laws, governance, democracy, and the liberties they protect, so they may actively teach, practice, and advance liberty and democracy.

Ultimately, a constitutional democracy can be no better than the people themselves. But when properly implemented constitutional democracy can give the people an opportunity to take control and responsibility for their own government; to strive to "form a more perfect union"; to "secure the blessings of liberty"; and to work toward greater justice, social progress, and a better future for themselves and their communities.

The primary mechanisms for achieving these goals are an educated and informed citizenry; fair and regular elections; separation of powers; the rule of law; and other constitutional checks and balances. When you learn about our system of laws and governance, and its democratic purposes, you become a stronger citizen and we become a stronger nation and democracy. This chapter explains essential principles of law and governance.

Federal Powers, Limits, and Sources of Federal Law

The federal government is by design a government of limited powers. Under the Tenth Amendment to the U.S. Constitution the federal government may exercise only those powers expressly delegated to the federal government in the text of the U.S. Constitution. The Tenth Amendment declares:

The powers not delegated to the United States by the Constitution, nor prohibited by it to the States, are reserved to the States respectively, or to the people.

All powers not expressly delegated to the federal government remain with the states (with their own internal systems of separation of powers and other checks and balances), or ultimately to the people.

Division of Powers under the U.S. System of Law and Governance

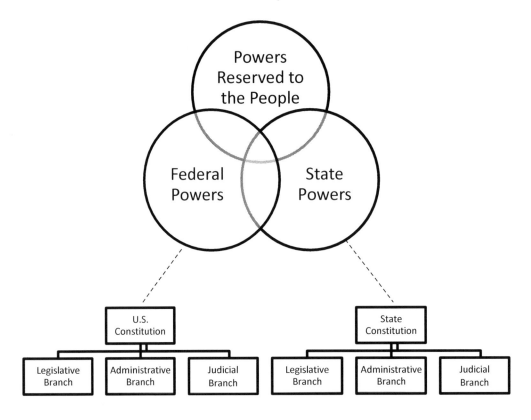

© **Dayton**

Rather than relying on government officials to independently respect the limits of their powers, the constitutional system relies on each branch of government to jealously guard its own powers from intrusion, and relies on the people to stand up against government intrusions on their rights. State governments can contest federal expansions of power beyond constitutional limits; the federal government can object to any intrusions on federal powers or any state intrusions on the rights of federal citizenship; and citizens can use free speech and the ballot box to protect their rights and help assure that no one is able to accumulate so much unchecked power that they become above the law and unaccountable to the people.

The federal government only has those powers delegated to it through the Constitution. Education is not mentioned in the U.S. Constitution, therefore it is a power reserved to the states and the people. Although public education is a state function, through civil rights legislation under the Fourteenth Amendment (e.g., Title VI, Title VII, Title IX, etc.), federal conditional funding grants (e.g., IDEA, ESEA, etc.), and federal court decisions (e.g., *Brown v. Board*; *Goss v. Lopez*, etc.), in practice the federal government exerts significant control over the daily operations of public schools. Accordingly, those responsible for the daily operation of public schools must know and understand applicable federal laws, as should all persons associate with schools.

In the federal legal system Congress passes statutes governing education at the federal level. The U.S. Department of Education issues federal regulations guiding the administration and oversight of federal statutes in educational institutions. And federal courts interpret federal laws and rule on disputes under federal laws and the U.S. Constitution.

Sources of Federal Laws

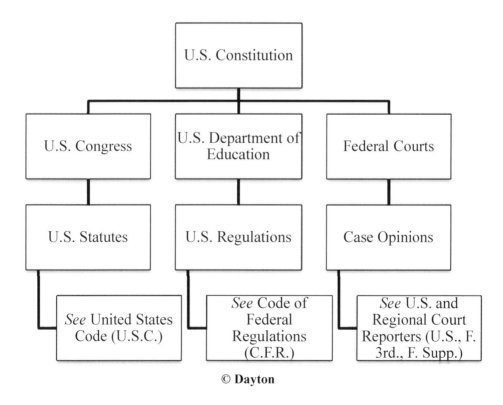

© **Dayton**

3

State Powers, Limitations, and Sources of State Law

Although the U.S. Constitution imposes some limits on state powers under the Fourteenth Amendment, states still exercise broad powers in those areas outside of the scope of the U.S. Constitution and legitimately within the realm of state authority. Education is a power generally reserved to the states through public systems of education, or to the people themselves through private schools and home study programs. There are variations among the 50 U.S. states, but generally concerning public education plenary authority is vested in the state legislative branch, the general assembly.

The constitutions of all 50 states make it the responsibility of the state's general assembly to create and support a public system of education. The general assembly has broad authority over education in the state, subject only to the limits of the U.S. Constitution, the state constitution, and the expressed will of the people through their free speech and periodic elections. The state general assembly enacts appropriate legislation necessary to create a system of public schools, including, for example, statutes governing school finance; attendance; curriculum; student discipline; and teacher employment, tenure, and dismissals.

The administrative branch of state government, including the governor, the state board of education, the state superintendent, and the state department of education establish administrative policies and regulations for the state-level administration of the general assembly's education statutes. Because education is the largest single item in most state's budgets and the administration of a state-wide system of public education is an enormous, complex, and politically sensitive undertaking, governors and state departments of education are generally actively involved in the administration of public schools at the state level.

The state judicial branch rules on disputes under state laws and the state constitution. While federal courts are courts of limited jurisdiction (hearing only federal issues) state courts are courts of general jurisdiction and may rule on state or federal issues. State courts have been called on in many states to interpret the state's education clauses in the state constitution and to define the scope of educational rights students are entitled to under the state constitution. State courts are the ultimate authority on state law questions.

Public schools are locally governed by a local school board. While important in function, these local boards have no independent sovereign authority. Under the U.S. system of governance there are two dual sovereigns: The federal and state governments, each with their own constitution and independent areas of authority. Local governments and school boards, while critical to the daily operations of local institutions, exist under the supervision and authority of the state government.

Sources of State Laws

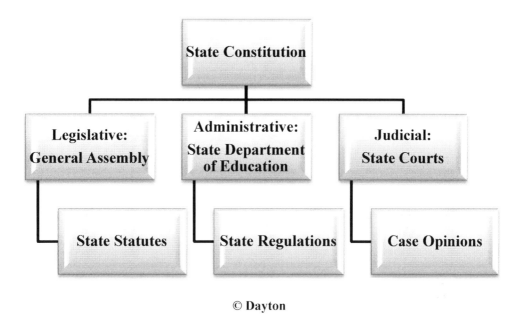

© Dayton

Local School Boards

Local school boards are responsible for local compliance with federal and state education laws. Having local schools governed by community members allows for a stronger community voice in local school decisions to accommodate unique community needs and preferences in local school operations. Generally, school board members are elected by local voters and are politically accountable to community members. In a few states and cities, however, school board members are appointed by elected officials, making them less directly accountable to the public, but still accountable through public pressure on the elected officials who appointed them.

The primary functions of the local school board are district level oversight of resources and personnel, and local policy enactment and implementation. The school board is granted broad powers to achieve these important missions and courts generally grant broad judicial deference to local school boards in making discretionary decisions about local matters.

It should be noted, however, that there are clear limits to these powers and limits to judicial deference. School board members must comply with all applicable federal and state laws. And school board members must respect the functional limits of their official roles. School board members are not school administrators or teachers. The school board hires professional administrators and teachers for the daily operation of local schools and to deliver the board approved instructional program. But while allowing administrators and other employees to do their jobs, school board members must not become overly deferential to any employee, e.g., a superintendent, board attorney, or anyone else in exercising the board's proper oversight or making appropriate policy decisions for the school district.

In the performance of official duties the local school board exercises powers from all three branches of government: Quasi-legislative authority in enacting local policies; quasi-administrative authority in school district oversight and legal compliance, and quasi-judicial authority in hearings and rulings on disciplinary actions involving school employees and students. The specific powers and duties of school boards are further defined in state constitutions, statutes, and regulations.

The school board has the authority to enter into legally binding contracts for all services and goods necessary for the effective and efficient operation of local schools. Local school boards review and approve matters including local school tax rates, annual budgets, contracts, hiring and firing, and district policies on facilities, curriculum, extracurricular programs, personnel policies, student discipline policies, etc.

School board members must understand their roles and properly exercise their legal authority. School board members have no individual legal authority and may only exercise legitimate legal authority by acting collectively as the school board. All actions taken by the board must be in full compliance with federal and state constitutions and laws, and must be in the best interests of the students and community. School board members are also generally bound by state level ethical mandates and the entire district is generally subject to review and evaluation by external accrediting agencies.

Local governance of education is highly valued in most states. Nonetheless, the state retains plenary authority over public education. Local school board members and all school employees are state officials ultimately governed by and accountable to the state. Further, all local public school property and funds ultimately belong to the state. Official school board business is conducted in meetings subject to state open meetings laws, open records laws, and other applicable state laws.

Essential Questions & Answers

Do state public school employees have to comply with the U.S. Constitution?

Yes. Art. VI of the U.S. Constitution requires all public agents, including public school board members, administrators, and teachers to swear (or affirm) they will respect the Constitution. Violations of the Constitution may result in dismissal from public office and financial liability for violations of individual rights and related damages caused by these violations.

What does the U.S. Constitution require from public school employees?

All public school employees, from the superintendent to the newest teacher, must respect all persons' constitutional rights including rights of religious freedom, free speech, freedom of assembly, privacy, due process of law, and equal protection of the laws.

Do students, parents, and community members have to comply with the U.S. Constitution?

No. The Constitution only limits the actions of government agents and does not apply to or set any limits on private citizens. But citizens employed by the government must comply with the Constitution while acting in their official capacities and exercising government powers. As a private citizen, for example, a public school teacher could be an active minister on Sunday, but on Monday as a public employee the Constitution requires religious neutrality and prohibits religious proselytizing while on duty.

If public school employees and other state employees must comply with the U.S. Constitution, why do we need state constitutions?

State constitutions address issues not addressed in the federal constitution, including education. The state constitution establishes a state system of public schools and general standards and rights to education under state law. Further, on issues addressed by the federal constitution, such as freedom of speech, religion, etc., state constitutions may protect these rights at higher levels. States may not, however, protect these rights at lower levels than they are protected under federal law. The U.S. Constitution establishes a floor of protections for rights of federal citizenship that must be respected by all government agents and agencies, federal, state, and local, but state constitutions may add additional rights and protections.

Are private schools bound by federal or state education laws?

Concerning federal education laws, generally, no. Non-government schools (private schools; home schools; etc.), are not bound by the U.S. Constitution. The U.S. Constitution only limits government agents and agencies. Further, unless private schools take federal funding and conditional funding grants from the U.S. Department of Education, they are not bound by most other federal education mandates. State governments, however, may reasonably regulate private schools, and to a lesser degree, home schools. The extent to which the state regulates private and home schools is at the discretion of the state general assembly. Generally, however, state regulation has been minimal, leaving private schools and home schools great latitude to act independently. But states do commonly set minimum standards for attendance, curriculum, etc. State standards for private and home schools can be found online at your state department of education (DOE) website.

How can I get information about public school policies and practices?

First check online resources. You can find state DOE regulations and resources on your state DOE website. Various issue specific advocacy organizations (e.g., special education; home school; civil liberties; etc.) provide helpful information on their websites. Local school policies should be available to the public online. Or you may want to simply ask teachers, administrators, or board members to help you find the information. But always ask to see a copy of the policy. Don't rely on the school official's interpretation only, as the interpretation could be inaccurate or self-serving. In the event information is available but not voluntarily provided you can generally file an open records request for the information at little or no cost.

What can I do if I object to a local school policy or practice?

If you believe you have a legitimate complaint concerning a local school policy or practice, exercise your constitutional rights of free speech and petitioning of government for a redress of grievances. Local school policies likely provide a process for filing complaints. Unless doing so is clearly futile you will want to follow the established process. In general start local and less formal in attempting to resolve an issue efficiently. But if necessary write formal complaints up the chain of authority to state and federal officials if local officials are unresponsive to legitimate complaints.

Essential Practice Skills

To operate effectively and efficiently, group leaders must be prepared to conduct effective and efficient meetings, whether these are meetings of the school board; teacher, parent or student groups; or other meetings. Common sense rules of procedure are necessary to maintain order and to assure a full and fair discussion of issues. *Robert's Rules of Order* may be useful in managing organizational business and debates, especially in larger meetings. But democratic organizations may adopt any procedural rules deemed best by the majority. In establishing procedural rules, generally, procedural simplicity is superior to procedural complexity. Procedural rules should facilitate and not complicate meetings.

The meeting Chair should not allow procedural rules to be used as strategic weapons to silence substantive debate on the merits of an issue, or to impede organizational business. There is no organizational benefit to allowing members with disproportionate expertise in the rules of procedure to strategically stifle good faith debate by other members with less procedural expertise, or to manipulate procedural rules to block organizational progress. The purposes of procedural rules are to maintain order; assure full and fair debate on important questions; and to facilitate the efficient conduct of business. Procedural rules should be adopted, interpreted, and applied with these purposes in mind.

Different types of meetings require different leadership styles by the Chair. Larger formal meetings require more formal procedural rules and styles of leadership, while less formal procedures and leadership styles work better in smaller and less formal meetings. A large formal public meeting of the school board, for example, with hundreds of participants, could quickly devolve into chaos without a consistent adherence to appropriate procedural rules, while an overly rigid adherence to *Robert's Rules* in a small informal meeting will seem absurd and likely only get in the way of completing the necessary business.

In chairing meetings, follow a leadership style that is appropriate for the context and consistent with the institutional culture and purposes. All but the most informal meetings, however, generally follow this basic format:

1) Call to Order
2) Approval of the Minutes
3) Committee Reports
4) Unfinished Business
5) New Business
6) Adjournment

Preparing a guiding script in advance of the meeting can be very useful, especially for less experienced meeting Chairs.

Example script for chairing a formal business meeting:

> "The [DATE] meeting of the [ORGANIZATION] is now called to order."
>
> "We will begin business with the approval of the minutes. Are there any necessary corrections or amendments to the minutes?" [PAUSE TO ADDRESS ANY CORRECTIONS]. "If there are no (additional) corrections the minutes are approved."
>
> "We will now hear any committee reports. The Chair recognizes [NAME OF COMMITTEE CHAIR] reporting on behalf of the [NAME OF COMMITTEE]" (and when the speaker's time has expired announce: "Thank you [NAME OF SPEAKER]").
>
> ADDRESS ANY MOTIONS/DEBATES/CALL QUESTION/ VOTE/REPORT RESULT
>
> "We will now address any unfinished business. The Chair recognizes [NAME OF MEMBER WISHING TO SPEAK] concerning [ISSUE OF BUSINESS].
>
> ADDRESS ANY MOTIONS/DEBATES/CALL QUESTION/ VOTE/REPORT RESULT
>
> "We will now address any new business. The Chair recognizes [NAME OF MEMBER WISHING TO SPEAK].
>
> ADDRESS ANY MOTIONS/DEBATES/CALL QUESTION/ VOTE/REPORT RESULT
>
> "The Chair finding that there is no further business for this meeting, this meeting is adjourned."
>
> > *Addressing motions*: To be recognized a member rises and addresses the Chair. "The Chair recognizes [NAME]." The member states the motion. Another member seconds the motion (or the motion fails for lack of a second). "It is moved

and seconded that [STATE MOTION]. Shall we call the question?"

Managing debates: After the Chair states the motion any member may stand and be recognized by the Chair for purposes of debating the motion. The Chair only recognizes one speaker at a time for the time allowed by the Chair. Interruptions of speakers are ruled out of order by the Chair. The Chair assures that there is a fair opportunity for a full and fair debate by members, and that the debate is focused on issues relevant to the motion. No member should be recognized to speak for a second time until all members wishing to speak have been recognized once. The Chair is responsible for efficiently moving through the agenda while maintaining order and civility. Any *ad hominem* attacks, irrelevant issues, unrecognized speakers, etc., are ruled out of order by the Chair.

Calling the question: If there is no debate, or after sufficient time for debate has been allowed, the Chair calls the question: "The question is on the adoption of the motion to [STATE MOTION]."

Voting and reporting the result: A quorum must be present (as defined in organizational bylaws) to cast legally binding votes. "Those in favor of the motion shall signify by [saying "aye" [PAUSE FOR COUNT] those opposed say "no" [COUNT] [OR CHAIR RULES ON VOICE VOTE; e.g., "In the opinion of the Chair the "ayes" have it"]; *or* raising the right hand; [PAUSE FOR COUNT] those opposed [COUNT]; *or* voting by roll call, ballot, etc. [FINAL COUNT IS CERTIFIED BY A NEUTRAL PARTY]. "The motion is adopted/has failed."

General guidelines for managing effective meetings

1) *Promote a local culture that values and supports highly capable and responsible local governance*: The quality of the meeting and the quality of the decisions and actions resulting from the meeting are always a function of the quality of the participants. Be proactive in recruiting the best people for governing boards. Of course, all highly capable, responsible, and productive people are busy, and it is human nature that busy people tend to avoid

additional responsibilities. But these are commonly the persons you most need for your local governing boards. Also, as Plato warned: Those who most seek power are those who can least be trusted with it. Because local governance plays such a vital role in educational institutions and the welfare of the local community, work to promote a local culture in which local governance is highly valued, and highly capable and responsible participation is encouraged and supported. Understand that incompetent or self-interested board members gone rogue can do enormous damage to the schools and the community. Therefore it is essential to encourage the most capable and responsible persons to serve on governing boards, and not just default to the status quo; those with little else to do; a personal axe to grind; the desire to exercise petty authority; etc. In the absence of the best local persons serving on the governing board, you open the door to the worst persons, and personnel related governance problems are far easier to prevent than to fix. Good local governance is a necessary prerequisite to good local schools. The local school board oversees the local school system and has a strong voice in critically important decisions concerning school mission, policy, personnel oversight, and student discipline. These decisions affect the educations, careers, lives, and future of the entire community. Capable and responsible board members and school leaders carefully consider the likely consequences of their decisions, both intended and unintended, and act wisely to advance the common good. You want only the most capable and responsible governing board members, so be proactive in recruiting the best persons, because no matter how well you run your meetings, bad people make bad decisions, and bad decisions result in bad consequences for the schools and community.

2) *Respect everyone's time with fewer and more efficient meetings*: Meetings consume time and energy. If a meeting isn't necessary, don't meet, or find a more efficient alternative. Formal school board meetings must comply with state meetings laws which may somewhat limit creativity and flexibility. But for faculty meetings and other less formal meetings always seek the most efficient means of completing the necessary tasks. Communicate information though memos instead of meetings; meet with individuals or small groups when the full group isn't needed; excuse persons from parts of meetings that are unnecessary for them; have informal, brief, stand up meetings when formal sit down meetings are not required; etc. Regrettably, education institutions have a long and wasteful tradition of scheduling regular, long, faculty meetings whether they are necessary or not. If you must schedule meetings far in advance in order to get them on everyone's calendar, cancel any unnecessary meetings to free up time and energy for more pressing needs. Always start meetings on time and end on time or

sooner (as soon as all necessary business is completed), building a reputation for running effective, efficient meetings that respect participants' time. If you commonly start meetings late, people are likely to begin showing up even later, further delaying the start of the meeting and making those who arrived on time wait even longer for the start of the meeting and less likely to arrive on time in the future.

3) *Thoughtfully plan and execute the agenda*: Well planned and executed agendas are the keys to effective, efficient meetings. Plan the agenda to maximize the use of participants' time and efforts. Make meeting agendas concise and clearly focused on outcome-based objectives. Remember that the way the agenda item is phrased influences participants responses to the agenda, so phrase action items to stimulate active involvement and effective outcome-based actions (e.g., instead of "Vote on ad" try "Identify strategies for the most effective implementation of our marketing plan"). Phrase discussion items to stimulate productive brain-storming and problem solving (e.g., instead of "Review of student data" try "How can we maximize student learning and outcomes using student data?"). Keep to the agenda. Persistently refocus the discussion on agenda items. As soon as the agenda has been satisfactorily completed, adjourn the meeting. Meetings scheduled for two hours do not have to last for two hours, and the realistic possibility of completing necessary work and early adjournment encourages cooperation and more efficient use of time by meeting participants.

4) *Understand that the physical environment shapes behavior*: Given available facilities and resources, what can you do to create the most welcoming, professional, and functional environment for the meeting? With the purposes of the meeting in mind, set up the room in advance to facilitate and support meeting participants in efficiently achieving those purposes. Have necessary media materials loaded, tested, and ready to go. If supplies or break-out areas are needed have these ready in advance. Take advantage of strategic seating and furniture placements to improve communications or prevent potential social interaction problems (e.g., mix up seating options to avoid persistent groupings that reinforce factions; if someone persistently opposes you as Chair in meetings, provide no chair opposite you at the table, thereby eliminating the symbolic position of opposition and requiring that person to be seated among the other participants; if some participants tend to sit at the back and be unengaged, remove all seats from the back so they will join the group; etc.).

5) *Assure that everyone has a fair opportunity to contribute*: Meetings are for group interaction. Allowing anyone to dominate the meeting will defeat that

purpose. Make sure everyone who wants to speak has a reasonable opportunity. But discourage or cut short unnecessary monologues and lectures. When you must cut someone short, do so as kindly and respectfully as possible. Be careful not to engage in viewpoint bias as the Chair. Everyone understands that the person serving as the Chair also has perspectives and opinions on important issues. But participants will respect a meeting Chair who assures that all persons and all viewpoints are treated fairly and without bias in the meeting.

6) *Keep the meeting focused, efficient, civil, and productive*: It is the responsibility of the Chair to keep meetings focused, efficient, civil, and productive. If anyone introduces a distraction, politely but firmly refocus the meeting on agenda items. Be sure that all meeting time is being used as efficiently as possible. Discussions and votes may require the participation of the larger group, but delegate more time-consuming and complex tasks to smaller committees or individuals who can report back to the full group as necessary. Never allow uncivil or disrespectfully treatment of anyone in the meeting. Professionally but firmly refocus the meeting on the legitimate purposes. When meetings are focused and efficient there is less room for incivility and productive outcomes are more likely.

7) *Maintain control of the meeting*: Be prepared to respectfully but firmly set reasonable limits on anyone who is disruptive, obstructionist, or otherwise out of order during the meeting. As the meeting Chair, always remain professional and take the moral high road, even when others do not. It is up to the meeting Chair to set and maintain the professional tone of the meeting and to assure that all meetings are respectful and productive events.

8) *End the meeting with a review of important decisions and a clear plan for necessary action*: Before the meeting is adjourned clearly restate in summary what was decided. This helps to promote goal oriented meetings and solidify group consensus. End the meeting with a concise statement of the plan for necessary next actions, and clearly assign responsibility for all necessary tasks to appropriate individuals or committees. Follow up with a written summary including names, tasks, and deadlines. Send a polite reminder prior to deadlines. Be certain the action plan is accurately recorded in the minutes. Provide regular status reports to members to encourage and recognize progress. Send out minutes of the meeting for review prior to the next meeting.

Essential Practice Tips

Read your school policies: Your local school has publically available operating policies governing the daily operations of the school including policies on curriculum, extra-curricular activities, attendance, discipline, personnel management, complaints, hearings, etc. The best place to start in understanding the operations of your local school is to review your school policies. You can find answers to many of your questions directly in school policies. School employees must know and follow their own policies. There is no legitimate excuse for not knowing and following your own policies.

Learn about state Open Meetings and Open Records laws: All 50 states have some form of Freedom of Information Act (FOIA)/open records laws concerning meetings and information held by state or local government agencies. State laws vary concerning what is subject to disclosure; what is exempted; and the process for acquiring access to government records. But generally these laws start with the assumption that all information held by government officials is public information subject to disclosure. And in most cases any citizen may view public information at little or no cost.

Keep good records concerning important matters: Document important matters. Ignore unimportant matters; keep basic records on routine matters; but when an issue has the potential for future litigation keep thorough, accurate, and objective records. Good documentation is what wins litigation. Understand that if you are a public official many of your records may be subject to public scrutiny through open records requests, etc. If you records are objective and professional, however, public disclosure is not a problem. If you are a public employee draft your records anticipating that they are public records and you may be asked to defend them in a hearing.

Avoid unnecessary conflicts and litigation: Disputes are inevitable, but ugly conflicts and litigation are not. To avoid unnecessary conflicts and litigation know the law and apply it fairly. Even when you must take negative actions, treat others fairly and respectfully. Most people can accept negative decisions if they believe they have been treated fairly and respectfully. And few people really want to be engaged in stressful and expensive conflicts and litigation if they can be reasonably avoided. In "The Art of War" Sun Tzu advised building a golden bridge for your enemy to retreat on, and said that the greatest victory comes in the battle that was never fought. Look for wise ways to achieve your necessary objectives without unnecessary conflicts.

Essential Points

- Ignorance of the law is no excuse: All professionals are accountable for knowing the laws that govern their profession, and all citizens are responsible for compliance with applicable legal mandates.
- Art. VI of the U.S. Constitution requires public employees, including public school employees, to swear to support the Constitution.
- Violations of the Constitution by public employees may result in employment sanctions, termination, and monetary damages for violations of well-established law.
- The U.S. Constitution is the Supreme Law of the Land. All laws and all actions of government officials must be consistent with the Constitution.
- "Power tends to corrupt, and absolute power corrupts absolutely." Lord Acton. Effective checks and balances are always necessary to limit any unaccountable accumulation of excessive power by any individual or group, allowing only the powers necessary to the duties.
- The Constitution established a system of checks and balances to limit abuses of government powers. We must insist these are respected.
- The Bill of Rights and subsequent amendments to the Constitution set limits on government and government agents, in order to protect citizens' religious freedoms; political freedoms; privacy; and rights to fair treatment and equality under the laws.
- The Constitution only limits government actions. Public employees are bound by the Constitution while acting in their official capacities. The Constitution does not apply to private actions by private citizens.
- The rule of law is essential to justice and democracy. Under the equal rule of law no one is above the limits of the law, and no one is below the protections of the law.
- In a democracy all government officials, including those in the highest offices, are public servants not rulers.
- As Hammurabi's Code of Law recognized nearly 4,000 years ago the essential purpose of the law is "to bring about the rule of righteousness in the land . . . so that the strong should not harm the weak." The powerful need the limits of the law; the weaker need the protections of the law. It is the responsibility of all of us, as citizens in a just democracy, to assure that all government officials respect the rule of law, and that the equal rights of all persons are protected. As Mahatma Gandhi said: "The true measure of any society can be found in how it treats its most vulnerable members."

Essential Terms

Rule of law: Power and status are irrelevant to legal rights. The same just laws must govern all persons, and all persons are equally bound by the laws.

Stare decisis: The Common Law tradition of standing by and following sound decisions in prior cases to promote judicial predictability and equal justice.

Jurisdiction: A court's legal authority to hear and decide a case and to exercise legal authority over the parties. Parties are only bound by court decisions in their jurisdiction.

Legal standing: Defines whether a party has a legal right to bring a case to the court for resolution.

Essential Cases

Marbury v. Madison, 5 U.S. 137 (1803): This case established the principle of judicial review and the U.S. Supreme Court as the final authority in interpreting the U.S. Constitution. This case arose from a dispute over who had the final authority to make federal appointments. Holding: The federal judicial branch interprets the Constitution and its decisions are binding on those under its jurisdiction.

Gibbons v. Ogden, 22 U.S. 1 (1824): A challenge to the authority of Congress to regulate interstate commerce. Holding: When state and federal laws are in conflict and the federal government is acting under a constitutional grant of authority federal law is supreme.

United States v. Nixon, 418 U.S. 683 (1974): President Nixon did not want to turn over potentially incriminating audio tapes under court order. Nixon's attorney argued to a federal court of appeals: "The President wants me to argue that he is as powerful a monarch as Louis XIV, only four years at a time, and is not subject to the processes of any court in the land except the court of impeachment." In a unanimous opinion, the U.S. Supreme Court disagreed. Holding: No one is above the law.

A Closer Look at the Law

Our nation's founders were students of the Age of Enlightenment and sought to create a just government committed to openness, functional checks and balances, and decisions based on evidence, facts, truth, and reason. Those who doubt the importance of these principles should consider the saga of warning involving the Soviet Union's Trofim Lysenko.

Lysenko may have been the uneducated son of peasants, but what he lacked in education he more than made up for in zealous commitment to political dogma, ambition, and an attitude of absolute certainty. Based on his interpretation of Marxist theory, Lysenko rejected Western "bourgeois" scientific methods in general, and specifically rejected the work of Mendel, the founder of modern genetics, whose field-based scientific observations established that inherited variations in organisms resulted from combinations of genes from parent organisms.

Lysenko rejected Mendelism in favor of Lamarckism (i.e., the belief that organisms could inherit the acquired traits of progenitors). Under the theory of Lamarckism, for example, dogs with cropped ears and tails would in time produce pups with cropped ears and tails, and human body builders could pass the massive muscle development acquired through exercise on to their children. Lamarckism has been proven false: Genetic traits are inherited; acquired traits are not. Nonetheless, Lamarckism fit much better with Soviet ideology, which taught that through Communism's acquired life experiences of ideal collectivism, future generations of humans could be purged of human tendencies toward Capitalism and individual greed.

Lysenko also fit the model of the "peasant genius" the Soviets wished to promote over academics trained in Western science. And importantly, while scientific theories, debate, and testing take time; produce only degrees of certainty; and may raise unwanted questions about the status quo and political dogma; Lysenko offered regime supporting immediate answers with absolute certainty.

Based on his untested but politically useful theories, Lysenko quickly gained favor with Stalin and became the Director of Biology in the Soviet Union. Lysenko combined his political ideology and his theories into a political/agricultural movement known as Lysenkoism. Using the power of his position, Lysenko implemented his theories nation-wide in Soviet controlled agriculture with disastrous results.

In his failed "cluster planting" theory, for example, Lysenko insisted that seeds, trees, etc., should be planted very closely together, to increase the yield per acre. Lysenko reasoned that in uncorrupted nature it must surely be true that plants of the same type would never compete with others of their kind (as do the corrupted Capitalists) but would instead coexist and thrive

18

collectively. Simple field tests would have proven his theories false. Plants that are growing too closely together necessarily compete for space, light, water, and nutrients, reducing yields and wasting expensive seeds and seedlings. But field testing and the scientific method had been rejected and discredited by Lysenko as tools of Western sedition.

Rather than allowing the truth to interfere with useful propaganda, Soviet controlled media touted Lysenko's genius and ignored the consequences of his theories. Lysenko was even given his own "scientific" journal to provide an additional facade of credibility to his work. And before the failures of his last theory could be confronted, his prior failed mandate would be superseded by his next theory as the essential missing step in his great plan. For example, cluster planting would work, it was argued, if only the seed had been properly prepared, or the soil had been tilled deeper, and yet deeper the next year. In practice, however, the seed treatments failed to produce greater yields, and tilling too deeply was crushingly labor intensive; energy inefficient; turned under fertile top soil; and brought poor quality sub-soils and rocks to the surface.

Any scientists who dared to question Lysenko's theories were attacked as Western sympathizers and purged from government controlled science and academia. The fact that the Nazis had so thoroughly embraced Mendelian genetics and Western scientific methods (albeit with the darkest of motives) made these attacks very easy for Lysenko and his supporters. The final blow to truth came when the government made it illegal to challenge Lysenko's theories. Scientists and academics practicing or advocating orthodox genetics, science, or agriculture were imprisoned and killed. Lysenko's chief academic rival was starved to death in prison.

In 1964 the famous Soviet physicist and human rights advocate Andrei Sakharov wrote that Lysenko was "responsible for the shameful backwardness of Soviet biology and of genetics in particular, for the dissemination of pseudo-scientific views, for adventurism, for the degradation of learning, and for the defamation, firing, arrest, even death, of many genuine scientists." Lysenko's pseudo-science theories are also blamed for contributing to millions of deaths from famine when China adopted Lysenko's failed theories; theories which had been disproven in practice, but were politically protected from challenge.

In the absence of strong and effective checks and balances, there will always be another "Lysenko" ready to exploit unchecked government powers for personal gains. Strong protections for free speech and a free press are necessary to protect against the proliferation of dangerous lies. Openness is the remedy for corruption. The U.S. system works, but not on its own. Democracy and the rule of law are the necessary tools. Be we the people must learn to effectively use these tools in our own governance.

Law & Professional Ethics in Practice

All government agents, including public school employees, have sworn to comply with our Constitution as a condition of holding a public position. Further, many states have state employee "code of ethics" statutes that require state employees to support the federal and state constitutions and all applicable laws, and to report any known violations by other state agents. Some states have ethical codes specifically for educators. If you become aware of a violation of the law by a public school educator, what do you do? What constitutes a reportable offense in your state? Are you required to report? Who do you report to? Can anyone make a voluntary report? An anonymous report? What happens if you don't make a report?

Questions for Further Exploration

1) *Governance and law*: What are the legitimate purposes of government? What are the legitimate purposes of law? What distinguishes good and bad government; good and bad laws? How should the common government reconcile minority rights with majority rule; freedom with security; individualism with the common good? Did the Founders believe that we could answer these questions definitively by following their original intent? Or was their intention to provoke perpetual public dialogue about how to address these issues under changing circumstances consistent with our foundational values? What do the values evidenced in the Declaration of Independence and the Constitution suggest to you concerning these issues?

2) *Control of education policy*: What is the proper role of the federal government in public education? Should states; local school boards; or parents and students have more or less control over public education?

3) *Judicial duty and activism*: If judges neglect their judicial duties justice is denied and the rule of law is jeopardized. But if judges overstep their constitutional bounds through judicial activism judges intrude on legislative powers and the rule of law is jeopardized. What checks and balances are needed to keep judges from straying out of their constitutional lane in either direction (neglect of judicial duty or judicial activism)? Should judges be granted lifetime tenure? Should judges be appointed or elected? Should judges be subject to popular recall? Should different policies apply to federal and state judges?

4) *Open Forum*: What other related issues or current events would you like to discuss?

Suggested Activities for Further Learning

1) Read the U.S. Constitution (*see*, an abridged copy in the Appendix to this book; copies of the full document can be found online). Discuss what you learned from reading the Constitution.

2) Find your state's constitution (available online) and read through your state's bill of rights and the sections governing education. Discuss what you learned.

3) Contact your U.S. Senator and your Representative in Congress concerning an issue of importance to you.

4) Contact your State Senator and your State Representative in the State General Assembly concerning an issue of importance to you.

5) Visit a local federal or state courthouse and sit in on part of a trial. Most trials are open to the public and visitors are welcomed to watch the proceedings.

6) To improve your meetings, incorporate the Essential Practice Skills tips from this chapter in your meetings.

Chapter 2: Children, Families, and the State

Children are an especially vulnerable group that must be rigorously protected by the law. While respecting legitimate family privacy and parental rights, there is a collective social responsibility to protect children and to provide necessary services in the best interests of the child. The first right and responsibility to care for and protect the child resides with parents or other legal guardians.

If parents fail in these obligations, however, centuries old common law recognizes an obligation for the common government to assume these obligations under the *parens patriae* (i.e., parent of the nation; pronounced "parenz pa-tree-aye") doctrine. The *parens patriae* doctrine holds that while rights and responsibilities concerning the child are first vested in the parents, the common government also has a role as *parens patriae* when parents fail in their responsibilities to the child.

Parents may also voluntarily delegate some of their parental authority to school officials or others under the *in loco parentis* (i.e., in place of the parent; pronounced "in lo-co pa-rent-us") doctrine. Under the *in loco parentis* doctrine school officials may exercise reasonable quasi-parental authority while the child is in the care and custody of school officials, subject to the limits of the law and guided by the best interests of the child.

When acting *in loco parentis* school officials have a duty to supervise and protect children as a reasonable parent would under the circumstances. And children have a duty to follow the reasonable orders of school officials just as they must follow reasonable orders from their parents.

Children necessarily rely on the protection of adults both at home and at school. It is therefore the responsibility of adults to ensure that homes and schools provide a safe haven for children. Educators must protect the safety and well-being of students in schools so that the students may focus their full attention on learning and growing into well-adjusted, responsible, productive citizens through their studies and healthy social interactions in schools.

Children have legal rights from the moment of their birth. But the degree to which a child may exercise these rights necessarily depends on the maturity of the child. As the child grows closer to maturity, the child increasingly enjoys the full scope of rights belonging to mature adults. For example, children generally have the following rights at these ages:

AGE	EXAMPLE RIGHTS OBTAINED AT EACH MINIMUM AGE*
13	May be alone or "baby sit" younger children for a reasonable time
14	May select among otherwise fit and proper custodial parents
15	May obtain a learner's permit to drive
16	May legally consent to sexual contact (in some states)
17	May join the military with parental consent
18	Reaches the age of legal majority and is no longer a minor
21	May legally purchase and consume alcohol

* These are example minimum ages. Laws vary among states.

© **Dayton**

Parental Rights

Parents have both the legal right and responsibility to care for and make decisions on behalf of their minor children. Parental rights are taken very seriously under U.S. law and are protected by both the U.S. and state constitutions. Parents may, however, voluntarily give up parental rights by consenting to adoption or requesting a termination of parental rights.

In order to involuntarily terminate parental rights, however, the state must generally show: 1) Clear and convincing evidence that the parent is unfit; and 2) That it is in the best interests of the child to terminate parental rights.

Legal grounds for involuntary termination of parental rights may include child abandonment; neglect; abuse; mental incapacity of the parent; and other acts and conditions inconsistent with performing parental responsibilities, including the commission of serious felonies and resulting long-term incarceration.

Child Protective Services

Child protective services are the state agencies responsible for protecting the health, safety, and welfare of children when parents fail in these duties. These agencies act under the *parens patriae* doctrine. They have legal authority to investigate claims of child abuse and neglect; seek remedial court orders; and when necessary remove children from the home and seek termination of parental rights. Child protective services agents act under the dual goals of: 1) Pursuing the best interests of the child; and 2) Preserving the family.

In practice, however, these goals may sometimes conflict and prove mutually impossible when preserving the family is clearly not in the best interests of the child. Child protective services agents constantly face the danger of doing too little or too much in their efforts to protect children, either failing to adequately protect the child, or over-stepping their legal authority and intruding on family privacy and parental rights.

When there is clear and convincing evidence that children are in immediate danger, state officials have the authority to forcibly remove children from their parents on an emergency basis when necessary. This is, however, an extraordinary power that should only be used under extraordinary, emergency circumstances. Further, state officials must comply with state statutes and due process of law in this process.

Reporting Suspected Abuse or Neglect

It is the moral duty of all adults to protect children. In recognition of this obligation, all 50 U.S. states have enacted statutes mandating reports to state officials of suspected abuse or neglect of children. For persons subject to these statutes protecting children from abuse or neglect is not only a moral obligation: It is a legal duty. These statutes provide criminal sanctions if mandated reporters fail to make a timely report of child abuse or neglect.

> *If the Facts and Circumstances would cause a Reasonable Person to Suspect Child Abuse or Neglect, there is a Legal Duty to Report*

Mandatory reporting statutes were enacted in recognition of the general duty of adults, and child services professionals in particular, to protect children. In enacting these statutes lawmakers made a policy decision that when children may be in danger it is better to have too many reports rather than too few. Over-reporting consumes resources, and sometimes causes unnecessary intrusions. But under-reporting presents a serious danger that children may be unprotected. Therefore the legal standard is generally knowledge of "suspected" abuse and not just "known" abuse. There is a legal duty to make a report when a reasonable person would have suspected abuse under the facts and circumstances within the knowledge of the individual.

This is an objective legal standard, not a subjective standard. The "reasonable person" standard is based on the expected conduct of the ordinary person under the circumstances, a person with average knowledge, skills, and judgment. If a reasonable person would have made a report under those facts and circumstances, there is a legal duty to report. Further, the report should be made as soon as practicable avoiding any unnecessary delay that could interfere with the timely provision of help for the child.

Levels of Evidence of Abuse or Neglect and the Duty to Report

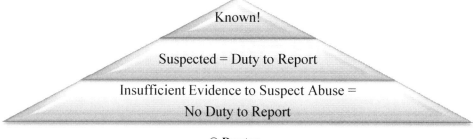

© Dayton

If there is insufficient evidence to cause a reasonable person to suspect abuse there is no duty to report. If there is evidence sufficient to cause a reasonable person to suspect child abuse, there is a legal duty to report and willful failure to do so may be subject to criminal punishments. Known abuse calls for immediate action to protect the child including a referral to law enforcement officials for immediate intervention.

If abuse or neglect are suspected the witness must comply with state laws for reporting abuse or neglect. For failing to report suspected abuse or neglect child care professionals could lose their professional licenses and be convicted of a misdemeanor (i.e., up to a year in jail). But if it can be proven that an adult actually knew about criminal child abuse and allowed the abuse to continue by failing to report, that person could be subject to prosecution as an accessory to the crime. In cases of child sexual abuse this could be a felony level crime punishable by significantly more than a year in prison.

When a report is made under the state reporting statute state child protection services personnel will investigate the report and make an initial determination whether the child is in danger or whether the child and family are in need of services, acting to protect the child as indicated. If the report turns out to be unfounded, however, as long as the report was made in good faith, persons reporting suspected abuse or neglect are generally shielded from any liability under state law by good faith immunity. Knowingly making a false report, however, is a crime. A person who knowingly makes a false report for purposes of harassment or defamation could be subject to both criminal prosecution and civil liability.

Abusers rarely abuse children in public view. Instead, child care professionals and community members may see signs and behaviors indicating that a child may be abused or neglected. It is also important to remember that while children must be protected from abuse or neglect, parents may also be in need of counseling, social services, or support. Not all marginal or bad parenting is legally actionable abuse or neglect.

Continuum of Parental Care

© Dayton

Optimal care for all children is ideal. Due to family, parental, or economic circumstances, however, optimal child care will not occur in many families. Child abuse and neglect laws seek to strike a proper balance between family privacy and public concern; parental autonomy and legal accountability; private economic realities and available public resources. Limited public resources mean that the state must establish a system of triage, directing resources to the children in greatest danger and need first.

Juvenile Law

Juvenile laws are primarily defined by state law. In most instances children under the age of 18 are subject to juvenile laws. Juvenile laws allow greater restrictions on the rights of children, restrictions that would be unconstitutional if applied to competent adults. Children, for example, must obey the lawful orders of their parents and school officials. They are subject to compulsory school attendance and curfew rules. And children are prohibited from engaging in many activities that would be lawful rights if they were adults including driving; living independently; working; marriage; voting; and the purchase of alcohol, tobacco, adult literature, or weapons.

Juvenile laws sometimes restrict children's rights. But they also protect children from known dangers, and generally make them subject to less severe punishments than adults. Although children can commit criminal acts and be held accountable for criminal conduct, criminal culpability requires proof of both *actus reus* (i.e., a guilty act; pronounced "act-us ray-us") and *mens rea* (i.e., a guilty mind; pronounced "mens ray-ah"). Establishment of *mens rea* for juveniles requires proof that the child understood the consequences of the actions under the circumstances. It must be proven that the child knew the difference between right and wrong, and that the child was capable of conforming behavior to avoid the prohibited act.

Children under the age of 7 are deemed incapable of sufficiently understanding the criminality of their acts. There is a rebuttable presumption that children age 7-14 are incapable of sufficiently understanding the criminality of their actions. But this presumption could be rebutted with compelling evidence in a particular case. Children ages 14 and over are presumed capable of understanding the criminality of their actions. But this presumption may be rebutted with evidence that a particular child was incapable of understanding the criminality of his or her actions as a juvenile. For children under the age of 18 the focus of the law is on rehabilitation rather than on punishment.

Child Custody

Serious situations involving abuse and neglect may result in termination of parental rights and a change in child custody. More commonly child custody changes result from a change of family circumstances including dissolution of marriage. When family circumstances change and these changes affect parent-child relationships and living circumstances, appropriate decisions must be made concerning the continued care and custody of minor children.

Child custody is generally divided into: 1) Physical custody; and 2) Legal custody. Parents with physical custody have the legal authority and responsibility to make daily decisions concerning child care and discipline, including emergency decisions when necessary. Parents with legal custody generally have rights to participate in longer-term decisions for the child including decisions on education, religious instruction, and other non-emergency decisions.

Concerning parental rights regarding students, state laws generally presume custody rights belong to the enrolling parent. Others may rebut this presumption, however, by presenting a valid court order. When school officials encounter a dispute between parents over parental rights, access to student records, etc., the party challenging the status quo must document the claim by presenting a court decree concerning child custody, etc. Otherwise, parents must take any unresolved issues to the court for resolution.

School officials should comply with a valid court order, but otherwise avoid direct involvement in contentious custody disputes between parents. Child custody disputes are decided by judges, not school officials. Parents must take their dispute to the court, not the principal, for resolution.

Access to Student Records

In 1974 The Family Educational Rights and Privacy Act (FERPA), 20 U.S.C. § 1232g, was enacted. FERPA applies to all educational institutions that receive federal funds. FERPA provides parents and eligible students access to their own educational records, and prohibits the disclosure of these records to third parties without parent or eligible student permission.

Parents generally hold FERPA rights on behalf of their minor children and have a right to access their child's educational records unless there is a court order, etc., concerning child custody that specifically revoked a parent's right to access these records. The right to access educational records transfers to a student who has reached age 18 or who is attending any institution of postsecondary education.

Parents or students have a right to a copy of their own records. School officials may charge a reasonable fee for the production of copies, but they cannot charge a fee for the retrieval of these records. Parents or students have a right to challenge any errors in the record and request amendments.

The educational institution must respond to the request for amendment in a reasonable time. If school officials refuse to amend the record the parent or eligible student must be informed of the right to a hearing to challenge the decision. Parents and students do not have a right to review documents that contain confidential information concerning other students or to access letters of recommendation for which the student waived the right to access.

School officials with a legitimate need to access student records may access these records internally without permission, but only for legitimate educational purposes. They may also share information from these records with other educational institutions or government agencies either with the permission of the parent or eligible student, or consistent with certain exceptions under FERPA including the disclosure of directory information (i.e., student name; phone; address; academic major; dates of attendance; and participation in school activities); health or safety emergencies; or in compliance with a court order or other lawful request from state or federal government officials.

Compulsory School Attendance Laws

All 50 U.S. states have compulsory school attendance laws making it the duty of parents to assure that children between the designated ages participate in an appropriate educational program of study. Parents may satisfy this requirement by having their children attend a qualifying public school, private school, or home school program of study.

Public schools are governed by state laws and regulations. Until the rise of public schools in the states, private and home school programs were largely unregulated. States now apply differing levels of regulations to private and home schools, ranging from virtually no active regulation to much more detailed requirements concerning teacher qualifications, minimum curriculum requirements, periodic attendance reports, and requirements for periodic standardized testing of children. Failure to comply with attendance requirements may be subject to criminal prosecution including fines or incarceration.

Private schools

Private schools have existed as long as civilization, with parents paying teachers tuition to educate their children. Many of these private schools were rooted in religious education, but increasingly more prestigious private schools focused on excellence in academics, becoming secular in nature. Private religious schools may use religion as a factor in admissions and employment when religious faith is essential to the mission of the school. Secular private schools, however, have no legitimate basis for religious discrimination in admissions or employment.

Home schools

Home learning is the original school. But by the 20th Century in the U.S. public schools were the dominate force in education. In the 1960s and 70s a growing anti-establishment movement began to see public schools as overly restrictive, authoritarian, school "factories" treating children like raw materials to be pushed into molds of conformity for the convenience of the military and industry, but at the expense of children's individuality and natural love for learning. John Holt, the "unschooling" pioneer, and others argued for a child-centered learning approach in which children were exposed to a rich learning environment, seamlessly connected to the real world, with the freedom to grow in their own natural directions. Home schools and private schools must comply with legitimate state regulations, but otherwise they control their own education programs and schedules.

Essential Questions & Answers

How do I report suspected child abuse or neglect?

Visit your state's child protective services department website for information on specific requirements in your state. For emergencies child protective services generally provide a 24-hour hotline, or you can contact a law enforcement agent directly for help. For non-emergencies involving students you can generally report to your school administrator who will then contact child protective services or law enforcement as appropriate. Always document your report to prove compliance with mandatory reporting laws.

If I report abuse but no abuse is found can I be sued or punished?

If you made the report in good faith (i.e., at the time of the report you sincerely believed there was cause to suspect abuse or neglect) state law generally provides good faith immunity from legal liability. The legal standard is "suspected" abuse or neglect, and not confirmed. There may be a legitimate explanation for the situation and not every investigation will find evidence of abuse. Bad faith reports (i.e., a report that is knowingly false and made with malicious intent) are subject to legal sanctions.

Does a public school principal have the right to question a student about school related events?

School administrators have the authority and responsibility to investigate and question students for purposes of maintaining a safe and orderly school environment. Though it is important to inform parents about issues of significant concern, school officials generally do not need parental consent to question students about ordinary school related events.

Do law enforcement agents have the right to question a student at school?

If state law permits, school resource officers (SROs) and probation officers of the juvenile court investigating school related issues may be allowed to reasonably question students at school concerning school events without prior parental notification. Law enforcement officers from other agencies investigating non-school related matters do not have the right to interview students at school simply for convenience. In such cases, the interrogation of students is not permitted without the consent of the parent unless the officer presents a valid court order or warrant for arrest, or states that the situation involves hot pursuit of a suspect linked to a felony crime.

Can public school officials force children to recite or stand for the pledge of allegiance to the flag?

No. In *West Virginia v. Barnette*, 319 U.S. 624 (1943), the U.S. Supreme Court declared: "If there is any fixed star in our constitutional constellation, it is that no official, high or petty, can prescribe what shall be orthodox in politics, nationalism, religion, or other matters of opinion or force citizens to confess by word or act their faith therein." Children can be invited to participate in pledges to the flag, and punished for any willful disruptions or other violations of legitimate codes of student conduct. But they cannot be coerced to participate or punished for declining to participate by word or act (e.g., not repeating the pledge; standing, saluting, etc.). Civil refusal to participate in public professions of creed is a constitutionally protected right in a free society. Students have the right to remain seated, take a knee, or otherwise engage in other non-disruptive symbolic protests.

How do I find out what the legal requirements are for a home study program in my state?

Search "home school" and your state name and you can easily find resources from your state department of education and public interest groups. Many states also offer free online educational support for home school families.

Can home school students participate in public school activities?

Some states have passed "equal access" laws giving home school students legal rights to participate in curricular and extracurricular activities. If state law does not address this issue, whether home school students may participate without being enrolled as full-time students is up to local school boards.

What do home school students have to do to apply to colleges?

Home school students may provide proof of college readiness through SAT or ACT scores; Advanced Placement (AP) credits; College Level Examination Program (CLEP) tests; success in online or dual enrollment courses; or through home study records and portfolios. Higher education is increasingly home school student friendly as many of these students have already developed the independent discipline and self-motivation necessary for success in higher education. But also check any specific admission requirements with individual institutions of higher education.

Essential Practice Skills

Child care professionals are on the front lines of defense in protecting children from abuse or neglect. For this reason it is essential that child care professionals recognize signs of abuse or neglect. Below are examples of warning signs and red flags. Note that the lists below are only illustrative lists intended to raise awareness of possible signs of abuse or neglect. These are not the only indicators of abuse or neglect, nor does an indicator of possible abuse or neglect necessarily mean a child is being abused or neglected. Each case must be independently evaluated in consideration of the totality of the circumstances.

General indicators of child abuse or neglect:

• Sudden behavioral changes
• Dramatic declines in school performance
• Becoming socially withdrawn
• Unexplained anxiety or anger
• Troubling conduct when with a parent
• Unusual desire to stay at school
• Substance abuse
• Bullying or abusing other children
• Running away
• Self-harm or attempted suicide

Indicators of child neglect:

• Unsupervised
• Poor hygiene
• Dirty or insufficient clothing
• Stealing or begging food or money
• Untreated dental or medical problems
• Excessive school absences
• Falling asleep in school
• Frequent illnesses or injuries

Indicators of verbal or emotional abuse are too often dismissed as merely regrettable. But a child can be severely and permanently harmed without anyone touching the child physically. In severe cases psychological and emotional pain can be worse than physical pain, and leave deeper and longer lasting scars. Severe verbal or emotional abuse may also drive a child to self-injury or other reactions to abuse that may endanger the child or others.

Indicators of verbal or emotional abuse:

• Low self-esteem
• The child repeating abusive comments
• Public disparagement of the child
• Intentional humiliation of the child
• Grossly disproportionate punishments
• Exposure to domestic abuse
• Displays of extreme anger directed at the child
• Throwing or destroying objects near the child
• Threats, intimidation, or attempts to frighten the child
• Threats to withhold necessities, abandon, or force the child out of the home
• Threatening to harm loved personal possessions or pets
• Other evidence of emotional manipulation of the child or intentional cruelty

Indicators of physical abuse:

• Unexplained marks (e.g., bruises; cuts; scalds; burns; bite marks; etc.)
• Any suspicious injury (e.g., broken ribs; spiral fracture on long bone; cigarette burn; etc.)
• Any suspicious pattern of recurrent minor injuries
• Bruise in the shape of an object
• Bruises on both sides of the face or body (i.e., accidents generally injure only one side)
• Injury in protected/hidden area (e.g., foot sole; inside the mouth; inner thigh; buttocks; back; etc.)
• Fingertip marks on neck (choking)
• Fingertip marks on upper arm or inside underarm (shaking)
• Rope burns or bruise marks on wrists or ankles suggesting restraint
• Broken or missing teeth
• Eye injury or hemorrhage
• Bruised outer ear (from being pulled or "boxed")
• Missing patch of hair (from pulling)
• Sickness or diarrhea from being forced to eat soap, salt, or other substances

Indicators of sexual abuse:

• Sudden change in behavior
• Low self-esteem
• Unexplained crying, anxiety, anger, social withdrawal
• Age-inappropriate sexual knowledge
• Overreaction to normal physical contact

- Inappropriate interactions with adults
- Sexual abuse of other children
- Discomfort in sitting or walking
- Sudden reluctance to disrobe for P.E. or showers
- Self-injury or attempted suicide
- Venereal disease or pregnancy

Based on an evaluation of the evidence and the totality of the circumstances concerning the child, the child care professional or other adult must decide on an appropriate course of action. Appropriate responses may range from an immediate emergency report to continued monitoring of the circumstances.

Emergency or imminent danger: Report to police for immediate intervention.

No emergency but red flags indicate abuse or neglect: Report as soon as possible consistent with statutory mandates for reporting.

No emergency or red flags but the totality of the circumstances would lead a reasonable person to suspect abuse or neglect: Make a timely report consistent with the state reporting statute.

Suspicious circumstance noticed but does not meet reporting criteria: Ask appropriate, reasonable questions, engaging in a non-intrusive investigation to assure child safety.

Questioning children concerning suspicious circumstances:

- Ask open-ended questions (e.g., "are you alright?"; "what happened?"; etc.)
- Follow up with more focused questions (e.g., what; how; who; when; why; etc.)
- Give the child time to respond
- Do not suggest conclusions
- Do not suggest abuse or neglect
- Do not act shocked
- Make the child feel safe and assure protection if needed

When possible, have another child care professional present to verify events and the child's statements. If at any point

34

evidence of abuse or neglect exceeds the legal threshold under the reporting statute, make a report. Child protective services agents, law enforcement officers, or medical personnel may need to engage in a more thorough and intrusive interview or search. Do not exceed the appropriate bounds of your professional role in questioning or searching a child.

Uncertain what to do: Call child protective services for a consultation.

Child, parent, or family is in need of assistance but there is no abuse or neglect: Direct to support services and resources in the community.

No current evidence of abuse or neglect, but a lingering concern remains: Continue to appropriately and discreetly monitor the child's health and safety.

The parent's reaction to an injury may provide important clues in separating naturally occurring injuries from abuse. Factors that may enhance suspicion are an intentional delay in seeking medical treatment when obviously needed; the explanation of the child's injury is vague; the parent seems more concerned about personal issues than the child's health and safety; the parent is curiously evasive or hostile; or the parent and child provided conflicting accounts of what happened.

Parental problems with money, lifestyle, substance abuse, or physical or mental health issues may increase risks for abuse or neglect. Parents' incomes of course have no correlation with their love for their children. But extreme poverty or homelessness can increase family stress and make it very difficult for parents to properly care for children.

Concerning lifestyle choices, a parent's lifestyle can have severe impacts on the health and safety of the child. Unhealthy or unsafe home conditions threaten the health and safety of the child. A parent's promiscuity or engaging in prostitution in the home may bring strangers into private contact with the child. To gain private access to a child, pedophiles sometimes target a parent with young children under the guise of a relationship with the parent. Substance abuse or drug dealing may also introduce dangerous people and conditions into the home. Domestic violence is a further threat to the child's mental and physical health and safety.

A parent struggling with serious mental health issues may be more prone to neglect and abuse or may be unfit to care for the child. If the parent is capable of child care, support should be provided to preserve the family when possible. But if the child is endangered by the parent's mental health problems the child must be protected.

For example, an uncommon by serious danger that must be recognized when present is Munchausen Syndrome by Proxy. This is a psychiatric disorder where the parent, most commonly the mother, causes or falsely claims injury or illness of the child. The parent may inflict an injury on the child, fabricate a "mystery" illness, or falsely claim to have observed seizures, high fevers, signs of internal bleeding or other medical concerns that cannot currently be proven or disproven, often with an over-eagerness to have medical tests and procedures conducted on the child. Medical records may be falsified and test samples intentionally contaminated by the parent. The parent's behavior may be motivated by acquiring personal sympathy or attention, or a desire to appear to "save" the child and be recognized as a hero while actually endangering the child. A parent with serious mental illness needs help, but the child must be protected first.

Essential Practice Tips

Protecting children: Learn to recognize the signs of child abuse and neglect, and teach your colleagues and other adults to recognize clear signs that children may need help. In most cases of abuse and neglect physical or behavioral signs are present and discernable to an alert observer. Nonetheless, sometimes a bruise is just a bruise; and sometimes unusual behavior is just unusual behavior. If, however, there is a pattern of signs of abuse or neglect, or any serious sign that cannot be reasonably dismissed as benign under the circumstances, a prompt report and appropriate professional intervention are warranted to protect the child.

Protecting the family: Willful and intentional abuse or neglect of children must be dealt with appropriately, including removal of the child from the home and filing criminal charges when warranted. Do not, however, assume that all child neglect is willful. Sometimes otherwise loving parents are overwhelmed by financial, health, or other problems and are in need of services themselves. With appropriate assistance and support the parent may be able to improve child care standards to healthy levels for the child. If it is possible to safely allow the child to remain with a parent who loves the child and is capable of providing appropriate care with assistance and support, preserving the child's family is a priority both legally and ethically.

Protecting yourself: Failure to report suspected child abuse and neglect is a crime in all 50 states. If you must report suspected abuse, also appropriately document your report including the facts and circumstances you reported;

who you reported to; the date of your report; and any other relevant information. Most administrators will promptly and responsibly forward and follow up on your report. But be warned: Someone who is unethical enough not to forward your report to the proper authorities is likely also unethical enough to claim that you never made the report if threatened with criminal charges for failing to forward your report. Documentation of your report protects you from any future false claim that you failed to report. Keep your documentation confidential and in a safe location. Also, be very cautious about getting overly involved in any domestic disputes between warring parents, etc. These disputes can be highly emotional, volatile, and even dangerous. An appropriate professional distance is called for, functionally and emotionally. And if there are any threats or other serious signs of danger notify law enforcement authorities to protect yourself and others.

Essential Points:

- Children have a right to protection, education, and other necessary provisions for their healthy development into adulthood.
- As the child develops toward maturity the child increasingly possesses the full scope of rights and responsibilities belonging to mature adults.
- Parents have the first right and responsibility to care for the child. But under the doctrine of *parens patriae* if parents fail in their responsibilities to the child, the State may assume these duties consistent with the best interests of the child.
- Child protective services agencies act under the dual (and sometimes conflicting) goals of: 1) Pursuing the best interests of the child; and 2) Preserving the family.
- When parents place a child in school they temporarily delegate some of their parental authority to educators.
- Educators have a responsibility to supervise and protect the children in their care as a reasonable parent would.
- Children have a duty to follow the lawful orders of educators while under school authority.
- School officials can question students concerning civil matters including potential violations of school codes of conduct. But special care is required in questioning a child about any criminal matters without parental notice and other appropriate due process protections.
- In all government proceedings potentially impinging on their life, liberty, or property, children must be given fair hearings and adequate due process of law.

- Until age 18 children are generally subject to juvenile laws which provide greater protections for children, but also allow for greater restrictions on children.

Essential Terms:

FERPA: The Family Educational Rights and Privacy Act, 20 U.S.C. § 1232g, provides parents and eligible students with access to their own educational records, and prohibits the disclosure of these records to third parties without parent or eligible student permission.

In loco parentis: Latin, meaning in place of the parent. School officials may exercise reasonable quasi-parental authority while the child is in the care and custody of school officials, subject to the limits of the law and guided by the best interests of the child.

Parens patriae: Latin, meaning parent of the nation. Rights and responsibilities concerning the child are first vested in the parents. But the government also has a role as *parens patriae* if parents fail in their legal responsibilities to the child.

Essential Cases:

In re Gault, 387 U.S. 1 (1967): A child was arrested and incarcerated based on questionable evidence and inadequate due process. The Court declared: "Under our Constitution, the condition of being a [child] does not justify a kangaroo court." Adequate due process and other constitutional protections apply to children as well as adults.

J.D.B. v. North Carolina, 564 U.S. 261 (2011): A 13 year old was subjected to interrogation by two police officers in a closed room at school for 45 minutes without parental notice. The child was given no *Miranda* warning; not informed he was free to leave; or informed that he did not have to respond to questions about criminal guilt. Held: The unique age-related vulnerabilities of children must be considered in determining whether children reasonably believed they were in custody when questioned by police and whether any confession obtained under those conditions was valid.

Pierce v. Society of the Sisters, 268 U.S. 510 (1925): The state passed a law requiring public school only attendance. A private religious school sued. Held: The state may mandate education for all children, but not public school attendance only. Parents may choose public, private, or home school options to satisfy state compulsory education requirements.

Roper v. Simmons, 543 U.S. 551 (2005): The death penalty was assigned as punishment for a murder committed by a 17 year old. Held: It is unconstitutional to impose the death penalty on juveniles.

West Virginia v. Barnette, 319 U.S. 624 (1943): Children of Jehovah's Witnesses sincerely believed flag salutes were religiously prohibited as idol worship. School officials punished the children for not participating in the flag salutes. Held: School officials may invite participation in pledges, flag salutes, etc. But they cannot coerce participation or punish anyone for declining to participate "by word or act" (e.g., not repeating the pledge; not standing; not saluting; etc.). Refusal to participate in state sponsored public professions of creed is a constitutionally protected right in a free society.

Yoder v. Wisconsin, 406 U.S. 205 (1972): Amish parents argued state compulsory attendance laws conflicted with sincerely held religious beliefs and their agrarian lifestyle. The U.S. Supreme Court allowed Amish children a limited exemption from otherwise valid public school attendance laws finding that Amish children were receiving an appropriate education through Eighth Grade or age 14 which sufficiently prepared them for work and citizenship in their community.

A Closer Look at the Law

State governments have both enormous responsibilities and powers. For this reason it is essential that states hire highly competent people, persons who can administer the law with common sense, and who are capable of striking a proper balance between the duty to protect children and the duty to respect family privacy and constitutional rights. Children and families are harmed when the state does too little or too much in protecting children.

In *DeShaney v. Winnebago*, 489 U.S. 189 (1989), for example, child protective services officials had received many complaints that Joshua, a minor child, had been subjected to severe beatings by his father. Nonetheless, state social services agents did not remove the child from the custody of his father. His father eventually beat Joshua so severely that the child suffered permanent brain damage and was left profoundly and permanently mentally impaired. Joshua's mother sued state child protective services on Joshua's behalf.

Nonetheless, in *DeShaney* the U.S. Supreme Court ruled against Joshua and his mother stating "had [state agents] moved too soon to take custody of the son away from the father, they would likely have been met with charges of improperly intruding into the parent-child relationship." In a dissenting opinion, however, Justice Blackmun declared:

> Poor Joshua! Victim of repeated attacks by an irresponsible, bullying, cowardly, and intemperate father, and abandoned by [state social services agents] who placed him in a dangerous predicament and who knew or learned what was going on, and yet did essentially nothing except, as the Court revealingly observes, "dutifully recorded these incidents in [their] files."

At the other extreme end of the spectrum of state reaction, in March 2008 a local domestic abuse hotline reported receiving a call from a "16 year-old girl" who identified herself only as "Sarah." The caller claimed physical and sexual abuse at the "Yearning for Zion" (YFZ) Ranch in a rural area near Eldorado, Texas. Four days later Texas Department of Family Protective Services and Texas law enforcement officials conducted a military-style raid on the YFZ Ranch. State agents were armed with automatic weapons, helicopters, and armored vehicles. They were not, however, met with any resistance from residents.

Texas officials were there to forcibly remove children from the YFZ Ranch based on their theory that the religious beliefs of the Fundamentalist Church of Jesus Christ of Latter Day Saints (FLDS) created a danger that children could be indoctrinated in harmful beliefs, and therefore the children must be removed from their parents' homes now for their future safety. The belief system in question allegedly included a history of polygamy involving under-age brides, and a culture of socialization and coercion into under-age marriages. State officials searched the Ranch and 468 children were taking from their homes and placed in state custody. State officials had not obtained a court order or provided individual parents with due process of law prior to seizing their children.

It was later learned that "Sarah" the complainant who provided the basis for this action was not a 16 year-old abused child, but was in fact a much older woman who had prior arrests for false reports in which she impersonated an abused girl. Further, the search of the Ranch and police interviews of children and parents did not produce any credible evidence of mass child abuse.

The forced removals caused great emotional distress to FDLS children and parents. And many of the children who were not vaccinated because of sincerely held religious beliefs became seriously ill when exposed to communicable diseases while in state child care facilities. FDLS parents sued state officials for the return of their children.

The Supreme Court of Texas, in *In re Texas Department of Family and Protective Services*, 255 S.W.3d 613 (Tex., 2008), held that the Texas Department of Family and Protective Services' allegations concerning FLDS religious beliefs and a culture of polygamy did not justify emergency removal of all 468 children prior to the provision of adequate due process of law. Parents had a right to adequate, individual notice of any specific charges and evidence against them, and a right to an individual hearing concerning matters related to their child. Mass removals of children from their parents based on little more than unproven theories about their religious beliefs and guilt by association were constitutionally prohibited.

If there is clear and convincing evidence that children are in immediate danger, state officials have the authority to forcibly remove children from their parents on an emergency basis when necessary. This is, however, an extraordinary power that should only be used under extraordinary, emergency circumstances. Further, state officials must comply with state statutes and due process of law in this process.

Law & Professional Ethics in Practice:

Many states have legally binding ethical codes expressly setting out the ethical duties of educators to students. Further, many professional organizations have similar ethical codes (e.g., NEA, ASCA, etc.). What these ethical codes have in common are ethical mandates to: Not in any manner harm or endanger students; only engage in appropriate relationships with students; never exploit student relationships for personal gain; be honest in academic matters and records; respect confidential student information; and respect the legal rights of students including rights to non-discrimination. Find and review the ethical standards in your state (e.g., search your state and educator code of ethics). What are the specific provisions addressing legal and ethical duties to students? What are the possible sanctions? How does one file a complaint if these provisions are violated by an educator? Can you define the lines between simple bad practice, unethical behavior, and illegal conduct, all of which should be addressed, but some of which must be reported to state officials?

Questions for Further Exploration:

1) *International children's rights*: Only two nations declined to ratify the United Nations Convention on the Rights of the Child (1990), Somalia and the United States. Should the U.S. ratify the United Nations Convention on the Rights of the Child? Why or why not? What is the current status of children's rights in the U.S. and in other nations? Do children have adequate

protections for safety and access to clean water, air, and a toxin free environment; food; shelter; clothing; medical care; education; and a chance for a healthy, happy, and productive future? What can be done to improve children's chances for a healthy, happy, and productive future?

2) *Home school and alternative education*: Millions of children receive a high quality, highly individualized education through home school studies, and go on to subsequent success in college, work, etc. For some children, however, home schooling is little more than legalized truancy. State laws governing home schooling range from what some consider far too intrusive on family privacy to what others consider far too lax in protecting children's rights to education. What laws govern your state's home school programs? Are these laws appropriate, too intrusive, or too permissive? Private and home school parents pay public school taxes. Should private and home school students be allowed to participate in public school academic and extra-curricular programs? Why or why not? Public schools were born in the Industrial Age and are based on a factory model that seems increasingly antiquated. What modifications or alternatives to this increasingly archaic factory model of schooling hold the greatest promise for the future?

3) *Group solidarity and individual free will*: Children have a right to decline participation in flag salutes and pledges, and they are not required to provide school officials with any explanation for their decision. Further, it would be inappropriate and possibly unlawful for school officials to question a student's religious beliefs related to these activities. If the student volunteered, however, that the refusal to participate was based on political or philosophical objections only, these are lawful topics of discussion with students. Would you want to attempt to persuade the student to participate? What would you say? Is our tolerance for dissent and diversity of belief a national strength or weakness? What did the Court say in *West Virginia v. Barnette*, 319 U.S. 624 (1943)?

4) *Open forum*: What other related issues or current events would you like to discuss?

Suggested Activities for Further Learning:

1) Read the United Nations Convention on the Rights of the Child (available online). Talk with educators or others with international experiences to compare and contrast the realities of children's rights in different nations.

2) Talk with a juvenile court judge, social worker, or other child services agents. What are the greatest challenges they face in helping children? How can educators, parents, and child services personnel work together more effectively to help children?

3) Read your state's statute mandating reports of suspected child abuse and neglect. What constitutes child abuse or neglect under your state's laws? Who is required to report? Who do you report to? What are the potential consequences for failing to report? Discuss the application of this statute in protecting children in your schools and community.

4) Although children are commonly asked to say the "Pledge of Allegiance" to the U.S. flag, few educators have explained to them what the pledge means and why it is important. What does it mean and why is it important? What is the history and meaning of the pledge? *See*, James Clavell, THE CHILDREN'S STORY (1964) (a short story exploring the meaning of the pledge). What is the history and meaning of protests during the pledge including remaining seated; "taking a knee"; etc.?

Chapter 3: First Amendment Freedoms and Religion

Regarding religion the U.S. Constitution's First Amendment states: "Congress shall make no law respecting an establishment of religion, or prohibiting the free exercise thereof" protecting individual rights of religious belief and practice from government interference. As James Madison, the author of the First Amendment recognized, efforts to use the force of government to coerce and compel religious beliefs and practices have caused great pains to individuals throughout human history, and served as the basis of countless conflicts and wars.

In recognition of these concerns, the First Amendment's "Establishment Clause" prohibits government officials from establishing any favored or disfavored religion. The "Free Exercise Clause" mandates that government officials must respect individual free exercise of religion and provide reasonable accommodations for the free exercise of religion when necessary. The First Amendment's religion clauses have been interpreted as requiring official governmental neutrality concerning religion, and establishing a reasonable "wall of separation" between church and state thereby protecting both private religious free will and the integrity of the common government.

This wall of separation between church and state is not, however, an absolute wall of separation. Religion plays a central role in many peoples' lives, and it has been a driving force throughout much of human history. Religion cannot be banned from the public square without also banning the free expression of people who hold religious beliefs. On the other hand, history shows that few issues are more divisive than whose religion will be officially recognized and favored in the public square and government.

The purpose of the symbolic wall of separation between church and state is to set appropriate boundaries between private religion and public power. This protects the individual and the church from state interference. And protects the common government from the disruption and divisiveness of conflicts over whose religion should receive official endorsement and have the power to compel others to express belief or face state imposed sanctions.

The height and strength of the wall of separation increases or diminishes in each case depending on the degree of danger presented by the co-mingling of church and state. For example, the U.S. Supreme Court has rejected challenges to the use of the phrase "In God We Trust" on money and "so help me God" in the Presidential oath of office. The passive, benign use of these phrases by government presents little real danger that anyone's religious freedom is jeopardized. Therefore the wall of separation is low enough, and flexible enough, to allow for the continued lawful use of these religious terms by government. At the other end of the continuum, however, public school sponsored prayer has been repeatedly rejected by the Court as a genuine danger to individual religious freedom and the essential maintenance of religious neutrality by the common government.

The wall of separation between church and state is at its highest in public schools where highly impressionable children are subject to compulsory attendance laws enforced by criminal sanctions. The Court has recognized that captive audiences of highly impressionable children are vulnerable to state sponsored religious indoctrination when they are away from the guidance and protection of their own parents in public schools.

Further, few issues are more potentially divisive and disruptive than battles over whether the political majority should have the authority to compel their religious beliefs and practices on other people's children through compulsory school attendance. The temptation to use public schools for the mass religious indoctrination of other people's children is enticing to zealous proselytizers, but intolerable to minority faith parents seeing teachers and coaches abusing their unique authority and access to other people's children, and manipulating peer pressure, to coerce religious conformity.

To help determine whether a particular government action violates the Establishment Clause the Court developed a legal test for answering this question in *Lemon v. Kurtzman*, 403 U.S. 602 (1971). Under the *Lemon* test, a government action challenged as violating the Establishment Clause will be constitutionally valid only if it satisfies each of the following conditions:

> 1) *Purpose*: There must a legitimate secular (non-religious) purpose for the challenged government action. The primary purpose underlying the government action cannot be religious in nature.
> 2) *Effect*: The primary effect of the government action must be religiously neutral. It must neither advance nor inhibit religion.
> 3) *Entanglement*: The government action must not foster excessive entanglement between church and state.

If a government action is found to have violated any of the three-prongs of the *Lemon* test, the challenged statute, regulation, policy, or practice is declared unconstitutional. Government officials have no lawful authority to continue any unconstitutional act and they may be held liable for monetary damages under 42 U.S.C. § 1983 for violations of constitutional rights.

The *Lemon* test can be used to assess the likely outcome of a potential case and as a guide in planning lawful future actions and policies. Whenever there is a question about whether a government action may violate the Establishment Clause the relevant facts can be measured against the *Lemon* test's three-prongs: 1) Purpose; 2) Effect; and 3) Entanglement:

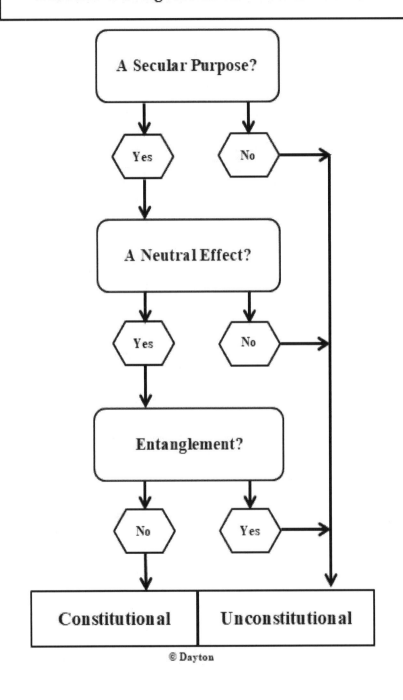

Establishment Clause *"Lemon* Test"
Does the Challenged Government Action Have:

A Secular Purpose?

Yes   No

A Neutral Effect?

Yes   No

Entanglement?

No   Yes

Constitutional   Unconstitutional

© Dayton

Free Exercise of Religion

Otherwise valid governmental actions may sometimes conflict with individual free exercise of religion. For example, deciding to serve pork products in the public school cafeteria because of favorable costs and demand is a valid governmental decision. But some students and faculty may be religiously prohibited from eating pork. While no one can be required to eat the pork products, of course, a reasonable accommodation for the religious free exercise observance of dietary restrictions may be offering an alternative menu item or an opportunity to bring lunch from home.

In many cases, respecting the free exercise of religion is as simple as granting an exemption to the individual, or providing a reasonable accommodation such as an opportunity for an alternative assignment, etc. If a reasonable accommodation can be provided without undue costs, administrative burdens, disruptions, or health and safety risks to others, a simple exemption or other reasonable accommodation is generally in everyone's best interests, and may be required by law.

The more difficult cases are those in which school officials believe they must refuse to grant an exemption or that the requested accommodation is unreasonable. In these cases, plaintiffs may attempt to force official recognition of the free exercise right and obtain a requested accommodation through litigation. To prevail in these cases plaintiffs must establish:

> 1) *The belief is religious*: Only religious beliefs are entitled to free exercise protection. Political or philosophical beliefs may be advanced through free speech, but they are not protected under the Free Exercise Clause;
> 2) *The belief is sincerely held by the plaintiff*: The plaintiff must prove by a preponderance of the evidence that the religious belief is sincerely held and not a sham belief only for purposes of obtaining the exemption or reasonable accommodation;
> 3) *The belief is central to the plaintiff's faith*: The belief impacted by the government action must be a core element of the plaintiff's faith, and not merely tangential.
> 4) *The government action is a direct burden on free exercise*: The government action must impose a direct burden on the free exercise of religion, and not merely an incidental burden.

If a plaintiff meets this burden of proof, the plaintiff has established a prima facie case (i.e., sufficient evidence to support the initial claim; pronounced "pry-ma fay-she" case) for a protected free exercise right unless the government can establish:

5) *There is a compelling governmental interest*: Government officials can prove a compelling governmental interest (e.g., protecting public security, health, safety, or respecting the Establishment Clause) for denying the exemption or other reasonable accommodation; and

6) *Government actions are narrowly tailored to achieving that interest*: The government's means of achieving the compelling interest must not be over-broad in limiting individual rights beyond what is necessary.

If the plaintiff ultimately prevails, the plaintiff is entitled to an exemption or other reasonable accommodation, but the government action remains valid for everyone else. The free exercise test can provide useful guidance in helping sort out which requests are valid and which ones are not entitled to protection under the Free Exercise Clause.

For example, if a Native American student presented credible evidence that her Tribe prohibited the use of vaccinations based on religious convictions, and that she also sincerely held this religious view, the objection to the state immunization policy is a religious belief under the Free Exercise Clause and sincerely held.

In contrast, if parents request an exemption because they are concerned about possible links between vaccinations and health consequences, this is not a religious belief protected under the Free Exercise Clause. State law or local policy may provide a process for exemption for health concerns, or an exemption may be argued for through free speech. But non-religious beliefs are not protected by the Free Exercise Clause.

While the U.S. Supreme Court's free exercise cases do provide some guidance, the law in this area is complex, controversial, and in some respects unsettled. The Court's 5-4 decision in *Employment Division v. Smith*, 494 U.S. 872 (1990), further complicated the law in this area. In *Smith*, the Court redefined the fourth-prong of the free exercise test, holding that "direct burden" does not refer to the impact of the government's actions in obstructing the individual's free exercise of religion, but to the intent of government officials. Under this interpretation, government actions only burdened free exercise if the plaintiff can prove that the religious practice was intentionally targeted by government officials. Rules of general application that do not target religious practices do not violate the Free Exercise Clause. Note, however, state constitutions and laws may require accommodations beyond federal legal requirements. In general, if a reasonable accommodation for religion can be provided without undue burden, it is good legal and ethical policy to provide it.

Free Exercise Test and the Plaintiff's Right to Religious Exemption/Reasonable Accommodation

© Dayton

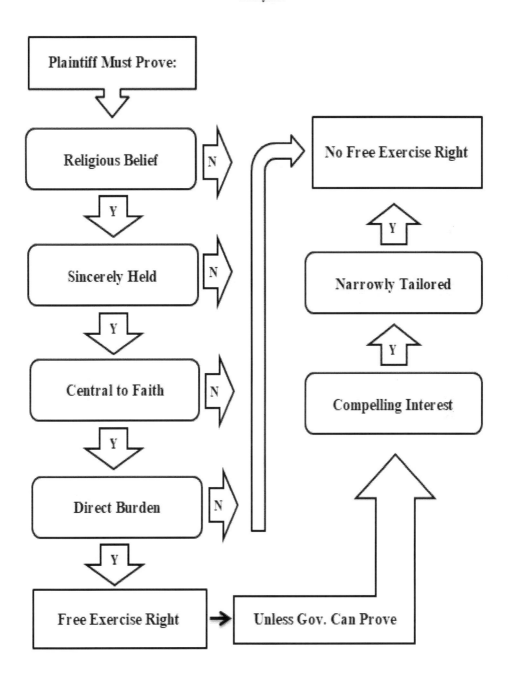

Essential Questions & Answers

Do public school students have a right to pray in schools?

Yes. The Establishment Clause only applies to agents of the government. Students are private citizens. School employees are limited by the Constitution. Students are not. Concerning prayer during non-instructional time, the U.S. Department of Education's *Guidance on Constitutionally Protected Prayer in Public Elementary and Secondary Schools* states that: "Students may pray when not engaged in school activities or instruction, subject to the same rules designed to prevent material disruption of the educational program that are applied to other privately initiated expressive activities."

Is it lawful for public school coaches to lead students in prayers?

No. Coach led prayers were a tradition, especially in rural areas of the South. Local tradition, however, does not trump the U.S. Constitution. Article VI of the U.S. Constitution requires all state officials (including coaches) to swear to respect the Constitution and individual rights. At least since *Engel v. Vitale*, 370 U.S. 421 (1962), the Establishment Clause has been recognized as prohibiting public school employees from leading students in prayer while acting in their official capacities. Nor can coaches actively participate in student led prayers. Public schools are religiously diverse institutions. Allowing a coach to endorse a particular religion and prayer puts students who do not share that particular faith in the position of either participating against their conscience or not participating and being subjected to the consequences of non-participation from the coach and other students. Under these circumstances the religious peer pressure is unreasonably coercive. Further, state led prayer is contrary to the command of the Establishment Clause that government officials remain neutral concerning religion while acting in their official capacities and not endorse any one religion or prayer over others. All public school employees must respect private choices concerning religion and not use their public positions to impose their personal religious beliefs on other people's children.

Can student athletes in a public school vote to have a coach lead the team in prayers?

No. Getting a local majority to vote in favor of an unlawful practice does not change an unlawful act into a lawful act. In *Engel* the U.S. Supreme Court declared: "Our Founders were no more willing to let the content of their prayers and their privilege of praying whenever they pleased be influenced by the ballot box than they were to let these vital matters of personal conscience depend upon the succession of monarchs." Further, having the majority of students vote in favor of the unlawful practice increases the coercive impact of peer pressure on any student objecting to the state sponsored prayers. In *Lee v. Weisman*, 505 U.S. 577 (1992), concerning peer pressure to participate in prayer, the Court stated: "This pressure, though subtle and indirect, can be as real as any overt compulsion . . . Finding no violation under these circumstances would place objectors in the dilemma of participating, with all that implies, or protesting . . . the State may not, consistent with the Establishment Clause, place primary and secondary school children in this position . . . While in some societies the wishes of the majority might prevail . . . The Constitution forbids the State to exact religious conformity from a student as the price of [participation in public school activities]."

Can public school students lead and participate in team prayers?

Yes. As private citizens the students have a constitutional right to pray if they choose to. But prayers in public schools must be genuinely initiated and conducted by students and not by state officials acting in their official capacities. Students may choose to continue a tradition of pre-game prayers with other students who wish to participate. But as a state official, the coach cannot lawfully control or lead the prayers, or actively participate while acting in an official capacity. Nor can the coach lawfully bring in an outside "chaplain" to lead the team in prayers, effectively doing by proxy what the coach could not lawfully do directly. This too is endorsing a favored religion or endorsing religion generally in violation of the Establishment Clause.

May a public school offer students a course on the Bible?

Yes, if the course presents an objective academic study of the Bible and is not just a pretext for religiously proselytizing public school children. In *Abbington v. Schempp*, 374 U.S. 203 (1963), the U.S. Supreme Court declared "it might well be said that one's education is not complete without a study of comparative religion or the history of religion and its relationship to the advancement of civilization. It certainly may be said that the Bible is worthy of study for its literary and historic qualities. Nothing we have said here indicates that such study of the Bible or of religion, when presented objectively as part of a secular program of education, may not be affected consistently with the First Amendment."

May public schools ask students to observe a daily moment of silence?

Yes. Courts have generally upheld the practice of observing a moment of silence as long as it is not conducted as a religious exercise where prayer is encouraged or discouraged, or there is entanglement with the church (e.g., led by a member of the clergy) in violation of the Establishment Clause.

If a public high school allows other student groups to meet, does a religious student group have a right to meet as well?

Yes. The Equal Access Act, 20 U.S.C. § 4071, makes it "unlawful for any public secondary school which receives Federal financial assistance and which has a limited open forum to deny equal access or a fair opportunity to, or discriminate against, any students who wish to conduct a meeting within that limited open forum on the basis of the religious, political, philosophical, or other content of the speech at such meetings."

May public schools excuse students to attend off-campus religious instruction during regular school hours?

Yes. The U.S. Supreme Court has upheld the discretionary practice of "release time" in which requesting students are allowed to attend periodic religious instruction sessions during regular school attendance hours at an off-campus location. In *McCollum v. Board of Education,* 333 U.S. 203 (1948), the U.S. Supreme Court struck down the practice of allowing clergymen to use public school classrooms for religious instruction of students during the school day. But in *Zorach v. Clauson,* 343 U.S. 306 (1952), the Court upheld a program that provided religious instruction to public school students during the school day in locations off of school property. The off-campus location may be, for example, a separate building not on school property or a van or other vehicle parked just off-campus. School officials, however, must remain neutral. Release time cannot be a pretext for endorsing or advancing any religion or religious group.

Is it lawful for public school teachers to meet with other teachers at the school before or after working hours for voluntary Bible study?

Yes. Peers may meet voluntarily. But there cannot be any element of state coercive authority related to religious activities in the public school. To avoid situations involving state power and religious coercion teachers cannot meet with students and administrators cannot meet with employees they supervise. Concerning teachers, administrators, and other school employees, the U.S. Department of Education's *Guidance on Constitutionally Protected Prayer in Public Elementary and Secondary Schools* states: "When acting in their official capacities as representatives of the state, teachers, school administrators, and other school employees are prohibited by the Establishment Clause from encouraging or discouraging prayer, and from actively participating in such activity with students. Teachers may, however, take part in religious activities where the overall context makes clear that they are not participating in their official capacities. Before school or during lunch, for example, teachers may meet with other teachers for prayer or Bible study to the same extent that they may engage in other conversation or non-religious activities."

Are public school teachers and administrators allowed to wear an unobtrusive symbol of their religious faith while on duty?

Yes. If the symbol is unobtrusive and would not cause a reasonable person to see the teacher as unlawfully coercing students or endorsing a particular religion as favored in the classroom. Reasonable persons generally do not see the wearing of an unobtrusive religious symbol, such as a small crucifix or Star of David necklace, as an attempt to religiously coerce students.

Are religious symbols allowed in the public school?

If the religious symbols belong to students and represent only the student's speech, then yes. But no if the religious symbols are reasonably viewed as school officials endorsing religion. Courts have consistently ruled that public school officials cannot display a copy of the Ten Commandments or other religious symbols in public schools. Nor can public school teachers lawfully display an obtrusive religious symbol, such as a crucifix on the teacher's desk or classroom wall, or Bible or scriptural display in the classroom. A teacher may carry a Bible for personal use but not for intentional display to students.

Are students allowed to include religious themes in their assignments?

Yes. The U.S. Department of Education's *Guidance on Constitutionally Protected Prayer in Public Elementary and Secondary Schools* states: "Students may express their beliefs about religion in homework, artwork, and other written and oral assignments free from discrimination based on the religious content of their submissions. Such home and classroom work should be judged by ordinary academic standards of substance and relevance and against other legitimate pedagogical concerns identified by the school."

How must public schools treat religious holidays?

School districts are commonly closed during religious holidays observed by the majority of students and faculty. These school closing policies recognize that the majority of students and faculty would not be present at these times and continued operation of the school would be inefficient. For students and teachers who practice minority faiths, however, school officials must provide reasonable accommodations for their free exercise of religion to avoid charges of religious discrimination. What accommodations are reasonable depends on the circumstances in each case. But a policy that clearly treated members of minority faiths unfairly in comparison to the treatment of the religious majority would constitute religious discrimination.

Are public schools allowed to include school sponsored prayers in graduation ceremonies?

No. In *Lee v. Weisman*, 505 U.S. 577 (1992), the U.S. Supreme Court ruled that public schools may not sponsor graduation prayers. In addressing "whether a religious exercise may be conducted at a graduation ceremony" the Court found in *Weisman* that: "No holding by this Court suggests that a school can persuade or compel a student to participate in a religious exercise. That is being done here, and it is forbidden by the Establishment Clause of the First Amendment."

What should I do if school officials refuse to respect religious freedom and the religious provisions of the U.S. Constitution's First Amendment?

Unfortunately, some public school teachers and coaches are ignorant of the law and the harms done to minority faith students through violations of religious rights. When possible, try to educate these persons. But if the violation is willful or is tolerated by school administrators or board members, contact the American Civil Liberties Union (ACLU); Americans United (AU); and/or the Freedom From Religion Foundation (FFRF) to report the violation. These organizations will keep your identity confidential. They will first try to persuade school officials to voluntarily respect the law and the equal rights of all persons. But if that fails, they will obtain an order from a federal court to force legal compliance in order to vindicate the rule of law and the equal rights of all persons. The law in this area is well-established and clear. Lawlessness by public school officials cannot be tolerated without endangering the rule of law and the equal rights of all persons. Willful violations may be punished with contempt sanctions and monetary judgments for violations of well-established law.

Essential Practice Skills

Church-state law and its application in public schools can be a complex and sometimes confusing area of practice. To help in better understanding the application of these complex legal principles the U.S. Department of Education's *Guidance on Constitutionally Protected Prayer in Public Elementary and Secondary Schools* (*see*, below) provides useful guidance on applying the First Amendment's religion clauses in public schools:

Constitutionally Protected Prayer in Public Elementary and Secondary Schools: U.S. Dept. of Education

Prayer During Non-instructional Time

Students may pray when not engaged in school activities or instruction, subject to the same rules designed to prevent material disruption of the educational program that are applied to other privately initiated expressive activities. Among other things, students may read their Bibles or other scriptures, say grace before meals, and pray or study religious materials with fellow students during recess, the lunch hour, or other non-instructional time to the same extent that they may engage in non-religious activities. While school authorities may impose rules of order and pedagogical restrictions on student activities, they may not discriminate against student prayer or religious speech in applying such rules and restrictions.

Organized Prayer Groups and Activities

Students may organize prayer groups, religious clubs, and "see you at the pole" gatherings before school to the same extent that students are permitted to organize other non-curricular student activities groups. Such groups must be given the same access to school facilities for assembling as is given to other non-curricular groups, without discrimination because of the religious content of their expression. School authorities possess substantial discretion concerning whether to permit the use of school media for student advertising or announcements regarding non-curricular activities. However, where student groups that meet for non-religious activities are permitted to advertise or announce their meeting--for example, by advertising in a student newspaper, making announcements on a student activities bulletin board or public address system, or handing out leaflets-- school authorities may not discriminate against groups who meet to pray. School authorities may disclaim sponsorship of non-curricular groups and events, provided they administer such disclaimers in a manner that neither favors nor disfavors groups that meet to engage in prayer or religious speech.

Teachers, Administrators, and other School Employees

When acting in their official capacities as representatives of the state, teachers, school administrators, and other school employees are prohibited by the Establishment Clause from encouraging or discouraging prayer, and from actively participating in such activity with students. Teachers may, however, take part in religious activities where the overall context makes clear that they are not participating in their official capacities. Before school or during lunch, for example, teachers may meet with other teachers for prayer or Bible study to the same extent that they may engage in other conversation or non-religious activities. Similarly, teachers may participate in their personal capacities in privately sponsored baccalaureate ceremonies.

Moments of Silence

If a school has a "minute of silence" or other quiet periods during the school day, students are free to pray silently, or not to pray, during these periods of time. Teachers and other school employees may neither encourage nor discourage students from praying during such time periods.

Accommodation of Prayer During Instructional Time

It has long been established that schools have the discretion to dismiss students to off-premises religious instruction, provided that schools do not encourage or discourage participation in such instruction or penalize students for attending or not attending. Similarly, schools may excuse students from class to remove a significant burden on their religious exercise, where doing so would not impose material burdens on other students. For example, it would be lawful for schools to excuse Muslim students briefly from class to enable them to fulfill their religious obligations to pray during Ramadan. Where school officials have a practice of excusing students from class on the basis of parents' requests for accommodation of non-religious needs, religiously motivated requests for excusal may not be accorded less favorable treatment. In addition, in some circumstances, based on federal or state constitutional law or pursuant to state statutes, schools may be required to make accommodations that relieve substantial burdens on students' religious exercise. Schools officials are therefore encouraged to consult with their attorneys regarding such obligations.

Religious Expression and Prayer in Class Assignments
Students may express their beliefs about religion in homework, artwork, and other written and oral assignments free from discrimination based on the religious content of their submissions. Such home and classroom work should be judged by ordinary academic standards of substance and relevance and against other legitimate pedagogical concerns identified by the school. Thus, if a teacher's assignment involves writing a poem, the work of a student who submits a poem in the form of a prayer (for example, a psalm) should be judged on the basis of academic standards (such as literary quality) and neither penalized nor rewarded on account of its religious content.

Student Assemblies and Extracurricular Events
Student speakers at student assemblies and extracurricular activities such as sporting events may not be selected on a basis that either favors or disfavors religious speech. Where student speakers are selected on the basis of genuinely neutral, evenhanded criteria and retain primary control over the content of their expression, that expression is not attributable to the school and therefore may not be restricted because of its religious (or anti-religious) content. By contrast, where school officials determine or substantially control the content of what is expressed, such speech is attributable to the school and may not include prayer or other specifically religious (or anti-religious) content. To avoid any mistaken perception that a school endorses student speech that is not in fact attributable to the school, school officials may make appropriate, neutral disclaimers to clarify that such speech (whether religious or non-religious) is the speaker's and not the school's.

Prayer at Graduation
School officials may not mandate or organize prayer at graduation or select speakers for such events in a manner that favors religious speech such as prayer. Where students or other private graduation speakers are selected on the basis of genuinely neutral, evenhanded criteria and retain primary control over the content of their expression, however, that expression is not attributable to the school and therefore may not be restricted because of its religious (or anti-religious) content. To avoid any mistaken perception that a school

endorses student or other private speech that is not in fact attributable to the school, school officials may make appropriate, neutral disclaimers to clarify that such speech (whether religious or non-religious) is the speaker's and not the school's.

Baccalaureate Ceremonies
School officials may not mandate or organize religious ceremonies. However, if a school makes its facilities and related services available to other private groups, it must make its facilities and services available on the same terms to organizers of privately sponsored religious baccalaureate ceremonies. In addition, a school may disclaim official endorsement of events sponsored by private groups, provided it does so in a manner that neither favors nor disfavors groups that meet to engage in prayer or religious speech.

* * * * *

Essential Practice Tips

Religious neutrality: If you are a government agent, practice religious neutrality in your professional duties, neither advancing nor inhibiting religion. In your private capacity religious faith and practice are your choice and right. But as a government official always be certain that no reasonable person could perceive you as using your official power to reward or punish on the basis of religious belief. This is especially important when there is a power relationship between you and the other person. For example, peers may ask other peers if they would like to visit their church, etc. When there is a power relationship (e.g., administrator/teacher; teacher/student; etc.) this may be seen as misusing positional authority to coerce religious compliance.

Separation of church and state: The church and the state must stay in their respective lanes to protect both. Respect the rights of all individuals and families to make their own decisions concerning matters of faith free from state interference through the public school. The public school belongs to all persons equally and not just to those in the religious majority. All private citizens, whether they are in the majority or a minority of one, have rights to pray or not pray as they choose free from any government coercion.

Free exercise: State officials should avoid placing persons in circumstance where they have to choose between what their religious faith requires and what the state requires. Whenever possible, seek to provide a reasonable accommodation for the free exercise of religion. A requested accommodation is not reasonable if it would result in health or safety dangers to others; unreasonable costs; unreasonable administrative burdens; or necessitate a fundamental alteration of legitimate program requirements. But in most instances religious believers are merely asking to be exempted or allowed an alternative assignment, costing the state little or nothing. As an outsider to a minority faith, you may not understand the individual's religious belief, or their religious requirements. But try to see the situation through their eyes and treat that person as you would like to be treated under similar circumstances. This is both the right thing to do, and the legally safe thing to do. Accommodate religious freedom when possible. If a reasonable accommodation has been provided there is no legitimate basis for a complaint or law suit.

Respect for religious diversity: Practice genuine respect for the sincerely held beliefs of all persons. Learn about the religious beliefs and practices of others, and teach children about the World's many faiths, their cultural differences, their common purposes, and how all persons of good faith (regardless of their religious faith) can live together in peace.

Essential Points:

- The key for government institutions in navigating the Establishment Clause is to maintain neutrality concerning religion, neither advancing nor inhibiting religion in a public institution.
- In a government institution there must be no favored or disfavored religions, and religion cannot be favored over non-religion.
- While acting in their official capacities public school employees are strictly prohibited from endorsing religion or in any manner coercing participation in religious activities.
- On duty public school employees may not lead or participate with students in prayers; display religious symbols or scripture on their desks or classroom walls; or in any manner encourage or discourage students concerning religion.
- Choices concerning religious instruction belong to students and their families. Public school employees have no legal right to interfere in private family choices concerning religion.
- Reasonable accommodations for the free exercise of religion must be provided to individuals, including excusals for religious holidays with a reasonable opportunity to complete any missed work.
- When public school facilities are made available to students or members of the public, these facilities must be made available to all

eligible persons and groups on an equal basis, regardless of religious faith and affiliation.

- Public school employees can be members of the clergy off-duty if they choose to, exercising full rights of religious freedom. But while acting in their official capacities all government employees must respect the equal rights of all persons in the public institution and not take sides on matters of religious faith.

Essential Terms:

Coercion test: Judicial test that asks whether government officials are using the power or prestige of the state to coerce belief or practice concerning religion. Government officials may not use the force of law or the threat of penalty to coerce belief or practice concerning religion. But more subtle forms of religious coercion are also prohibited including psychological coercion or social pressure. Consistent with the *Lemon* test, governmental neutrality toward religion is required.

Endorsement test: Judicial test that asks whether based on the totality of the circumstances a reasonable observer would conclude that government officials have taken sides on religion by unlawfully using government authority to endorse a particular religious view. Consistent with the *Lemon* test, the endorsement test requires governmental neutrality towards religion.

Equal Access Act: Generally codified free speech rights for student initiated meetings (*see*, 20 U.S.C. § 4071). School officials create a limited open forum by opening school sanctioned student initiated meetings to any non-curriculum related student group. When the Equal Access Act applies, school officials must open the door to all student groups equally, regardless of their religious, political, philosophical, or other viewpoints and beliefs.

Lemon test: From *Lemon v. Kurtzman*, 403 U.S. 602 (1971). A government action challenged as violating the Establishment Clause will be constitutionally valid only if government officials can establish a legitimate secular purpose; neutral effect; and no excessive entanglement between church and state.

Reasonable accommodation: Public school students and employees must be provided with reasonable accommodations for the free exercise of religion including days off for required religious observances and exemptions from activities that conflict with sincerely held religious beliefs. Accommodations are unreasonable and not required if they impose unreasonable financial or administrative burdens or safety risks.

Essential Cases:

Abington v. Schempp, 374 U.S. 203 (1963): The state required that each school day begin with readings from the Bible. Held: Public schools may not lawfully require Bible readings or lead students in reciting the "Lord's Prayer" etc.

Allegheny v. ACLU, 492 U.S. 573 (1989): Declared a religious holiday display on public property unconstitutional.

Edwards v. Aguillard, 482 U.S. 578 (1987): State support of "Creation-Science" programs unlawfully used the symbolic and financial support of government to achieve a religious purpose.

Engel v. Vitale, 370 U.S. 421 (1962): State officials composed a prayer to be said aloud each day by students in the presence of a teacher. Held: Public school officials may not lawfully compose prayers and direct students to repeat those prayers.

Good News Club v. Milford Central School, 533 U.S. 98 (2001): Concerning student clubs, public school officials may neither favor nor disfavor student religious speech and viewpoints.

Lamb's Chapel v. Center Moriches, 508 U.S. 384 (1993): Concerning use of public school facilities by outside groups, school officials may neither favor nor disfavor religious viewpoints or groups. Facilities must be made available to all groups on an equal basis.

Lee v. Weisman, 505 U.S. 577 (1992): Public school officials invited a member of the clergy to read an approved prayer at a graduation ceremony. Held: Public schools may not sponsor graduation prayers.

McCollum v. Board of Education, 333 U.S. 203 (1948): Allowing clergymen to use public school classrooms for religious instruction of students during the school day is unconstitutional.

Rosenberger v. Rector, 515 U.S. 819 (1995): A public university could not exclude a religious student group from public funding intended to support student speech.

Santa Fe v. Doe, 530 U.S. 290 (2000): Public schools may not directly or indirectly sponsor prayers at athletic events.

Stone v. Graham, 449 U.S. 39 (1980): A state statute requiring the display of the Ten Commandments on the wall of every public school classroom was unconstitutional.

Zorach v. Clauson, 343 U.S. 306 (1952): The Court upheld a discretionary program that provided voluntary private sponsored (no school sponsorship or endorsement) "release time" religious instruction to students during the school day in locations off of school property.

A Closer Look at the Law

Few issues generate more impassioned debate than public school sponsored prayer. These disputes are generally not, however, the result of ambiguity in the law. For over a half-century the U.S. Supreme Court has clearly and consistently held that the U.S. Constitution's Establishment Clause mandates religious neutrality by public school personnel when they are acting in their official capacities. This has been well-established law at least since *Engel v. Vitale* in 1962 ("the constitutional prohibition against laws respecting an establishment of religion must at least mean that in this country it is no part of the business of government to compose official prayers for any group of the American people to recite as a part of a religious program carried on by government . . . government in this country should stay out of the business of writing or sanctioning official prayers and leave that purely religious function to the people themselves and to those the people choose to look to for religious guidance"), and arguably *West Virginia v. Barnette* in 1943 ("If there is any fixed star in our constitutional constellation, it is that no official, high or petty, can prescribe what shall be orthodox in politics, nationalism, religion, or other matters of opinion or force citizens to confess by word or act their faith therein. If there are any circumstances which permit an exception, they do not now occur to us").

In the U.S. it is common knowledge that public school sponsored prayer is unlawful. Nonetheless, in public school classrooms, in locker rooms, and on athletic fields throughout the U.S. Bible belt and other scattered mostly rural areas in the U.S., public school teachers and coaches regularly violate this well-established law. It is difficult to believe they don't know the law, because many of these same people bitterly complain about the Court's church-state decisions claiming that "the Court took God out of our schools!" when in fact the Court's decisions only took religious control over other people's children away from public school employees.

Students may pray anytime they wish to in public schools. And the only limitation on school employees is that they cannot lawfully use their official positions to coerce those under their state authority into religious conformity through direct teacher/coach pressure or school orchestrated peer pressure. As the Court said in *Lee v. Weisman* "the government may no more use social pressure to enforce orthodoxy than it may use more direct means."

The U.S. Supreme Court has recognized that acts of religious coercion by school officials are not victimless events, creating serious risks of harm to minority faith students and their families. In *Santa Fe v. Doe*, 530 U.S. 290 (2000), the Court noted that students holding minority religious beliefs had been insulted, intimidated, and harassed, even by school officials, and that therefore: "The District Court permitted respondents (Does) to litigate anonymously to protect them from intimidation or harassment." The Court also noted "that many District officials apparently neither agreed with nor particularly respected" that decision, and continued to try to discover and expose the students involved as plaintiffs, a potentially dangerous act of witness intimidation, requiring a federal court to issue this order:

> Any further attempt on the part of District or school administration, officials, counselors, teachers, employees or servants of the School District, parents, students or anyone else, overtly or covertly to ferret out the identities of the Plaintiffs in this cause, by means of bogus petitions, questionnaires, individual interrogation, or downright 'snooping', will cease immediately. ANYONE TAKING ANY ACTION ON SCHOOL PROPERTY, DURING SCHOOL HOURS, OR WITH SCHOOL RESOURCES OR APPROVAL FOR PURPOSES OF ATTEMPTING TO ELICIT THE NAMES OR IDENTITIES OF THE PLAINTIFFS IN THIS CAUSE OF ACTION, BY OR ON BEHALF OF ANY OF THESE INDIVIDUALS, WILL FACE THE HARSHEST POSSIBLE CONTEMPT SANCTIONS FROM THIS COURT, AND MAY ADDITIONALLY FACE CRIMINAL LIABILITY. The Court wants these proceedings addressed on their merits, and not on the basis of intimidation or harassment of the participants on either side.

The law is clear: Public school officials may not lawfully use their official positions and state authority to advance their personal religious views. Nonetheless, legal violations continue. For example, in 2015, in open contempt for the law, a public school football coach in Georgia set up a make-shift baptismal pool with a plastic pond liner and a garden hose, and conducted a mass baptism of students on the public school football field. This particularly brazen constitutional violation was posted on Youtube with the caption: "Take a look and see how God is still in our schools!" a not so subtle jab at federal judicial mandates of religious neutrality in schools.

The Freedom From Religion Foundation (FFRF) responded with a letter demanding that public school officials respect the Constitution they swore to uphold as a condition of holding their public offices, and that the coach cease unlawful religious endorsement and coercion, stating: "Football players are at the mercy of their coach and want to please their coach, and when they are being corralled to come and attend a religious worship service to be dunked and baptized, how can anyone not realize that's coercive?"

Similar cases are all too common, and the vast majority of violations go unreported because of fear of retaliation. Fear of retaliation is a serious concern for minority faith families living in an aggressive proselytizing community. A 2006 case in Oklahoma, for example, *Smalkowski v. Hardesty*, started with a Jewish public high school student being coerced by a basketball coach to say the Lord's Prayer, but resulted in her father being physically attacked by the principal who then falsely charged both the father and the daughter with felony level crimes in a conspiracy with local law enforcement agents to discredit the family and force them out of the community. Smalkowski, the student's father, said this about the case:

> Though I worried about being sent away for five years on bogus charges, my dread was the Christian mob. They knew I must be found guilty in order to slow or stop the civil case being filed in Federal court. Since the start of my daughter's stand against the public schools disregard for the law of the land, it was imperative to run us out of the county to make any civil action non–valid . . . The courtroom was packed, for it is the Bible belt. There was no love in this courtroom. The loving Christians brought their children to hear the verdict. They brought the town. They brought ministers. I even saw another Judge in the back of the room . . . It was lies then, it was lies now and the DA knew it! People prayed openly for a conviction. Many holding their Bibles . . . Yet the so–called victim [the school principal], the 325 lb. victim, the ex–Marine, was nowhere to be found. Neither was the assistant district attorney to be found—whose vindictive, bogus case this was from the start . . . This is a place where children write on their schoolbooks, "The South will rise again!" That "black people caused slavery!" . . . Where religious fanaticism is fused with political rhetoric and political leaders pander to this madness. This place has a sickness, a malignant disease and it is spreading.

Smalkowski continued that despite "all their praying, lies, crooked cops, warning that justice better be done, packing the courthouse with their followers" the religiously motivated frame-up was obvious and the jury ultimately had to find Smalkowski not guilty. Smalkowski concluded:

> Our forefathers are on our side in this fight . . . From Adams to Madison to Jefferson and Paine they all knew the dangers of a Theocracy . . . within the federal courts we can protect this nation from a Theocracy. The wall between church and state must stand. But the wall is being battered and cracks now appear. The [fundamentalists] are at the gate attempting to breach the wall and send us down the road to an age of darkness and fear.

The anti-Semitic motivated harms done to the Smalkowski family, in the name of "righteous" school prayer, were shocking to the conscience and clearly unlawful. School officials ultimately settled out of court with the Smalkowski family for constitutional violations and other harms.

Incidents like the *Smalkowski* case are most likely to occur in areas historically dominated by fundamentalist groups but transitioning into more religiously diverse areas because of rapid demographic changes. In these cases school prayer has too often been "weaponized" in the local culture wars to rally locals against the "outsider" invaders "threatening our culture." Although presented as an act of religious piety the goal is to unify local forces against the outsiders and let the outsiders know who is still in control. Outsiders can either submit to the religious authority of the locals or leave.

As a nation of immigrants, many of whom fled to the U.S. to escape religious persecution, the U.S. has always been a religiously diverse nation. That religious diversity is rapidly increasing, even in the U.S. South, which has historically been dominated by Evangelical White Christians. Research by the Public Religion Research Institute (PRRI) in 2014 found that because of rapid demographic changes White Christians had become a minority in 19 U.S. states, including the Bible belt states of Georgia, Louisiana, and Texas. Research by PRRI in 2016 found that White Christians had become a minority in the U.S. population overall.

As demographers and sociologists so commonly note, demographics are destiny. It will become increasingly difficult for public school employees to continue to engage in unlawful religious proselytizing in public schools as the number of plaintiffs willing to challenge them continues to grow, and the numbers of community members willing to defend unlawful proselytizing declines. For more on this subject *see* the PRRI publication, Robert P. Jones, THE END OF WHITE CHRISTIAN AMERICA (2016).

As the U.S. Supreme Court's cases make clear, our nation's founders understood the necessity of protecting our religious freedoms from those who would attempt to use the power and prestige of our common government to push their personal religious views on everyone else. And also the necessity of preventing government officials from cynically using exaggerated piety and grandstanding public show-prayers for personal political gains, thereby defiling the true sacredness of sincere prayer.

Many mainline and progressive Christians argue that these fundamentalist "show-prayers" in public gatherings are a sacrilege that Jesus warned against in MATTHEW 6:5 stating "when you pray, do not be like the hypocrites, for they love to pray . . . on the street corners to be seen by others."

Concerning state sponsored religion in the U.S., in *Engel v. Vitale* (1962) our Highest Court declared "religion is too personal, too sacred, too holy, to permit its 'unhallowed perversion' by a civil magistrate." The civil magistrates the Court was referring to in that case were public school employees, establishing a clear legal command in a nation dedicated to religious freedom: *A license to teach in our public schools is not a license to preach in our public schools.*

Would those who currently support public school sponsored prayers and other forms of religious proselytizing by public school employees still support this conduct if it was not their prayers and beliefs being taught in the public school? Would they so enthusiastically defend public school teachers and coaches leading children in the Jewish Shema or the Islamic Al-Fatiha and attempting to convert children in public schools to Judaism or Islam? Do we find them zealously championing the equal rights of non-fundamentalist mainline and progressive Protestants, Catholics, Buddhists, and non-believers to use the public school to convert other people's children to their beliefs? Or do they only support public school sponsored religion when it is their favored beliefs being taught to other people's children?

Respecting everyone's religious freewill in public schools is the law, and it is right ethically and morally. Decisions concerning religious education, practice, and belief belong to families and the children themselves, and not to public school employees abusing their authority over other people's children.

Law & Professional Ethics in Practice:

Art. VI of the U.S. Constitution requires all agents of government, including public school educators, to swear or affirm they will respect the mandates of our Constitution. Those mandates include the religion clauses of the First Amendment and the constitutional commands of Art. III that: "The judicial power shall extend to all cases, in law and equity, arising under this Constitution" as recognized in *Marbury v. Madison*, 5 U.S. 137 (1803).

The law is clear: The U.S. Supreme Court interprets the Constitution, and the Court has interpreted the Establishment Clause as requiring religious neutrality in official capacities. This mandate reaches its zenith in public schools where the dangers of religious coercion are greatest.

Standards of professional ethics require, at a minimum, that professionals respect well-established law and their oaths of office to comply with the Constitution and laws. The law has been clear and well-established since *Barnette* (1943) and *Engel* (1962). There is no valid legal or professional ethical basis for using one's state authority to proselytize personal religious beliefs to other people's children. Do you agree? Or are there valid arguments for ignoring well-established law and professional ethics?

Parents seeking religious education can enroll their children in religious schools or supplement public education with religious instruction consistent with their beliefs. Educators who feel called to combine religion and teaching can work in religious schools. But do religious proselytizers have the right to extend their private religious mission into public funded schools and target other people's children? There are national organizations devoted to encouraging and supporting public educators' religious proselytizing in public schools. The right to join one of these groups is protected by the First Amendment (i.e. free speech/freedom of association). Nonetheless, religious coercion in practice remains unlawful and unethical. Is there a legal/ethical duty to report these willful church-state violations? Why or why not?

Questions for Further Exploration:

1) *Prohibited endorsement v. protected free exercise/free speech*: State endorsement of religion is prohibited. But private free exercise of religion and free speech are protected. In the continuum between prohibited state endorsement of religion and protected individual free exercise/free speech, where is the legal line? Under what circumstances is prayer at a football game prohibited as state establishment or protected as individual free exercise/free speech? Who can and cannot lawfully pray overtly at a public school sponsored athletic event?

2) *Official state religion*: Imagine that the U.S. Supreme Court reversed its decisions prohibiting compulsory participation in public school sponsored prayers. Your local school plans to require participation in daily prayers. But whose prayer will you pray? Will you take a vote and pray the prayers of the majority? How will those in the religious minority react to having their prayers excluded and their children compelled to say the majority's prayer? Can you compose a generic prayer that would offend no one? Would a generic prayer satisfy anyone? What about non-believers and

atheists? Do your perspectives on these questions depend on whether you are in the religious majority or the minority?

3) *Shock the monkey*: Two very different world-views form the foundations for the ongoing debate over the teaching of evolution in schools. And like most "culture war" issues, nearly everyone has already taken a side and they have no intention of changing their minds, making these discussions often less of a debate and more of an argument. Generally the only persons who haven't chosen a side (yet) are young children, which is why schools are the battle ground of choice for these issues. Although you may not agree with those holding opposing views on these issues: Do you fully understand what they believe? Do you understand why they believe this? Can we find a way to respectfully disagree and to peacefully co-exist? Can we teach principles of respectful disagreement and tolerance to all children, regardless of which side they may be on concerning these issues? Can we find common ground by recognizing the Bible as a tool for exploring the spiritual realm and science as a tool for exploring the physical realm, the Bible describing humanity's spiritual origins and science describing physical origins? Would this approach work in your school and community? Why or why not?

4) *Open forum*: What other related issues or current events would you like to discuss?

Suggested Activities for Further Learning:

1) Regardless of any of our individual opinions concerning religion, the reality is that religious beliefs are a driving force for billions of people, shaping their world views. And the choices they make based on religious beliefs shape our common world. But how much do religious believers actually know about the histories and religious doctrines of their own faiths? How much do they know about the religious histories and beliefs of others? Whatever your beliefs, learn more about the history and ideas that form the foundations of your belief system. Learn more about the different religious beliefs of colleagues and friends and talk with them about what you have learned. Useful resources for exploring religious beliefs can be found at www.beliefnet.com.

2) Read a book about religious beliefs, such as STEPHEN PROTHERO'S RELIGIOUS LITERACY: WHAT EVERY AMERICAN NEEDS TO KNOW--AND DOESN'T (2008). Discuss what you learned with colleagues and if appropriate look for ways to incorporate this knowledge into lessons for your children or students.

Chapter 4: First Amendment Freedoms and Speech

Freedom of belief and expression are fundamental human rights. Humans are unique in their abilities to think abstract thoughts, formulate complex systems of belief, and communicate these ideals through speech, writing, and other means of expressive communication. To deny these rights of belief and expression to individuals is to deny their rights to be fully human.

Free speech is our means of expressing our unique humanity and protecting our common interests. It is the essential means through which we protect our other rights. Free Speech is a necessary tool for expressing dissent and perpetuating and advancing democracy and the rule of law.

Public schools serve an important role in teaching the lessons of freedom of expression, citizenship, and democracy. If public schools are to act as the functional nurseries of an enduring democracy students' free speech rights must be protected, respected, and encouraged so that students may mature into citizens well prepared to actively discuss ideas; ask necessary questions; speak out on important public matters; vote wisely; and participate fully in a democratic society. We won't graduate citizens willing and able to fully participate in a free democracy from totalitarian run schools. Free societies have schools that teach the essential lessons of freedom including respect for the free speech rights of all persons.

Education, free speech, civility, and civic courage are the four pillars of democracy. Totalitarian regimes are only possible when the people are kept ignorant, silenced, divided, and fearful of speaking up and making their own decisions. A closed culture of retaliation, fear, and silence is a breeding ground for corruption. The broad protection of free speech is the best means of shining the light of truth into every corner of our common society to assure honesty and accountability. As Justice Brandeis said: "Sunlight is the best disinfectant."

To protect essential free speech rights, the general rule under the U.S. Constitution's First Amendment is that government cannot limit individual speech unless there is a compelling public necessity for the limitation. The scope of potential expression protected by the First Amendment is as broad as the universe of human thought and human ability to express those thoughts.

At the core of these rights are protections for religious and political speech. Philosophical, satirical, commercial, and an infinite variety of other types of expression are also protected. However, in the potential universe of protected expression, speech that is illegal, obscene, defaming, or in a non-public forum does not receive First Amendment protection.

In summary, the general rule under the First Amendment is that speech is protected, but the scope of protection necessarily involves balancing the rights of the individual with legitimate public needs. You cannot, for example, yell "fire" in a crowded theatre because of legitimate public safety concerns. Further, the Court recognizes some special exceptions to general First Amendment protections for free speech.

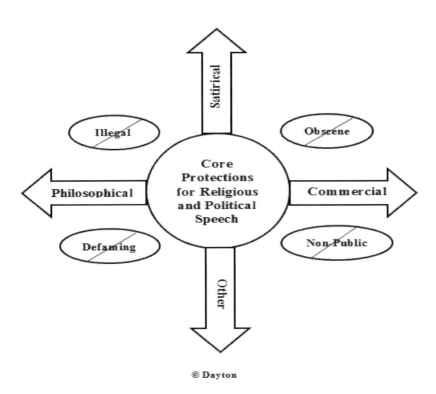

Potential Universe of Protected Speech

© Dayton

Speech that is unprotected:

a) Illegal or subversive speech, which can be controlled if it is:
    i) Directed towards inciting illegal or subversive action; and is
    ii) Likely to incite imminent lawless action (includes "fighting words" and "yelling fire in crowded theatre").
b) Obscene.
c) Defamatory.
d) Speech in a non-public forum (regulations must be reasonable in light of the purposes of the forum).

Student Speech Rights

In *Tinker v. Des Moines*, 393 U.S. 503 (1969), the Court declared:

> It can hardly be argued that either students or teachers shed their constitutional rights to freedom of speech or expression at the schoolhouse gate . . . In our system, state-operated schools may not be enclaves of totalitarianism. School officials do not possess absolute authority over their students. Students in school as well as out of school are "persons" under our Constitution. They are possessed of fundamental rights which the State must respect, just as they themselves must respect their obligations to the State. In our system, students may not be regarded as closed-circuit recipients of only that which the State chooses to communicate. They may not be confined to the expression of those sentiments that are officially approved. In the absence of a specific showing of constitutionally valid reasons to regulate their speech, students are entitled to freedom of expression of their views.

In harmonizing constitutional ideals with concrete operational realities the Court must strike a proper balance between essential individual freedoms and the legitimate needs of the public. Democracy is incompatible with both chaos and oppression. The school culture must be both free and orderly; both candid and civil. The Court has consistently recognized the authority and obligation of school officials to protect order and discipline in schools, while appropriately respecting free speech rights.

Concerning free speech in public schools the Court has distinguished between two different types of student expression: 1) Individual student expression; and 2) Public school sponsored student expression:

> 1) *Individual student expression* is speech not sponsored, controlled, or reasonably perceived as attributable to the school. The *Tinker* standard governs individual student speech. Tinker requires school officials to show through evidence of facts and circumstances that student expression would "materially and substantially interfere with the requirements of appropriate discipline in the operation of the school." Avoiding minor disruptions and discomforts are not sufficient justifications to limit individual expression.

> 2) *School sponsored expression* (e.g., school newspapers, forums, performances, etc.) that are sponsored, controlled, or reasonably perceived as attributable to the school. The *Fraser* (*Bethel v. Fraser*,

478 U.S. 675 (1986)) and *Hazelwood* (*Hazelwood v. Kuhlmeier*, 484 U.S. 260 (1988)) decisions govern school sponsored speech. School officials have broad discretion to control content where the expression is sponsored by the school. These limitations can be based on any legitimate educational rationale (e.g., age appropriateness; fit with the educational mission, etc.).

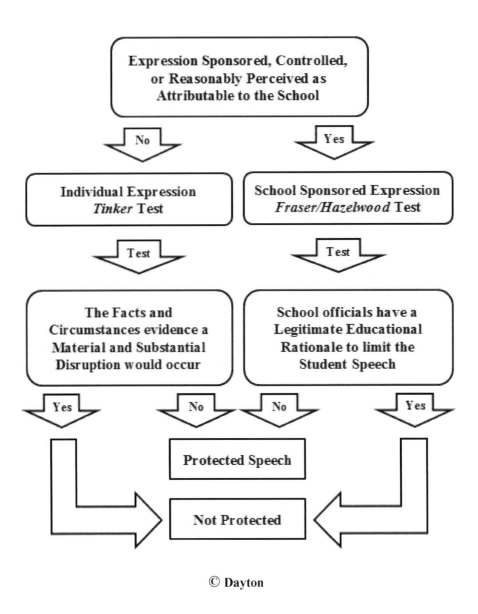

Student Speech: *Tinker & Fraser/Hazelwood* Tests

© Dayton

Employee Speech Rights

Generally, public employees have the same free speech rights as all citizens. If public school officials wish to sanction speech by school employees, including dismissal or other employment sanctions, school officials must be prepared to show that the speech negatively impacted the employment relationship, and that the speech was unprotected in the context. The *Pickering* test, from *Pickering v. Board of Education*, 391 U.S. 563 (1968), is used to distinguish between protected and unprotected speech by public employees:

> *Pickering test*: To determine whether speech is protected, courts generally balance the employee's speech rights against the employer's legitimate interests in efficient operation of the public institution. Questions considered in this balance include:
>
> 1) *Was the speech related to a legitimate matter of public concern?* Speech regarding legitimate public concerns (i.e., issues relevant to citizens) generally receives First Amendment protection.
>
> 2) *Was the speech true?* True statements receive more protection than false statements.
>
> > Note: Even if the speech is true, courts will also consider public officials' legitimate needs for: 1) Regular close contact and a working relationship of loyalty and trust with the speaker; 2) Appropriate office discipline; and 3) Harmony among co-workers.
>
> 3) *If false, was the false statement merely negligently made by the public employee?* False statements made only negligently may still receive First Amendment protection.

PURPOSELY
KNOWINGLY
RECKLESSLY
-----*Pickering Line*-----
NEGLIGENTLY

Note: Courts will also consider whether the false statements interfere with the performance of duties or the regular operations of the institution.

In "mixed motive" cases (there is both a legitimate basis for termination and a legitimate controversy over free speech) if a teacher merits termination independent of a subsequent free speech controversy, school officials do not have to continue the employment of an otherwise unfit teacher.

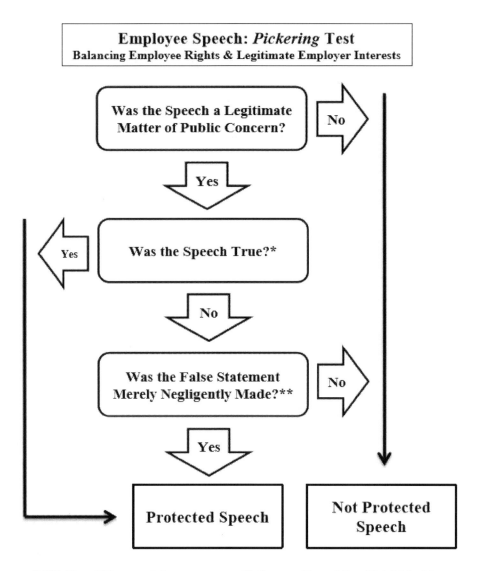

Employee Speech: *Pickering* **Test**
Balancing Employee Rights & Legitimate Employer Interests

Was the Speech a Legitimate Matter of Public Concern?

No

Yes

Was the Speech True?*

Yes

No

Was the False Statement Merely Negligently Made?**

No

Yes

Protected Speech

Not Protected Speech

* *N.B*: Even if the speech is true, courts will also consider public officials' legitimate needs for: 1) Regular close contact and a working relationship of loyalty and trust with the speaker; 2) Appropriate office discipline; and 3) Harmony among co-workers.
** *N.B*: Courts will also consider whether the false statements interfere with the performance of duties or the regular operations of the institution.

© Dayton

Lawful Limitations on Speech

The Court recognizes some universal exceptions to First Amendment protections, and these limitations are always available to government officials:

> a) Government officials can always apply reasonable time, place, and manner (TPM) restrictions on speech. TPM restrictions are held reasonable if they are:
> > i) Content neutral;
> > ii) Narrowly tailored to serve a significant governmental interest; and
> > iii) Leave open an adequate alternative channel of communication.
>
> b) Government officials can always limit free speech by establishing a compelling governmental interest for the intrusion on freedom of expression, and that no less restrictive alternative exists.

Reasonable Time, Place, and Manner (TPM) regulations are an important administrative tool for both respecting First Amendment rights and avoiding unwarranted disruptions or safety hazards. TPM restrictions are lawful when they are: 1) Content neutral (i.e., they focus on the TPM of the speech and not the content); 2) Narrowly tailored to serve a significant governmental interest (i.e., avoiding unwarranted disruptions; safety hazards; etc.); and 3) The alternative TPM leaves open an adequate alternative channel of communication for otherwise protected speech (i.e., allows speech in an alternative TPM).

For example, instead of protesting when buses are unloading (Time), blocking the main entrance way (Place), and using bullhorns (Manner) that are likely to frighten children and hurt their ears, protesters can be asked to move to a still visible side area and not use (or turn down) amplification to reasonable levels that do not cause undue disruption or safety concerns.

When fairly and effectively used by school officials reasonable time, place, and manner (TPM) restrictions can help to assure appropriate discipline and avoid disruptions in the operation of the educational mission while not discriminating based on the perspective of the speakers and leaving open other appropriate channels for them to communicate without disrupting the school. TPM regulations should not, however, be manipulated by school officials to discriminate based on the speaker's political message or point of view, as if challenged, a reviewing court will quickly see through any pretextual use of TPM regulations to in fact limit non-preferred speech.

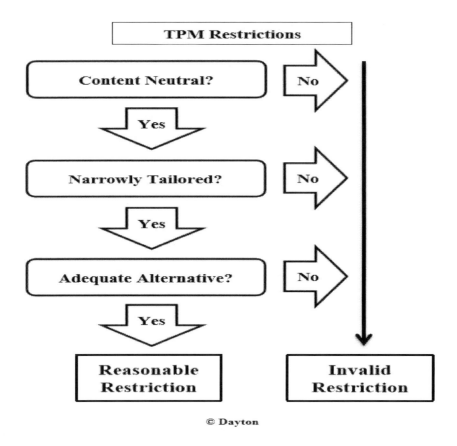

© Dayton

Essential Questions & Answers

Why should people who say offensive things have free speech protections?

As Justice Oliver Wendell Holmes, Jr., famously said concerning our First Amendment in *United States v. Schwimmer*, 279 U.S. 644 (1929) "it is the principle of free thought--not free thought for those who agree with us but freedom for the thought that we hate." If we can silence the speech of those we disagree with, those who disagree with us may be able to silence our speech as well. The price of protecting free speech for everyone is that we have to tolerate the free speech of others, even when we may find their speech offensive. We may, of course, use our own speech to express our objections to offensive speech. In a democracy the remedy for objectionable speech is more speech in response. But it is speech to point out error and not to silence the voices of others. Not all speech is protected under the First Amendment. But mere offense is not a lawful reason for silencing speech. Speech of any real importance is likely to offend someone.

What do public school officials have to prove to limit student speech?

According to the Court in *Tinker*, in cases involving individual student speech school officials may only limit the speech if they can establish it would "materially and substantially interfere with the requirements of appropriate discipline in the operation of the school." And "where there is no finding and no showing that engaging in the forbidden conduct" meets this standard "the prohibition cannot be sustained." To justify limiting individual student speech, school officials must show more than a desire to avoid the unpleasantness, discomfort, or minor arguments and disturbances that normally occur with the expression of unpopular views. Further, mere speculation or an abstract, undifferentiated fear of disruption will not suffice. When challenged, school officials must be able to articulate facts and circumstances that would convince a reasonable person that a material and substantial interference is likely to result if the speech is not limited.

What do school officials have to show to limit student speech in school sponsored forums?

Although the *Tinker* standard offers students engaged in individual speech significant protections against censorship by school officials, courts have granted school officials significant authority to control school sponsored speech. In a school sponsored forum school officials need only show that there was a legitimate educational rationale for limiting the speech (e.g., the speech was age-inappropriate; inconsistent with the school's basic educational mission; etc.). This *Fraser/Hazelwood* burden of proof (i.e., a legitimate educational rationale) for school sponsored speech is much easier for school officials to prove than the *Tinker* standard (i.e., a material and substantial interference) for individual student speech, giving school officials much broader control in a school sponsored forum.

What constitutes a "school sponsored forum" subject to greater control by school officials?

School sponsored forums include school convocations, performances, athletic events, school newspapers, and other expressive activities that students, parents, and other members of the public would reasonably perceive as bearing the "imprimatur of the school" even if they are not in fact school sponsored. If, for example, students do not wish to be subject to school authority in their publications they should not use the school's name or logo. And they should clarify that their publication is strictly private, with no school sponsorship, and that the publication includes only their own individual speech for which the students and not school officials are fully responsibility.

Can school officials prohibit students from expressing dissent at school events, such as "taking a knee" in protest during the national anthem?

No. The Court's decisions in both *Tinker* and *Barnette* deny school officials any lawful right to punish peaceful non-disruptive political dissent by students. As the Court said in *Tinker* students do not "shed their constitutional rights to freedom of speech or expression at the schoolhouse gate" and in *Barnett* "no official, high or petty, can prescribe what shall be orthodox in politics, nationalism, religion, or other matters of opinion or force citizens to confess by word or act their faith therein." Students may be punished for any legitimate violation of the student code of conduct, but not merely for expressing political dissent. Protecting the right to political dissent is a core purpose of the First Amendment.

Can school officials remove books from the library based on political or religious objections from the community or school board members?

No. Under the U.S. Supreme Court's decision in *Board of Education v. Pico*, 457 U.S. 853 (1982), once library materials have been officially placed in the library by school officials, whether the removal of library materials is lawful depends on the motivation for the removal. In using state power to censor, decisions cannot be motivated by partisan politics, religion, or any other improper personal bias. Books and other materials can be removed for legitimate educational reasons, e.g., a subsequent discovery that the library media contained vulgar materials; was not age appropriate; or other legitimate findings concerning the library material's educational value. Materials cannot be removed based on the political or religious views of individuals or groups. No reason is required, however, for simply declining to add materials to the school library, and materials may be removed for legitimate custodial reasons (e.g., damaged; outdated; etc.).

Can school officials lawfully prohibit the display of gang symbols in schools?

Yes. Gang symbols cloaked as free speech in schools are not protected under the First Amendment. School officials have a compelling interest in keeping gang-related crime and violence out of schools. School officials must, however, reasonably distinguish between gang-related uses of symbols and sincere religious expression. For example, while wearing a crucifix or a

Star of David is not protected speech when the clear purpose of the symbol is gang-related, observance of sincerely held religious beliefs is protected speech and protected free exercise of religion. In most cases, however, it is not difficult for school officials to distinguish between who is wearing the symbol because of gang-related activity and who is engaged in sincere, constitutionally protected free exercise of religion.

Can a public school teacher be fired for making a false statement about a school official on an issue of public concern if the false statement was an honest mistake?

No. A false statement on a matter of legitimate public concern made merely negligently is within the protections of the First Amendment. It is in the public interest to encourage government employees to address matters of legitimate public concern. However, false statements made recklessly, knowingly, or purposely by public employees are not protected. In *Pickering*, the Court determined that culpability greater than mere negligence was generally required before public officials could lawfully sanction false statements by employees on matters of legitimate public concern. To make a false statement "negligently" means that the speaker merely failed to use ordinary care in determining whether the statement was true. To make a false statement "recklessly" means that the speaker engaged in reckless disregard for the truth; "knowingly" means that the speaker knew the statement was false but made it anyway; and "purposely" is to make a statement known to be false for the purpose of inflicting harm.

Can public school educators be fired for belonging to political groups?

No, generally. Educators enjoy the same freedoms as all other citizens to participate in political parties, unions, professional associations, etc. Educators commonly belong to unions or professional education associations, and the state must respect their rights of freedom of association. Teachers generally cannot be required to disclose their private associations to state officials. These activities are outside of the jurisdiction of school officials unless it can be shown that they negatively affect job performance or fitness for duties. For example, membership in controversial but lawful, non-violent political groups are protected associations. But membership in a group that practices or advocates unlawful conduct, or that endangers children or the school community could be subject to employment action.

Essential Practice Skills

Powerful ideas have a viral nature spreading from one mind to another through effective communication. As Chris Anderson said in TED TALKS (2016): "Your number-one mission as a speaker is to take something that matters deeply to you and to rebuild it inside the minds of your listeners." When people's thoughts change, our collective reality begins to change.

You have free speech rights, but that does not guarantee effective communication of your ideas. Becoming a more effective communicator enhances your ability to help others and to improve our world. The following are practical suggestions for improving your presentation skills:

Know your audience

Learn what you reasonable can about your audience in advance so that you can plan a presentation that is a good fit for the needs of the audience. How many people can you expect? A presentation for a small group should be more intimate and informal than for a very large group. What is the group's knowledge level on the subject? You don't want to bore a knowledgeable group with basics or lose beginners with advanced details. What does this group need to learn about the subject? The closer your presentation fits with the intended audience's needs the more successful your presentation will be.

Plan a clear and concise presentation

Keep it simple and brief. In general, your presentation should not exceed 15-20 minutes (i.e., the normal limits for an adult attention span) before opening the floor for questions. If necessary break longer presentations into multiple shorter sections, giving the audience a chance to refresh and refocus between topics. Refer your audience to written works for further details.

Focus on your core message throughout the presentation. What do you really want the audience to understanding after the presentation? Repetition of your core message is essential. Plan to communicate your core message three times: Tell the audience what you are going to explain; explain it; and then summarize what you explained. Each time it is repeated (with appropriate variations) your core message will be clearer to the audience.

If you do not need visual aids to communicate your message don't use them. A speaker standing solo on the stage communicating person-to-person with the audience can result in a powerful presentation. If your message is clear and personal speak directly to the people without any distractions.

When it is necessary to communicate large amounts of information, however, a picture can truly be worth a thousand words. Use clear and simple charts, graphs, and other helpful visual aids to communicate data and trends, focusing on visually highlighting main points. Make the complete data available in a separate document rather than cluttering the visual aid.

If you plan to use visual aids, e.g., Powerpoint, etc., make your presentation materials as clear and concise as possible, generally 12 slides or less. Use short, concise text in large clear fonts. The text in slides should only be used to emphasize main points. Use the speaker notes feature for more detailed points you want to remember to convey for each slide.

Preview your entire presentation attempting to see it through the eyes of an audience member. Are all materials as clear and concise as possible? Is the presentation inviting and interesting to an audience member?

Prepare and practice the presentation

Prepare a presentation that is appropriate for the situation, and then practice it to improve your communication. There are two basic types of presentations: The prepared speech; and the spontaneous talk. Both styles have advantages and disadvantages and are appropriate for different settings. The prepared speech is safer and more likely to be thorough and accurate; but it can sound recited and boring. The spontaneous talk generally sounds fresher and facilitates audience connections; but it can be more risky (e.g., drawing a blank; forgetting to cover important points; inaccuracies; etc.).

To maximize success think of these two very different styles as extreme polar opposite ends of a continuum of presentation styles. Select your presentation style along this continuum based on your circumstances. Short technical presentations to large audiences; recorded presentations; etc., call for a more scripted approach (but not just robotically reading a script). Longer informal presentations to smaller groups call for a more informal approach (but not just speaking off the top of your head).

In preparing for your presentation remember that simple is better. Make your message as easy as possible to understand and as engaging to the audience as possible. You want to draw them into your thoughts and open their minds to the ideas you are communicating.

No one has unlimited time, but you can never be over prepared. Use the time you have wisely to prepare and practice, improving your presentation as you go. Whether the prepared materials are a full written text or just a basic outline go into every presentation knowing exactly what you want to communicate and how you need to do it. A clear, impactful, easy flowing presentation is always the result of good preparation and practice.

Presentation anxiety is normal and can be useful as a motivating force for thorough preparation. But if presentation anxiety is causing you undue stress or interfering with your presentation, you need to mitigate any excessive presentation anxiety. Step one is recognizing that the root causes of presentation anxiety are fear of the unknown and fear of negative judgment.

To mitigate fear of the unknown be well prepared and arrive early. You will know exactly what you need to do and you will be well prepared to do it. You will have avoided late arrival stress; you can become comfortable with the presentation room; make sure everything is ready; and greet participants as they arrive, changing most unknowns into knowns.

To mitigate the fear of negative judgments focus on serving the needs of participants and not on your own performance. Your audience cares about useful, accurate information, not your ego. That must be your focus too. You are there to help participants learn about your subject, not to be judged. Further, something as complex as a presentation cannot be reduced to simple failure/success. Every presentation has both successful and less than successful moments. To improve, learn the lessons of every experience.

Accept your imperfections and strive for improvement not perfection. Success is meeting the needs of your audience whether or not you receive rounds of applause. Be professional and gracious no matter what anyone else does or says and stay focused on your mission: Providing a useful and engaging presentation for your audience.

In the event you encounter a detractor or heckler (a common fear underlying presentation anxiety), just focus on doing your job. Stay firmly in the moral high ground. Never embarrass anyone, even if they invite it. A snappy comeback may feel good at the moment, but it will only distract from your presentation and lower you to the level of the heckler. In the longer run, you will never regret taking the moral high road and maintaining your professional composure even when that requires great patience.

Do not, however, allow anyone to hijack your presentation. If anyone attempts to monopolize your limited presentation time politely inform them you will be happy to continue the conversation after your presentation, but you have limited time and others want to see your presentation.

If someone asks a poor question simply thank them for the question and then tactfully rephrase it as a better question and response for the audience. If someone points out a legitimate error, thank that person and respectfully correct your error. Not having to be perfect greatly reduces anxiety.

You will gain trust and respect from an audience if they see that you always welcome the truth from any source and that you have no fear of admitting your imperfections and correcting any errors. If you make an error on something that matters, simply acknowledge the error and correct it or promise to follow up with the correct information. Otherwise, move on and learn from any errors for the next presentation.

Connect with your audience

The most important factor in connecting with your audience is to be genuinely enthusiastic about your topic and about helping your audience to learn more about it. Enthusiasm, or its absence, is obvious in a presentation.

Connect with your audience before, during, and after the presentation. Informally meet audience participants prior to your presentation and try to get a better understanding of their needs and interests. During the presentation make friendly eye contact with audience members, call people by name if you can, and whenever possible talk with audience members after the presentation to follow up on any questions.

Speak clearly, slowly, and in full voice. If your presentation isn't heard and understand it cannot be successful. Take your subject seriously, but don't take yourself too seriously. Usefully employ humor, current events, personal experiences, anecdotes, etc. to personalize and humanize your presentation. People want to engage with real and approachable people.

Be certain that you always leave open adequate time and opportunities for members of the audience to ask questions and to actively engage in the presentation. People most enjoy a presentation in which they were personally engaged and not just passive observers.

Final preparation for your presentation

Dress professionally and present yourself in a confident and friendly manner. First impressions are lasting. If you make a good first impression people will ignore a few less than perfect moments. As noted above, arrive early whenever possible to give you a safety buffer against unexpected delays. Preview your materials one last time just prior to the presentation so that the materials will be fresh in your mind and easy to recall as needed.

And finally, get excited about having the opportunity to talk with people about something that really matters to you. You have a chance to make a difference. Relax, and get focused on making a difference through a fun and engaging presentation of your ideas. For further information *see*: Chris Anderson, TED TALKS: THE OFFICIAL GUIDE TO PUBLIC SPEAKING (2016).

Essential Practice Tips

1) *Free speech and symbolic expression*: Individual expression through speech and symbolic communication is an essential part of being human. Trying to stop people from expressing themselves is like squeezing a handful of sand: The harder you squeeze, the faster it flows through your fingers. As a leader, don't squeeze any harder than you have to. Maintain proper order and discipline when necessary, but do so in a fair, respectful, and balanced way. Welcome the honest expression of all opinions. But build shared cultural expectations that require everyone to express their opinions in an appropriate and respectful time, place, and manner.

2) *Controversy and conflict:* Controversy is inevitable, but it can be destructive or constructive. Learn to steer controversy in healthier directions as creative tension that moves people toward positive change. Steer conversations toward a focus on the real core problems and not just the personalities; towards shared problem solving and not just blaming others. Rarely is a serious problem solely attributable to the actions of a single person or group. More commonly we all bear some responsibility for the problem, either through action or inaction. While blaming one person or group is easy, actually solving problems takes everyone's cooperation. When someone comes to you with a controversy, conflict, or other problem, generally, it is helpful to ask them what they can do to help in implementing a positive solution, empowering them to help themselves as well.

3) *Civility*: Cultural norms are generally learned through role models in the community. Be the role model for civility in your community. Learn to stay above the fray, and to maintain your perspective and not "take the bait" when provoked. No matter what the other person says, respond calmly, professionally, and respectfully. Take a deep breath before responding when necessary. You can speak firmly and resolutely in making your point while still modeling civility. Dishing back the same abusive treatment you received may be tempting in the moment. But it also lowers you to the level of the abuser. In the longer run you will never regret taking the moral and professional high road in your interactions with others. You can become the model of civility in your institution, positively changing the culture in your community and teaching others invaluable lessons about the real power of civility. The wise person knows that ultimately every struggle is about winning hearts and minds. You are not just trying to win arguments: You are trying to win the respect and long-term support of everyone for ideas and policies that will move the school and community forward.

4) *Redress of grievances*: Learn to listen to others. What most people really want is to be heard. They can often accept not getting what they wanted, if they feel they have been respectfully heard and treated fairly. Try to really hear what the other person is telling you, and attempt to demonstrate to them that you see their perspective, even if you do not agree.

5) *TPM restrictions*: Effectively use reasonable time, place, and manner (TPM) restrictions to avoid disruptions in the operation of the school while not discriminating based on the perspective of the speakers.

Essential Points:

- The First Amendment generally prohibits content-based censorship, with political and religious viewpoints receiving the greatest protections, commercial speech receiving less rigorous protection, and obscenity falling outside of the scope of constitutional protection.
- The Court recognizes some universal exceptions to First Amendment protection, and these limitations are always available to government officials: TPM restrictions and establishing a compelling interest.
- Concerning free speech in public schools the Court has distinguished between two different types of student expression: a) Individual student expression; and b) Public school sponsored expression.
- *Individual student expression* is speech not sponsored, controlled, or reasonably perceived as attributable to the school. The *Tinker* standard governs individual student speech. School officials must show through evidence of facts and circumstances that student expression would "materially and substantially interfere with the requirements of appropriate discipline in the operation of the school." Avoiding minor disruptions, discomforts, and unpleasantness are not sufficient justifications to limit individual expression.
- *School sponsored expression* (e.g., school newspapers, forums, performances, etc.) that are sponsored, controlled, or reasonably perceived as attributable to the school. The *Fraser* and *Hazelwood* decisions govern school sponsored speech. School officials have wide discretion to control content where the expression is sponsored by the school. Limitations can be based on any legitimate educational rationale (e.g., age appropriateness; fit with the educational mission, etc.).
- If school officials open the door to any non-curriculum related student group, then meetings during non-instructional time are governed by the Equal Access Act, 20 U.S.C. § 4071, which prohibits

discrimination on the "basis of the religious, political, philosophical, or other content of the speech at such meetings."

- Free speech in the school related cyber-world is governed by the same general legal principles that apply to the physical-world, with *Tinker* regulating individual student speech and *Fraser* and *Hazelwood* governing student speech in school sponsored electronic forums. The problem of jurisdiction in the cyber-world presents some unique challenges. In the cyber-world "on-campus" general means school controlled media (or use of any media while physically at school), and "off-campus" is the use of purely private media while not under the physical jurisdiction of the school.

- Generally, public employees have the same free speech rights as all citizens. If public school officials wish to sanction speech by school employees, including dismissal or other employment sanctions, school officials must be prepared to show that the speech negatively impacted the employment relationship, and that the speech was unprotected in the context. The *Pickering* test is used to distinguish between protected and unprotected speech by public employees. In "mixed motive" cases if a teacher merits termination independent of a subsequent free speech controversy, school officials do not have to continue the employment of an unfit teacher.

- Educators have rights to freedom of association and generally cannot be required to disclose their private associations to state officials. These activities are outside of the jurisdiction of school officials unless it can be shown that they negatively affect job performance or fitness for duties.

Essential Terms

Equal Access Act: The Equal Access Act, 20 U.S.C. § 4071, prohibits discrimination based on the "religious, political, philosophical, or other content" of speech at school sanctioned student initiated meetings. The Act applies when school officials subject to the Act create a limited open forum by allowing non-curriculum related student groups to meet.

Forum analysis: Determining the type of forum determines the scope of protected speech in that forum: *Open forum* (traditionally places of open public communication such as public streets, parks, etc. Government can only limit speech with reasonable TPM regulations or by establishing a compelling interest). *Limited open forum* (may be limited to designated groups, e.g., students; teachers; etc., and topics, e.g., age appropriate topics for students, announced agenda items, etc. Limitations may be based on reasonable TPM regulations in the context of the more limited forum or by establishing a compelling interest). *Closed forum* (not generally open for public speech, e.g., military facilities; prisons; meetings in lawful executive session, etc. Restrictions are upheld unless unreasonable or clearly aimed at suppressing a particular viewpoint).

School sponsored speech: Speech reasonably perceived as attributable to the school, even if not in fact school sponsored.

Student sponsored speech: Speech reasonably perceived as attributable to students acting as private citizens and not representing the school.

TPM regulations: Reasonable Time, Place, or Manner (TPM) regulations on otherwise protected speech, to regulate but not prohibit speech.

Essential Cases:

Bethel School District v. Fraser, 478 U.S. 675 (1986): A high school student intentionally presented a sexually suggestive "campaign speech" aimed more at humor than legitimate political speech. Held: School officials may lawfully impose sanctions on students engaged in lewd and indecent speech in a school sponsored forum.

Board of Education v. Pico, 457 U.S. 853 (1982): School officials have broad discretion in the acquisition of library materials, but the removal of library materials cannot be motivated by narrow partisan politics, religion, or other improper personal bias. Books and other materials may be removed for legitimate educational (e.g., age inappropriate content; indecent content; etc.) or custodial reasons (e.g., outdated, damaged, etc.).

Hazelwood School District v. Kuhlmeier, 484 U.S. 260 (1988): School officials sought to exclude certain controversial stories from the school sponsored newspaper. Held: In public school sponsored forums school officials need only establish "legitimate pedagogical concerns", i.e., there was a "legitimate educational rationale" for limiting student speech. School sponsored forums include school convocations, performances, athletic events, school newspapers, and other expressive activities that students, parents, and other members of the public would reasonably perceive as bearing the "imprimatur of the school" even if they are not in fact school sponsored.

Pickering v. Board of Education, 391 U.S. 563 (1968): School officials sought to take disciplinary action against a teacher who wrote a negative letter to the local newspaper about school issues. Held: Teachers have a First Amendment right to publicly comment on legitimate matters of public concern and "absent proof of false statements knowingly or recklessly made by him, a teacher's exercise of his right to speak on issues of public importance may not furnish the basis for his dismissal from public employment."

Tinker v. Des Moines, 393 U.S. 503 (1969): Mary Beth Tinker was punished by public school officials for wearing a black armband protesting against war. Held: In cases involving student political speech school officials may only limit this speech if they can establish it would "materially and substantially interfere with the requirements of appropriate discipline in the operation of the school" and "where there is no finding and no showing that engaging in the forbidden conduct" meets this standard punishments violate students' free speech rights and "cannot be sustained."

A Closer Look at the Law

Mary Beth Tinker, the plaintiff in the leading case on free speech in schools, *Tinker v. Des Moines*, was born into a family devoted to the "Social Gospel" of promoting human equality and social justice not just in theory but in practice. At age 13 she famously wore a black armband to school silently protesting against war and was suspended for her political expression. For a closer look at the events associated with *Tinker*, here is Mary Beth in her own words, from: Mary Beth Tinker, *Foreword: Free Speech in Public Educational Institutions*, Vol. 2 of the *Education Law & Policy Review*, a special issue on free speech available free online at www.edlawcon.org:

"In 1965, my brother John and I, along with Christopher Eckhardt and several other students in Des Moines, Iowa were suspended from school for wearing black armbands. We weren't experts on the Constitution. We were just sad about the Vietnam War. The message of our armbands was to mourn for the dead on both sides of the war, and to support a Christmas truce . . . When we wore our armbands to school we had no idea that we would make history . . . The road to the U.S. Supreme Court for my family and I began with our experiences during the Cold War and the Civil Rights Movement, and from there it was a fluke of history that we, and not some other students, ended up at the Supreme Court for the simple offense of expressing ourselves . . .

At school, things were not so heartwarming. We prepared for nuclear war by diving under our desks at the sound of an alarm, while air raid shelters popped up all over town. I wondered what Strontium 90 fallout was, and what would happen to us when we drank it along with our milk. My brothers and sisters and I kept hoping that the adults of the world had things under control, but my parents and others didn't seem convinced . . .

By Christmastime, the TV news was more and more about Vietnam--the burning huts, the body bags and caskets, and the body counts. About 1,000 U.S. soldiers had been killed by November, when my mother and brother, John, attended a march against the war in Washington D.C., along with Chris Eckhardt and his mother. Returning to Iowa, they talked about supporting Senator Robert Kennedy's call for a Christmas truce. They heard of the idea of wearing black armbands, possibly from a Quaker . . . Students in the Unitarian youth group became interested . . .

On December 14, 1965 our local school administrators announced a ban on black armbands. Now, I was torn about what to do. I didn't want to jeopardize my status as a "top student," but I remembered the popular saying "Eichmann only followed orders" referring to the Nazis. I thought of my parents, the Birmingham children, and the people in Ruleville [historic Civil Rights location]. Finally, I decided I would take a stand and wear the armband, along with Paul and Hope, our family friend Chris Eckhardt and several other students. John decided to try and reason with the administrators first.

At school, almost no one commented on my armband except some boys who teased me. But they always teased me. When I got to math class, though, my teacher, Mr. Moberly, was waiting with a pink slip directing me to the office. There, Mrs. Tarmann, the Girls' Adviser, asked me to take off the armband. I had been so nervous all day, but now, I looked at Mrs. Tarmann and took off my armband. I was suspended anyway, and walked home, full of apprehension about my controversial action.

At Roosevelt [High School], Chris Eckhardt was suspended after threats from students, a teacher, and an administrator, who asked if he wanted a busted nose. To my surprise, that evening the local media took an interest in our story. When the School Board President said that it was a trivial matter, John decided to wear an armband the next day, and was suspended as well. Five students were suspended, but not my siblings, Paul or Hope, whose elementary teacher instead taught a lesson on the Bill of Rights.

We received considerable support in Des Moines, but we were despised by others who accused us of being unpatriotic or Communists. Red paint was thrown at our house, and postcards with hammers and sickles came, saying: "Go back to China or Russia." A radio host threatened my dad on the air. On Christmas Eve . . . a bomb threat. A woman on the phone said she was going to kill me.

We thought this was nothing compared to what Blacks in the south were facing, or the Vietnamese and soldiers. Life went on. In 1967, the Lovings [*Loving v. Virginia*, 388 U.S. 1 (1967)] won their case for interracial marriage. The same year, Martin Luther King made a speech against the war, and was killed soon after, in 1968. Racial tensions escalated, as well as anti-war sentiment.

In November of 1968, when I was in 11th grade, we moved to St. Louis. Soon, we traveled to Washington, D.C. for the oral arguments in our case, now before the U.S. Supreme Court. Still shy, and now preoccupied with adjusting to a new school, I barely heard the arguments.

Several months later, I was surprised to hear that we had won by 7-2. We celebrated with ice cream and soda pop at home, but nothing was mentioned in my classes. In 1970, I graduated high school, oblivious to the far-reaching significance of our victory . . ."

* * * * * * *

Although unanticipated by Mary Beth in 1970, the reach of *Tinker* remains enormous. *Tinker* has been cited as controlling law over 10,000 times in cases and law reviews, and *Tinker* continues to be the leading case governing free speech in educational institutions, assuring that the free speech rights of both students and teachers are protected in schools.

Law & Professional Ethics in Practice:

As private citizens public educators have a right to express their political views and to participate in the political process. However, reasonable limits may be set on public employees' partisan political activities to protect the ethical integrity of public institutions and to maintain public confidence in the equal administration of the laws. Public schools must never become partisan institutions. No one should be allowed to use public powers or resources to advance their personal political agenda. Public educators may not use their classrooms to make partisan political speeches or to solicit votes, nor use state resources (e.g., school copier, public address system, official e-mail, etc.) to communicate partisan political messages. No one has a right to use captive audiences of students or employees in public schools to push their personal political views, or to favor or disfavor others based on their political beliefs. Where is the legal/ethical line between protected free speech and the abuse of public power and resources for partisan purposes?

Questions for Further Exploration:

1) *Free speech and democracy*: How important are rights of free speech in a democracy? How important is democracy? When the free speech rights of individuals conflict with public order, how should these conflicts be resolved?

2) *Free speech rights of students*: In *Tinker* the Court recognized that as students, children did not "shed their constitutional rights to freedom of speech or expression at the schoolhouse gate." But the Court has also long recognized that children's rights are not necessarily coequal with the rights of adults. In balancing students' rights to free speech and the interests of school officials in maintaining order did the Court strike the correct balance in *Tinker*?

3) *Free speech rights of teachers*: How important are teachers' free speech rights in schools? How should these rights be balanced with the competing interests of school officials, students, and the community?

4) *Open forum*: What other related issues or current events would you like to discuss?

Suggested Activities for Further Learning:

1) Words have the power to change people and change the world. When truth is needed but unwelcomed, the simple act of speaking the truth can become a great and enduring act of courage that inspires listeners and countless readers in future generations. Select a speech you find inspiring and share with your colleagues what you have learned from this speech, for example: Plato: *The Apology* (400 B.C.E.); Jesus: *The Sermon on the Mount* (33 C.E.); Patrick Henry: *Give me Liberty or Give Me Death* (1775); Sojourner Truth: *Ain't I a Woman?* (1851); Frederick Douglass: *What to the Slave is the Fourth of July?* (1852); Abraham Lincoln: *Gettysburg Address* (1863); Ghandi: *Quit India Speech* (1942); Nelson Mandela: *I am Prepared to Die* (1964); Dwight D. Eisenhower: *Farewell Address* (1961); John F. Kennedy: *The Decision to Go to the Moon* (1961); Martin Luther King, Jr.: *I Have a Dream* (1963); John Perry Barlow: *A Declaration of the Independence of Cyberspace* (1996).

2) Review your local school's policies related to free speech, including student and faculty speech, use of school technology, dress codes, academic freedom, etc.

Chapter 5: Search and Seizure

The Fourth Amendment to the U.S. Constitution was intended to protect against abuses of government powers involving unreasonable searches and seizures, while also allowing for reasonable and lawful searches and seizures when necessary. The Fourth Amendment states:

> The right of the people to be secure in their persons, houses, papers, and effects, against unreasonable searches and seizures, shall not be violated, and no Warrants shall issue, but upon probable cause, supported by Oath or affirmation, and particularly describing the place to be searched, and the persons or things to be seized.

The Fourth Amendment protects a broad range of human privacy rights while also recognizing legitimate government interests when searches and seizures are warranted. There is, for example, a fundamental right to privacy in the human mind protected by the Fourth Amendment. Your personal thoughts and beliefs belong to you alone, and are beyond the legitimate reach of government powers. Humans should enjoy complete freedom of individual thought and belief, free from governmental intrusions and interference, even if technology someday advances to enable such intrusions.

In the physical world, beyond the realm of pure thought, the right to bodily privacy must also be vigorously protected by the Fourth Amendment. To have government agents exposing, touching, probing, or removing anything from a person's body without consent is obviously a severe intrusion on individual privacy requiring a compelling justification.

Although an intrusion on the home is not as directly personal as an intrusion on the body, it is nonetheless a very serious intrusion on individual privacy. People's personal papers and effects are also protected under the Fourth Amendment. Today these rights extend not just to paper letters in leather purses, but also to our electronic versions of these papers and effects stored in our personal electronic devices.

Whenever there is a reasonable expectation of privacy, the Fourth Amendment protects against unreasonable intrusions by government agents. Outside of that reasonable expectation of privacy, however, there is no Fourth Amendment protection.

In summary the Fourth Amendment establishes that there is a core right of human privacy that is beyond the reach of government; bodily privacy is vigorously protected and requires strong justifications; courts vigorously protect the privacy of the home from unwarranted intrusions; our papers and personnel effects are protected; but at some point beyond these protections there is no longer any reasonable expectation of privacy and Fourth Amendment protections no longer apply.

The Core Right of Privacy and Associated Fourth Amendment Rights

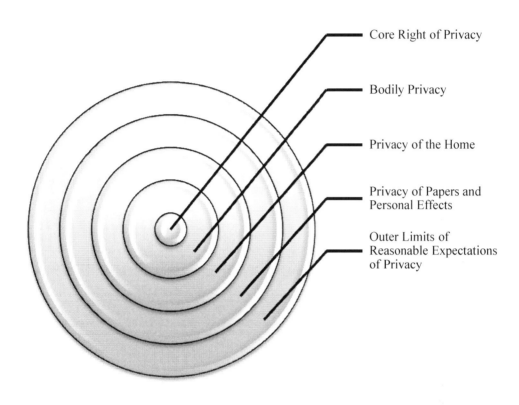

Core Right of Privacy

Bodily Privacy

Privacy of the Home

Privacy of Papers and Personal Effects

Outer Limits of Reasonable Expectations of Privacy

© **Dayton**

Beyond the reasonable expectation of privacy there is no protection. Individuals do not, for example, have any reasonable expectation of privacy in anything they place in plain view, leave unsupervised or abandoned in public areas, or otherwise fail to maintain reasonable privacy or control over.

To protect public safety and order government agents must sometimes conduct searches for evidence of prohibited activity or contraband, and seize property or persons. The command of the Fourth Amendment and similar state constitutional provisions is that these searches and seizures must be reasonable under the totality of the circumstances, appropriately balancing the rights of individuals against legitimate governmental needs.

Prior to conducting a lawful search the government is generally required to prove to a reviewing magistrate that there is "probable cause" for the proposed search:

Elements of Proof Leading to Probable Cause

© Dayton

Knowledge of Facts
and Circumstances

Based on Reasonably
Trustworthy Information

In a Quantum Sufficient to
Pursuade a Reasonably
Prudent Person

Of Probable Cause to
believe there is Evidence
Subject to Lawful Seizure

Exceptions to these general requirements include:

1) Searches incident to arrest;
2) Emergency situations;
3) Searches by consent;
4) International border searches; and
5) Items in plain view.

Establishing probable cause requires a relatively high burden of proof. In *New Jersey v. T.L.O.*, 469 U.S. 325 (1985), however, the U.S. Supreme Court held that because of the special context of public schools only "reasonable suspicion" of a violation of the law or school rules was required to conduct a reasonable search in schools, not the higher standard of probable cause.

To justify a challenged search, government officials must establish sufficient cause for the search (i.e. probable cause or reasonable suspicion). Courts evaluate these claims by weighing the individual's reasonable expectation of privacy under the circumstances against the government's legitimate need to search. Police searches are subject to the higher standard of "probable cause." But public school officials generally need only show that their searches of students were based on the lower standard of "reasonable suspicion" defined by the *T.L.O.* test. To be reasonable under the *T.L.O.* test the search must be:

> 1) *Justified in its inception*: The school agent had reasonable grounds to believe that a search would produce evidence of wrong doing (i.e., illegal activity or a breach of school rules).
> 2) *Reasonably related in scope to the objectives of the search and not excessively intrusive in light of the*:
>> a) Age of the student;
>> b) Sex of the student; and
>> c) Nature of the infraction.

Elements of Proof Leading to Reasonable Suspicion under *T.L.O.*

Search was Justified in its Inception, with Reasonable Grounds to Believe that the Search would Produce Evidence of Wrongdoing

Search was Reasonably Related in Scope to the Objectives of the Search, and not Excessively Instrusive in light of the Age and Sex of the Student and the Nature of the Infraction

Reasonable Suspicion of a Violation of the Law or School Rules Sufficient to Justify the Search as Reasonable under the Fourth Amendment

© Dayton

95

In all searches, school officials should carefully weigh the intrusiveness of the search against the legitimate need for the search. If the intrusiveness of the search outweighs the need for the search, the search is unreasonable and therefore unlawful.

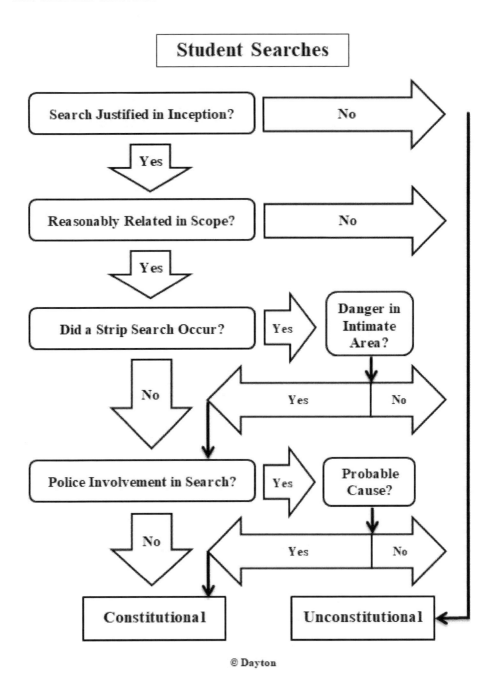

© Dayton

Strip Searches of Students

Strip searches of students are disfavored under the law and should be strongly avoided. As the U.S. Supreme Court noted in *Safford v. Redding*, 557 U.S. 364 (2009), strip searches of children by school officials are recognized as a distinct category of searches generally disfavored by courts. These highly intrusive searches require additional elements of proof beyond the *T.L.O.* test. For a strip search to satisfy the requirements of the second prong of the *T.L.O.* test (that the search be reasonably related in scope to the objectives of the search) the *Redding* test further requires that strip searches must be based on:

> 1) A reasonable suspicion of danger and;
> 2) A reasonable basis for believing that the danger is hidden in an intimate area.

A genuine need for urgency in preventing the danger (e.g., seizing an imminently dangerous weapon; explosives; etc.) would also bolster the case for an intrusive search by school officials. Strip searches falling short of these standards may result not only in institutional liability, but also individual liability for public school officials conducting strip searches contrary to well-established law after *T.L.O.* and *Redding*.

Strip searches are those searches that go beyond a search of personal belongings and outer clothing to reveal intimate garments and private bodily areas. In *Redding* the Court noted that if a strip search by school officials is ever lawful it would have to satisfy *Redding* and the *T.L.O.* test that "the search as actually conducted be reasonably related in scope to the circumstances which justified the interference in the first place" and "not excessively intrusive in light of the age and sex of the student and the nature of the infraction."

School Locker Searches

Public school lockers are property owned by the school and controlled and supervised by school officials. Unless a right of privacy is established by state law, policy, or local practice, there is generally no reasonable expectation of privacy in property owned, controlled, and supervised by the school. Further, school officials commonly provide students with official notice through student handbooks or signed consent forms that school lockers are the property of the school, and that there is therefore no reasonable expectation of privacy in items that students place in school lockers.

School officials may routinely examine the contents of school lockers for custodial, safety, or other legitimate purposes. Even where a reasonable expectation of privacy in the locker is recognized, under *T.L.O.*, a search by school officials would only require reasonable suspicion of a violation of the law or a school rule. Contraband items found in the process of a lawful custodial inspection of lockers may be seized and used as evidence in school disciplinary and law enforcement proceedings.

Metal Detectors and Administrative Searches

Government searches of individuals generally require: 1) Individualized suspicion; and 2) Sufficient cause to justify the search under the circumstances. Courts have, however, recognized legitimate "administrative searches" (e.g., use of metal detectors) as an exception to these general rules. To qualify as an administrative search, the search must be:

> 1) Aimed at a general danger (e.g., keeping weapons out of public gathering areas); and
> 2) Nonintrusive.

Metal detectors may be used for administrative searches, and when properly administered, the detectors may help prevent general dangers and do so in a nonintrusive manner.

Under the Fourth Amendment suspicionless administrative searches are limited to what is reasonably necessary to guard against an immediate general danger (e.g., nonintrusive screening for weapons, explosives, etc., in a public gathering area; *not* for an intrusive search for marijuana, etc.). A search exceeding the lawful limits of an administrative search must be justified as an individual suspicion-based search, or fall within a recognized exception under the Fourth Amendment (e.g., a search by consent, etc.).

Security Cameras

Conduct in plain public view is not within the scope of any reasonable expectation of privacy, and is therefore not protected by the Fourth Amendment. Government officials, including school officials, can place security cameras in public areas to promote public safety, security, and to record evidence of misconduct. Cameras should not, however, be placed in areas in which there is a legitimate expectation of privacy such as restrooms, showering and changing areas, etc. Other more private and appropriate means of supervision and security should be used in these areas.

In addition to the use of security cameras in school entrances, hallways, cafeterias, and other common areas, security cameras are increasingly being used on school buses. Uses on buses include supervision and discipline of students on the bus, and also cameras aimed at vehicles near the bus. Bus cameras aimed at surrounding traffic are used to document evidence of dangerous illegal passing of the school bus while stopped and children are crossing the road, and to generally deter unsafe driving that endangers students. Public streets are public areas, and there is generally no reasonable expectation of privacy on public streets or in other public areas.

Electronic Privacy

There is generally a legitimate expectation of privacy in the contents of personal electronic devices. The contents stored in individuals' personal electronic devices are the modern electronic equivalents of their "papers, and effects" protected under the Fourth Amendment and similar state laws. These electronic files receive the same legal protections accorded to hard copies of private documents.

While the contents of electronic devices may be protected, consistent with state law and local policy school officials may lawfully prohibit students from having or using cell phones or other electronic devises in school or under certain circumstances (e.g., testing rooms; etc.). If a cell phone or other device is lawfully confiscate, however, that does not grant school officials a legal license to go on a "fishing expedition" through private electronic devices.

School officials may only search the contents of students' personal electronic devices if there is sufficient justification to do so under the guidelines established in *T.L.O.* The scope of the search cannot exceed the parameters of the justification for the search. If there is only reasonable suspicion for searching recent text messages, for example, older saved messages or stored photos should not be searched. If there is no valid cause to search the electronic device, the device should be secured, stored, and returned to the student or parent consistent with school policy.

Materials that students or teachers publicly post on-line (e.g., social media, etc.) are not protected by any reasonable expectation of privacy. To legitimately claim a reasonable expectation of privacy, the individual's actions must be consistent with the maintenance of privacy. By posting materials on-line and available to the general public, any reasonable expectation of privacy is waived. School officials may search available online materials without violating the Fourth Amendment.

Further, any reasonable expectation of privacy is limited to private electronic devices. There is no reasonable expectation of privacy when using public school computers, school e-mail, or other school owned and controlled electronic devices and systems.

Searches Using Dogs

The U.S. Supreme Court has not yet directly addressed the legality of dog searches in public schools, and lower courts have issued conflicting opinions. The Court has, however, addressed dog searches in other contexts. By viewing these cases in conjunction with the Court's articulated Fourth Amendment standards in public schools, some general principles can be reasonably deduced in this still evolving area of the law:

General principles governing dog searches:

• Anything search dogs can smell in the open air of public areas falls under the "plain view" doctrine; no search was involved; the Fourth Amendment is inapplicable.
• Search dogs should not be allowed to poke and jab their noses into people.
• Search dogs should remain a reasonable distance from people.
• Individuals should not be required to submit to very close smelling of their person by search dogs.
• Individuals should not be detained for an unreasonable time.
• A search using dogs must not be administered in a way that is unreasonable, frightening, or embarrassing to people.

If the search dog "alerts" to an individual this action by a trained canine may serve as the basis for the individual suspicion and cause necessary for a further lawful search. The reasonableness of the subsequent search is determined by balancing the intrusiveness of the search against the government's legitimate justification for the search under the totality of the circumstances.

To help assure that any searches involving search dogs are lawful under the Fourth Amendment, school officials should:

• Be prepared to explain why search dogs were necessary.
• Searches should be aimed at protecting health and safety.
• Plan adequately and appropriately prior to initiating dog searches.
• Take steps to minimize the intrusiveness of the searches as much as is practicable under the circumstances.
• The search should be conducted by well trained and tested dogs and professional handlers.

Searches of School Employees

Like many other issues under the Fourth Amendment, the law governing searches of school employees remains unsettled. Some argue that the *T.L.O.* standard should apply to all school searches, even those of adult school employees. Others argue that the rules concerning private employers should apply when the government is merely acting as an employer and not with police powers. And yet others argue that government searches of adults with adult consequences should be subject to the general standard of probable cause under the Fourth Amendment. The Court addressed this issue in *O'Connor v. Ortega*, 480 U.S. 709 (1987), but in a 5-4 decision that produced no majority opinion, the standard of law remained unsettled. The Court again failed to settle this issue in *City of Ontario v. Quon*, 560 U.S. 746 (2010).

Nonetheless, many lower courts have applied Justice O'Connor's plurality opinion standard in *Ortega*, holding that when the government conducts a search in its capacity as employer the relevant standard is whether that intrusion on the privacy of the employee is one that a reasonable employer might follow in the ordinary conduct of business, or whether it is unreasonable in the context. Others suggest that until the law is more clearly settled in this area, following the higher standard of probable cause is a safer practice.

What is currently clear is that a search of a government employee (including their private papers and effects) by a government supervisor or other government agent is in fact a search within the protections of the Fourth Amendment. It is the standard of proof required to justify these searches that remains unsettled. When the law remains uncertain, complying with the higher standard of law is the safest option, as you cannot lose a lawsuit by providing more constitutional protection than was required. For this reason, school officials may choose to assume that the standard of law for searches of adult employees is probable cause until this issue is finally resolved by the U.S. Supreme Court.

The Court has also recognized that "operational realities" may reduce or remove any reasonable expectation of privacy in certain circumstances. For example, there is a lower reasonable expectation of privacy in an office or desk that is shared, open, and commonly used by other employees, than in an office or desk that is assigned solely to the employee, locked, or otherwise objectively regarded as privately used. The scope of the expectation of privacy must be determined on a case-by-case basis, considering the unique circumstances and balancing the individual's legitimate privacy interests against the employer's legitimate interests in work-place supervision, safety, and efficiency.

Seizure and Bailment

Seizure of persons by school officials should only occur when doing so is necessary to protect health, safety, or order in the school, and any seizure or restraint of persons must be consistent with state law. Seized persons must be supervised in a safe area, treated appropriately, and only detained for the time necessary.

Concerning seized property, school officials hold seized property in bailment. School officials must use ordinary care in protecting the seized property from damage, loss, or theft. And they must provide students and/or parents with a fair process for redeeming items of value.

Essential Questions & Answers

What are the potential consequences for government officials if they violate Fourth Amendment rights?

Penalties for violating the Fourth Amendment rights of citizens include the "exclusionary rule" and monetary damages under federal and state law. Under the exclusionary rule evidence that was obtained in violation of the Fourth Amendment (i.e., "the fruit of a poison tree") cannot be used against a defendant, reducing government incentives for violations. Monetary damages may be assessed against the institution and the individuals responsible for violations of well-established law.

What is the standard of law when police officers are involved in school searches?

In *T.L.O*, the U.S. Supreme Court allowed a lower standard ("reasonable suspicion") to govern searches conducted by public school officials. But for law enforcement agents the higher standard ("probable cause") still generally applies, even when police are acting with school officials.

Can school officials conduct a lawful search under the "reasonable suspicion" standard without police involvement, and then turn any discovered evidence over to police, even if there was not "probable cause" for police to conduct the search themselves?

Yes. If school officials decide to conduct the search themselves, under *T.L.O.*, the legal standard is reasonable suspicion. Any evidence of a crime found in a lawful search by school officials may be turned over to police.

Probable cause is only required when law enforcement agents are involved in the search process.

To avoid discriminating against anyone school officials equally searched all students in the classroom for the $20 that was believed stolen. Was this lawful?

No. Under these circumstances searching everyone in a mass "blanket search" is *per se* unreasonable. The Fourth Amendment was intended to prevent "fishing expeditions" and other mass suspicionless searches by government officials. Government officials must be able to articulate a reason for searching any individual or individuals. Everyone could not possibly have stolen the missing $20, so the mass search was unreasonable. The reasonableness of a search is judged by weighing the legitimate need to search against the intrusiveness of the search. For this reason, a search for a relatively trivial amount of money is always a very bad idea, as government has very little legitimate need to search for trivial amounts of money. And even if a $20 bill is found, it generally proves nothing. Money is a fungible commodity, and one $20 bill is usually indistinguishable from others. Being found in possession of $20 does not prove the person stole it. In most cases it proves nothing more than the person had $20. Searching everyone in a misguided effort at equal treatment only multiplies the number of potential plaintiffs. If the search goes beyond outer clothing to reveal intimate garments and private bodily areas, these types of searches qualify as "strip searches" further elevating the legal standard (*see*, "Strip Searches" section above), and assuring a losing case for school officials.

Do school officials or law enforcement officials have to inform students of their legal rights prior to conducting a search?

No. A "*Miranda* warning" (from *Miranda v. Arizona*, 384 U.S. 436 (1966)), is only required to inform a person of applicable rights prior to police interrogation when that person is in police custody. No warning or information is required when lawfully searching an individual. For this reason, it is essential that everyone know their rights. With few exceptions (e.g., *Miranda* warnings; notification of due process rights; etc.), government officials generally have no legal duty to inform citizens of their rights. It is up to citizens to know and defend their own rights. Further, while it is generally unlawful to lie to government agents, government agents may lie to citizens in the process of investigations and interrogations. It is wise to know your rights and understand that not everything you may be told in an investigation or interrogation by a government agent is true.

Backpacks and bags are commonly searched prior to entering athletic stadiums and other facilities. Can school officials lawfully search all student backpacks and bags daily prior to entering the school building?

No. There is a fundamental difference between entering into an athletic stadium, etc., and public schools. People may choose not to enter athletic facilities, etc., if they don't want to submit to a random search (i.e., search by consent). But for students public school attendance is compelled by penalty of criminal law. Students cannot be forced to waive their fourth amendment rights through mandatory attendance laws. Students lawfully suspended or expelled may be asked to submit to a search as a condition of returning, particularly if the disciplinary removal involved a weapon or other contraband. And everyone may be subjected to a non-intrusive administrative search (i.e., metal detectors) to guard against weapons in the schools. Otherwise searches of students' persons or papers and effects requires the establishment of individualized suspicion and sufficient cause.

School officials conducted a search of school owned computers and e-mail systems. Evidence found was used to support school media policy violation charges against students and faculty. Evidence of unlawful activities was turned over to police. Was this lawful?

Yes. Individuals have no reasonable expectation of privacy when using school owned computers, media, e-mail systems, etc. School officials may search the school owned systems anytime without providing any warning or justification. Evidence of school policy violations can be acted on by school officials, and evidence of crimes may be turned over to police.

Can school officials search faculty offices, desks, and personal belongings?

Generally, no, unless school officials can establish individualized suspicion and a lawful basis for the search. General "blanket searches" and "fishing expeditions" based on the theory that "someone somewhere must be doing something wrong" are unlawful. Public employees generally have a reasonable expectation of privacy in their offices, desks, files, personal belongings, etc. However, "operational realities" may reduce or remove any reasonable expectation of privacy where areas are shared, open, and commonly used by others. In general, the more private the area searched the greater the justification required, balancing the individual's legitimate privacy interests against the employer's legitimate interests in work-place supervision, safety, and efficiency. In most cases there must be individualized suspicion and sufficient cause to justify any search.

Can school officials lawfully search through employees personal electronic devices?

As noted above, school officials can search school owned devices, but not private electronic devices unless they can establish a lawful basis for the search. In *Riley v. California*, 573 U.S. 783 (2014), the U.S. Supreme Court unanimously ruled that there is a right to privacy in persons' private electronic devices. Any search of a private device would require the establishment of a legal justification for the search, generally probable cause.

Is it lawful to randomly drug test students in public schools?

In *Vernonia School District v. Acton*, 515 U.S. 646 (1995), the U.S. Supreme Court allowed random drug testing of students athletes. In *Board of Education v. Earls*, 536 U.S. 822 (2002), the Court extended suspicionless searches to all students involved in extracurricular activities. The Court has not approved of random drug testing of the general population of students (i.e., students consent to participation in extracurricular activities but are subject to mandatory general attendance; attendance laws cannot be used to force a waiver of constitutional rights). School officials may, however, seek to obtain a drug test from any individual student based on sufficient cause to suspect an individual student is abusing an unlawful substance in violation of the law and school policy.

Is it lawful to randomly drug test employees in public schools?

The U.S. Supreme Court has allowed suspicionless testing of public employees where government officials have established a special need. In *Skinner v. Railway Executives Association*, 489 U.S. 602 (1989), the Court allowed random testing of transportation employees. Tests for bus drivers, etc., can be justified under *Skinner*, but not random tests for classroom teachers who do not pose any similar immediate safety risk. Further, it is unlikely that illegal drug use is wide-spread among teachers. And if it is, there is likely sufficient evidence to justify testing based on individual probable cause. If school officials believe it is necessary to test particular teachers, it is much safer legally to establish individualized suspicion and test individual teachers, rather than to attempt to adopt a broad-based and legally doubtful suspicionless search policy for all teachers.

Essential Practice Skills

As noted above government searches of individuals generally require individualized suspicion and sufficient cause to justify the search under the circumstances. Courts have, however, recognized legitimate "administrative searches" (e.g., use of metal detectors) as an exception to these general rules and lawful if they are aimed at a general danger (e.g., keeping weapons out of public gathering areas); and nonintrusive. Administrative searches are common in entrance areas to public facilities. The section below provides an overview of reasonable operational practices for administrative searches:

Conducting a lawful search with a door-frame style metal detector in an administrative search:

Administrative searches should be:

- Used in response to a credible general danger in the area.
- Not used to search for evidence of individual misconduct.
- Strategically placed so that all persons entering must pass through the detector.
- Persons are notified in advance to remove metal objects.
- There are no further intrusions on individuals unless the detector "alerts" or an individual's conduct independently warrants further action.

Responding to an "alert" by the metal detector:

- Detector alerts are common and mostly benign (e.g., metal belt buckles; steel shanks in shoes; keys; coins; medical implants; etc.). Nonetheless, have a lawful emergency response plan prepared and practiced in the event of an imminent danger (e.g., drawing or use of a weapon by a suspect).
- Observe the individual's reaction to the alert and subsequent conduct and demeanor.
- If there is no cause for immediate intervention, the individual is simply asked to pass through the detector again to confirm the alert. Otherwise no bodily contact or unnecessary intrusions or delays are imposed.
- After a confirmed alert, a hand-held detector is used to pin-point the metal object.
- A properly trained school official asks appropriate questions about the detected object.

• A further lawful search may occur if warranted by the facts and circumstances.
• Assure that back-up security can be quickly contacted in the event of an emergency.

After a metal detector alert is confirmed, any more intrusive follow-up search of an individual student by public school officials must comply with the *T.L.O.* test, and the *Redding* test for any searches that go beyond a search of personal belongings and outer clothing to reveal intimate garments and private bodily areas, all of which should be avoided unless absolutely necessary and justified under *Redding*. Police involvement requires probable cause for follow-up searches and seizures.

Metal detector alerts may, however, serve as key elements in establishing a lawful basis for a follow-up search, supplemented with other relevant factors showing sufficient reason for the search under the totality of the circumstances (e.g., the metal detector alerted; the alert was confirmed; a hand-held detector also confirmed the presence of a metal object; the shape and location of the object was consistent with a concealed weapon; the suspect's explanation was not credible; the demeanor of the suspect indicated deception and extreme nervous tension; etc.).

Adequately document any searches exceeding the scope of an administrative search including all relevant facts and circumstances that made the search reasonable under the totality of the circumstances. Until the law is clarified, assume that the standard for searches of non-student adults and all searches involving law enforcement agents is probable cause.

Administrative searches cannot be a pretext for unlawful blanket searches or fishing expeditions aimed at finding general individual violations of the law or school rules. The focus must remain on deterring the presence of serious common dangers such as weapons. Further, metal detectors should not be used arbitrarily. The use of metal detectors should be in response to a demonstrable legitimate need. School officials may wish to make factual findings documenting a need to protect a common area (e.g., prior instances of weapons in the area); adopt a lawful policy for the use of metal detectors; and assure that assigned personnel are adequately trained in the lawful, non-discriminatory application of the policy.

In summary, to qualify as an administrative search the genuine purpose cannot be to find non-dangerous individual misconduct. The purpose must be a nonintrusive means of preventing a serious common danger (e.g., preventing anyone from bringing a dangerous weapon into the area). However, contraband found in the process of a lawful administrative search may be seized and used as evidence in subsequent school disciplinary and law enforcement proceedings.

Essential Practice Tips

1) *Student searches*: Always seek the most efficient and least intrusive means of achieving necessary discipline and safety objectives. For example, a search can often be avoided by simply asking the person to voluntarily hand over the prohibited object. Whenever possible seek cooperation; not confrontation. If searches are necessary avoid body contact whenever possible, especially any contact with private areas. An adult witness should be present. If a coat or other exterior garment (not essential clothing) must be searched, ask the person to remove the coat before searching it. Only go beyond exterior garments in an emergency (*see*, Strip Searches). If the object sought is believed to be a dangerous weapon, make sure proper security precautions are in place before anyone approaches the suspect, or attempt to keep the suspect from endangering others by calmly steering that person toward a safer area until law enforcement officials can arrive.

2) *Strip searches*: Generally, do not engage in strip searches. Strip searches are disfavored under the law, and should be avoided whenever possible. Strip searches of children are not only humiliating to the student searched, but they present grave professional dangers to school officials as well. If an intrusive search related to serious criminal conduct is warranted but there is no immediate danger, make a police report and allow law enforcement officials to assume responsibility for any necessary search after the suspect is taken into police custody and away from school. If necessary monitor the student until the police arrive to prevent disposal of evidence, etc. If an intrusive search is necessary because of an immediate danger, assure compliance with the *Redding* test and search no further than necessary. Never engage in an intrusive search for trivial items (e.g., candy, money, etc.) unrelated to dangerous criminal conduct. Neither judges nor community members are likely to accept strip searches of children over such trivial matters. Remember that your actions may be reviewed not only by a court of law, but also by the court of public opinion in your community.

3) *Employee searches*: Retrieving files and other office necessities from a common work area in the absence of the employee because they are reasonable needed at the time generally does not constitute a "search." If, however, the true purpose is seeking evidence against the employee; the employee was available to retrieve what was needed; or there is a reasonable expectation of privacy in the office area of the employee, Fourth Amendment protections should be respected.

4) *Objecting to an unlawful search*: Do not consent to a search that you believe is unlawful. Government officials don't need your permission for a lawful search. But giving your permission allows the government agent to treat the search as a search by consent in which you have waived your rights to privacy. Keep anything that you wish to keep private covered from plain public view because anything in plain public view is not protected by a reasonable expectation of privacy and may be subject to search or seizure.

Essential Points

- When there is a reasonable expectation of privacy, the Fourth Amendment protects against unreasonable intrusions by government agents. Outside of that reasonable expectation of privacy, however, there is no Fourth Amendment protection.
- The Fourth Amendment protects individuals' reasonable expectations of privacy in their "persons, houses, papers, and effects" and requires government officials to establish that a challenged search was reasonable in its inception and scope.
- To conduct a lawful search, the government is generally required to establish "probable cause" to obtain a valid search warrant prior to any search under the Fourth Amendment. Probable cause is established by proving to a reviewing judge that the government agents seeking the warrant have:
  > 1) Knowledge of facts and circumstances;
  > 2) Based on reasonably trustworthy information; and
  > 3) In a quantum sufficient to warrant a reasonably prudent person to believe that a crime has been committed or property subject to seizure is present.

  Exceptions to these general requirements include:
  > 1) Searches incident to arrest;
  > 2) Emergency situations;
  > 3) Searches by consent;
  > 4) International border searches; and
  > 5) Items in plain view.
- Penalties for failing to respect the Fourth Amendment rights of citizens include the exclusionary rule and monetary damages under federal or state law. Evidence that was obtained in violation of the Fourth Amendment cannot be used against a defendant. Monetary damages may be assessed against the institution and the individual for violations of well-established law.
- In *T.L.O.* the Court held that because of the special context of public schools, the legal standard for school officials under the Fourth

Amendment is reasonable suspicion. To be reasonable under the *T.L.O.* test the search must be:

> 1) *Justified in its inception*: The school agent had reasonable grounds to believe that a search would produce evidence of wrong doing (i.e., illegal activity or a breach of school rules).
> 2) *Reasonably related in scope to the objectives of the search and not excessively intrusive in light of the*:
>> a) Age of the student;
>> b) Sex of the student; and
>> c) Nature of the infraction.

- Strip searches are generally disfavored by courts and require additional elements of proof beyond the *T.L.O.* test. In *Redding* the Court required this test (*Redding* Test): A strip search of a public school student is only lawful if it satisfies the *T.L.O.* test, and there is:

> 1) A reasonable suspicion of danger; and
> 2) A reasonable basis for believing that the danger is hidden in an intimate area.

- Under the "plain view" doctrine there is no reasonable expectation of privacy in objects or conduct in plain public view. Contraband or misconduct government officials can detect with the use of the common senses in public areas including through sight, hearing, smell, feeling of vibrations, etc., are outside of the protections of the Fourth Amendment.

- There is generally no reasonable expectation of privacy in property owned and controlled by the school including school lockers and school computers.

- When search dogs smell the air in school parking lots, hallways, locker areas, etc., no "search" is involved (i.e., smelling the air is permissible under the "plain view" doctrine). Fourth Amendment limits may be breached if the dogs are allowed to poke and jab their noses into the students; come too closely to students; students are asked to individually submit to very close smelling of their person by dogs; students are detained for an unreasonable time; or the dog search is otherwise administered in a way that is unreasonable, frightening, or embarrassing to persons.

- The U.S. Supreme Court allowed a lower standard governing searches conducted by public school officials in *T.L.O.* For police officers, however, the higher standard of probable cause still generally applies, even when police are acting with school officials.

- Searches of individuals generally require individualized suspicion and sufficient cause. Administrative searches (e.g., metal detectors)

are an exception to this general rule. To qualify as an administrative search, the search must be:
> 1) Aimed at a general danger (e.g., keeping weapons out of public gathering areas); and
> 2) Unintrusive.

- The contents stored in students' personal electronic devices are electronic versions of their "papers, and effects" under the Fourth Amendment. School officials may only search students' personal electronic devices if there is sufficient justification to do so under the guidelines established in *T.L.O.*
- Public employees generally have a reasonable expectation of privacy in their office, desk, files, personal belongings, etc. They are protected from unreasonable searches by both law enforcement agents and supervisors. However, "operational realities" may reduce or remove any reasonable expectation of privacy in certain circumstances.
- Seizure of students should only occur when doing so is necessary to protect health, safety, or order in the school. Seized students must be supervised in a safe area, treated appropriately, and only detained for the time necessary.
- School officials must use ordinary care in protecting seized property from damage, loss, or theft, and they must provide students and/or parents with a fair process for redeeming items of value.

Essential Terms

Exclusionary rule: Evidence that resulted from an unlawful search is excluded from use in a hearing or trial in order to discourage unlawful searches by government agents (i.e., "fruit of the poisonous tree").

Justified in its inception: The government agent searching had reasonable grounds to believe that the search would produce evidence of wrong doing (i.e., illegal activity or a breach of school rules).

Plain view doctrine: There is no reasonable expectation of privacy in objects or conduct in plain public view (i.e., including normal sight, hearing, smell, feeling of vibrations, etc.).

Probable cause: Requires the establishment of: Evidence of facts and circumstances; based on reasonably trustworthy information; in a quantum sufficient to warrant a reasonably prudent person; to believe that a crime has been committed or property subject to seizure is present.

Reasonable expectation of privacy: The individual's conduct is consistent with an expectation of privacy (subjective); and the expectation is one that society is prepared to recognize as reasonable (objective) (*see, Katz v. U.S.*, 389 U.S. 347 (1967)), e.g., bodily privacy; home privacy; personal items; etc.

Reasonable suspicion: The search was justified in its inception, reasonably related in scope to the circumstances, and not excessively intrusive in light of the age and sex of the student and the nature of the infraction (*see, New Jersey v. T.L.O.*).

Essential Cases

Board of Education v. Earls, 536 U.S. 822 (2002): Extended the Court's decision in *Vernonia* (testing of athletes) to allow suspicionless random drug testing for students participating in all extracurricular activities.

New Jersey v. T.L.O., 469 U.S. 325 (1985): Held that the Fourth Amendment applied to searches of students in public schools, but that only the lower standard of reasonable suspicion (rather than the higher standard of probable cause) was required to establish a lawful search by school officials.

O'Connor v. Ortega, 480 U.S. 209 (1987): When the government conducts a search in its capacity as employer, the relevant standard is whether the intrusion on the privacy of the employee is one that a reasonable employer might follow in the ordinary conduct of business, or whether it is unreasonable in the context.

Safford v. Redding, 557 U.S. 364 (2009): Strip searches of students are disfavored and unlawful unless they meet both the standards of *T.L.O.* (i.e., justified in inception and reasonable in scope) and *Redding* (i.e., reasonable suspicion of a danger hidden in an intimate area).

Skinner v. Railway Executives Association, 489 U.S. 602 (1989): The Court allowed random testing of transportation employees (e.g., train and bus drivers; etc.) based on legitimate public safety concerns.

Vernonia School District v. Acton, 515 U.S. 646 (1995): Allowed suspicionless random drug testing of students voluntarily participating in athletic programs.

A Closer Look at the Law

The Fourth Amendment established strong limitations on government officials engaged in the exercise of police powers, requiring that searches must generally be based on probable cause and a warrant. Parents, however, act as private citizens not bound by the Constitution. A police officer needs probable cause, but parents need no legal justification to search their own children's belongings in the exercise of legitimate parental authority.

The Constitution protects individuals from abuses of power by state agents. It is understood that when the police search you they are looking for evidence against you in an adversarial process. The Fourth Amendment keeps state agents honest in this process. In contrast, it is assumed that parents are acting in the best interests of the child. Which model more accurately describes the role of public educators in searching a student? School officials are government agents and they sometimes act like law enforcement agents in dealing with crimes in schools. But they sometimes also act like parents in trying to help children learn and improve conduct.

In *New Jersey v. T.L.O.*, the U.S. Supreme Court was asked to decide what rules apply to searches by public school officials. Should searches of students by school officials be subject to the same rules that apply to police officers; should school officials be allowed to search as "parents" under the *in loco parentis* doctrine; or should some intermediate standard of law apply?

In *T.L.O.* the Court adopted a middle ground between the police and parent legal standards. The Court recognized that the Fourth Amendment protects students because school officials are government agents. But the Court decided that because of the special context of public schools only "reasonable suspicion" of a violation of the law or school rules was required for school officials to conduct a reasonable search in schools, not the higher standard of probable cause.

In practice, a key to proving the lawfulness of a search is being prepared to present a persuasive narrative detailing what happened before and during the search that justified the actions of school officials and made these actions reasonable under the circumstances. It is advantageous to focus on professional knowledge and experience as an educator. Judges know the law and will not defer on matters of law. But judges generally defer to educators on matters where educational expertise and experience are relevant. The narrative justifying a search should be supported by the evidence, logical, and guided by common sense experience and good professional judgment.

To better understand this process, a review of the facts in *T.L.O.* illustrates how to conduct a lawful search, while a review of the facts in *Redding* shows what can go wrong in an unlawful search. Review the transcripts below, regularly referring back to the *T.L.O.* test on p. 95 and the *Redding* test on p. 97, to learn how to conduct a lawful search and how to avoid an unlawful search. The Court's recitation of the facts from *T.L.O.* and *Redding* appear below [*with illustrative instructional points added in brackets and italics*]:

A Case Study in Conducting a Reasonable Search
From: New Jersey v. T.L.O.

On March 7, 1980, a teacher at Piscataway High School in Middlesex County, N.J., discovered two girls smoking in a lavatory. One of the two girls was the respondent T.L.O., who at that time was a 14-year-old high school freshman. Because smoking in the lavatory was a violation of a school rule, the teacher [*initial inquiry is justified in its inception by a credible witness report of a breach of school rules*] took the two girls [*witness identification provided individualized suspicion*] to the Principal's office, where they met with Assistant Vice Principal Theodore Choplick. In response to questioning by Mr. Choplick [*Best Practice: Unless there is an emergency situation establish a factual justification prior to any search; a search must be justified in its inception*], T.L.O.'s companion admitted that she had violated the rule [*verification of witness report*]. T.L.O., however, denied that she had been smoking in the lavatory and claimed that she did not smoke at all [*use experience and logic; educators familiar with student smoking practices know it is a social activity; if two students were seen smoking together by a credible witness; one admitted smoking and the other denied it; it is likely the latter student is concealing/lying*].

Mr. Choplick asked T.L.O. to come into his private office [*Best Practice: Have another adult present*] and demanded [*Best Practice: First politely ask the student to voluntarily hand over an item or consent to search; cooperation and search by consent are preferred*] to see her purse [*connect suspicion to search object; must have reasonable grounds (based on evidence, experience; logic) to believe that a search of a particular object would produce evidence of wrong doing; i.e., girls usually conceal cigarettes in a purse*]. Opening the purse, he found a pack of cigarettes, which he removed from the purse and held before T.L.O. [*evidence of rule violation*] as he accused her of having lied to him [*additional rule violation*]. As he reached into the purse for the cigarettes [*only search as far as the current evidence and suspicion warrant; have a logical explanation justifying each step forward in the search*], Mr. Choplick also noticed

114

a package of cigarette rolling papers [*searcher is following a logical trail of evidence; using evidence and experience to justify further search; T.L.O. already had tobacco cigarettes; ergo, rolling papers were not for tobacco cigarettes; student may possess marijuana*]. In his experience, possession of rolling papers by high school students was closely associated with the use of marihuana. Suspecting that a closer examination of the purse might yield further evidence of drug use [*a logical extrapolation based on professional experience and current evidence, justifying further search*], Mr. Choplick proceeded to search the purse thoroughly. The search revealed a small amount of marihuana, a pipe, a number of empty plastic bags, a substantial quantity of money in one-dollar bills, an index card that appeared to be a list of students who owed T.L.O. money, and two letters that implicated T.L.O. in marihuana dealing [*evidence of rules violations and criminal violations; the trail of evidence led from likely violating the no smoking rule; to possession of drugs; to evidence of selling drugs; but when the trail of evidence and reasonable suspicion stopped, the search stopped; i.e., there was no reasonable suspicion of danger or reasonable basis for believing that the danger is hidden in an intimate area, so no strip search; no further search; searcher preserves evidence and notifies police consistent with school policy and state law*].

* * * * * * *

School officials prevailed in *T.L.O.* because they presented logical, credible evidence that the search was justified in its inception, reasonably related in scope to the objectives of the search, and not excessively intrusive. And when the trail of evidence stopped the search stopped. In short, their actions were reasonable under the circumstances. School officials failed in *Redding* because the search was questionable in its inception and then took an unreasonable and illogical leap into a highly intrusive strip search:

A Case Study in Conducting an Unreasonable Search
From: Safford v. Redding

The events immediately prior to the search in question began in 13-year-old [*age is relevant under T.L.O.; Redding is old enough to merit a high degree of personal privacy; young enough to be highly traumatized by an intrusive strip search at school*] Savana Redding's math class at Safford Middle School one October day in 2003. The assistant principal of the school, Kerry Wilson, came into the room and asked Savana to go to his office. There, he showed her a day planner, unzipped and open flat on his desk, in which there were several knives, lighters, a permanent marker, and a cigarette [*contraband justifying the inception of an investigation*]. Wilson asked Savana whether the planner was hers; she said it was, but that a few days before she had lent it to her friend, Marissa Glines [*calls into question knowledge and ownership of the contraband; best practice: Not an emergency situation; resolve factual disputes before proceeding*]. Savana stated that none of the items in the planner belonged to her [*if there is no credible evidence to rebut her denial, investigate or question further to guide further action*].

Wilson then showed Savana four white prescription-strength ibuprofen 400-mg pills, and one over-the-counter blue naproxen 200-mg pill, all used for pain and inflammation but banned under school rules without advance permission [*see T.L.O. test "nature of the infraction" element: a violation of school rules but otherwise lawful to possess*]. He asked Savana if she knew anything about the pills. Savana answered that she did not. Wilson then told Savana that he had received a report that she was giving these pills to fellow students; Savana denied it and agreed to let Wilson search her belongings [*search by consent; cannot exceed scope of consent; still no conclusive evidence of any wrongdoing by the subject of the search*]. Helen Romero, an administrative assistant, came into the office [*another adult witness; consistent with best practice*], and together with Wilson they searched Savana's backpack, finding nothing [*any further search must be justified*].

At that point, Wilson instructed Romero to take Savana to the school nurse's office to search her clothes for pills [*logical connection? Justification? RED FLAG: a strip search requires reasonable suspicion of danger and a reasonable basis for believing that the danger is hidden in an intimate area; see Redding test*]. Romero and the nurse, Peggy Schwallier, asked Savana to remove her jacket, socks, and shoes, leaving her in stretch pants and a T-shirt (both without pockets), which she was then asked to remove [*now escalated to a full strip search without lawful justification*]. Finally, Savana was told to pull her bra out and to the side and shake it, and to pull out the elastic on her underpants, thus exposing her breasts and pelvic area to some degree [*extremely intrusive nude body search without lawful justification*]. No pills were found [*highly intrusive search produced no evidence of violations; not justified by the nature of the infraction; no reasonable suspicion of danger or any reasonable basis for believing that the danger is hidden in an*

116

intimate area; intrusiveness of the search far outweighs any reasonable justification resulting in an extreme violation of the Fourth Amendment].

* * * * * * *

In all searches, school officials should carefully weigh the intrusiveness of the search against the legitimate need/justification for the search. If the intrusiveness of the search outweighs the legitimate need for the search, the search is unreasonable and therefore unlawful.

In *Redding* the Court declared:

> We do mean . . . to make it clear that the *T.L.O.* concern to limit a school search to reasonable scope requires the support of reasonable suspicion of danger or of resort to underwear for hiding evidence of wrongdoing before a search can reasonably make the quantum leap from outer clothes and backpacks to exposure of intimate parts. The meaning of such a search, and the degradation its subject may reasonably feel, place a search that intrusive in a category of its own demanding its own specific suspicions.

N.B.: Strip searches are disfavored under the law and should only be resorted to in situations where there is a reasonable suspicion of danger, and a reason to believe the danger is hidden in an intimate area. In summary, all school searches must at a minimum comply with the *T.L.O.* test. If a strip search of a public school student is ever lawful, it must satisfy both the *T.L.O.* test and the *Redding* test.

Law & Professional Ethics in Practice:

Even if school officials believe they can survive the court of law, would school officials survive the court of public opinion in your community if they engaged in a mass strip search of children, or a highly intrusive body search of any child? If you were ordered to assist with a strip search, what would you do? Consistent with the Nuremberg principles, if you follow an unlawful order it is no defense to claim you were only following orders. There is a legal and ethical duty to refuse to follow an unlawful order. On the other hand, it is insubordination to refuse to follow a lawful order. How can you determine whether the order is a lawful? *See, T.L.O.* and *Redding*. If you have time to check the law before making an important decision, always check the law to be certain. Otherwise, you must have a sufficient working knowledge of the law and professional ethics to make the right decision at the time. Learn the law now, and learn the applicable standards of professional ethics, so that you will be ready to make the right decision even under challenging circumstances.

Questions for Further Exploration:

1) *Janie's got a gun?*: There is a rumor that Janie has a gun. There is a noticeable bulge in the area of her left breast. What do you do?

2) *How far is too far?*: Should public school officials ever conduct strip searches of students? If yes, how far is too far? Down to underwear; removal of underwear; a search of a body cavity? If no, what are the alternatives if students are believed to be hiding contraband in intimate areas?

3) *Employee privacy rights*: What privacy rights should employees have while at work? If a principal is looking for a key, should the principal be allowed to search a teacher's desk? If the teacher's purse is in the desk, can the principal look in the purse for the key? What if the principal finds contraband in this process? What factors would tend to make this a lawful search; and what factors would tend to make this an unlawful search?

4) *Open forum*: What other related issues or current events would you like to discuss?

Suggested Activities for Further Learning:

1) Review your local school's search related policies including rules concerning searches of individuals; lockers; work areas; use of metal detectors; dog assisted searches; etc.

2) Review your local school's seizure policies including policies and processes for emergency detention; seizure and bailment of property; and return of seized items.

Chapter 6: Due Process of Law

Due process is the framework and lifeblood of any legitimate legal system, establishing substantive standards for fundamental fairness and a procedural system for conducting impartial hearings. In schools, due process plays an essential role in the just resolution of disputes over student discipline, personnel issues, and other significant controversies between individuals and school officials.

In its most basic form due process requires that government agents must treat individuals fairly in actions that significantly affect their life, liberty, or property rights (*see*, U.S. CONST. amend. V; XIV). Due process guards against two significant dangers: Abuses of power; and erroneous decisions.

Concerning due process protections against abuses of power, history demonstrates that absent a firm requirement of due process of law, government officials acting in bad faith can too easily exercise their official powers arbitrarily and abuse governmental powers to threaten and punish their personal enemies and dissenters.

Concerning due process protections against erroneous decisions, even when government officials are acting in good faith, due process of law helps to guard against errors and preventable mistakes by introducing procedural and substantive checks and balances into the process, i.e., procedural (fairness in procedures) and substantive (fairness in substance) due process.

Procedural due process refers to *how* the proceedings are conducted, while substantive due process concerns *what* is done. Procedural due process requires fair and adequate processes, including adequate general notice of the law; specific notice of charges and evidence to individuals accused of breaching the law; and a fair opportunity to be heard in response to the charges and evidence.

Substantive due process requires that government actions must be fundamentally fair; supported by an adequate justification; and must not unjustly intrude on protected liberties. Among practices prohibited by substantive due process requirements are: Rules beyond the scope of legitimate government regulation; arbitrary or grossly disproportionate sanctions; conflicts of interests by adjudicators; and other government actions so inconsistent with basic fairness as to deny fundamental liberties.

Government may impinge on a protected life interest through capital punishment, and liberty through imprisonment. Impingements on life through capital punishment or liberty in the form of imprisonment are limited to criminal proceedings and do not directly involve school officials. The constitutional concept of liberty, however, extends far beyond the scope of liberty under criminal law. As the U.S. Supreme Court recognized in

Board of Regents v. Roth, 408 U.S. 564 (1972): "In a Constitution for a free people, there can be no doubt that the meaning of 'liberty' must be broad indeed."

The Court has recognized that official civil sanctions far short of criminal punishments may significantly impinge on protected liberty interests. Civil sanctions that require due process for protected liberty interests include employment actions that suggest individual moral turpitude, dishonesty, professional incompetence, or otherwise impose a personal stigma on individuals, potentially limiting future opportunities. In *Roth* the Court stated: "Where a person's good name, reputation, honor, or integrity is at stake because of what the government is doing to him, notice and an opportunity to be heard are essential." Similarly, student disciplinary sanctions may impinge on protected liberty interests.

Protected property interests in public schools include employees' contractual rights and students' rights to a free public education. Educators' property rights to payment consistent with their state contracts are protected by the Due Process Clause. The U.S. Constitution grants no educational rights, but the Constitution's Due Process Clause protects the educational property rights granted to students by their state constitutions. These rights can only be denied through adequate notice and hearing under due process of law.

To provide adequate notice, all government rules must be at a minimum publicly enacted, published, and available for review. Government officials may not enact or enforce secret rules. Further, to avoid being unconstitutional vague and therefore void, government rules must be defined clearly enough so that persons of ordinary intelligence can reasonable know what is required or prohibited.

School officials may, for example, establish a lawful dress code for students and teachers, and they may enforce that dress code with appropriate sanctions. But everyone subject to the rules must have a fair opportunity to know the rules, and the rules must clearly define what constitutes a violation of the dress code. Rules are constitutionally inadequate if they are not publicly available or the rules are so vague that they give too much discretion in enforcement to government officials, or give too little notice to citizens concerning what is required or prohibited.

Individuals accused of violating government rules must be provided with specific information about the charges against them, and any witnesses or other evidence the government plans to use to prove its case so that the individual has a fair opportunity to prepare a response to the charges and evidence. Government officials must not hide exculpatory evidence or use hidden evidence to ambush the accused. Hearings must be conducted as good faith efforts to get to the truth and fairly enforce the common rules.

A determination of how much process is due is based on balancing the magnitude of the potential loss of rights by the individual against the magnitude of the burden on the government in providing due process. The smaller the individual interest at stake, the less due process is required; the larger the interest at stake, the more due process is required.

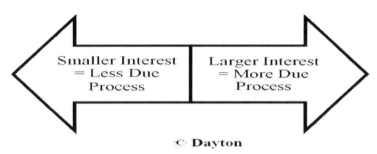

Determining How Much Process is Due

Smaller Interest = Less Due Process

Larger Interest = More Due Process

© Dayton

For example, a permanent expulsion of a student, or the dismissal of a tenured teacher, involves a significant impingement on individual property and liberty interests. Formal and comparatively extensive due process procedures are required in these situations. School officials must provide thorough written notice of the charges and evidence, and notify the individual of applicable procedural rights including the right to obtain copies of relevant documents, to call and confront witnesses, to be represented by legal counsel, etc.

In contrast a short suspension from school may only require an informal notice and hearing. For example: "Johnny, your teacher Ms. Smith reported to me that she saw you push and hit Jimmy [notice of evidence]. The student handbook says that the punishment for this violation of the code of conduct is a three day suspension from school [notice of charges/consequences]. What do you have to say for yourself Johnny? [opportunity to be heard]."

Informal due process proceedings can be quick, simple, and inexpensive. In this example, Johnny was given notice of the evidence and witnesses against him; informed of the charges and the proposed consequences; and he was given an opportunity to be heard, as required by due process.

Courts view some disciplinary actions as *de minimis* (i.e., trivial) in nature, for example the seizing of inexpensive prohibited items such as candy, balloons, etc., or minor punishments such as an informal reprimand, a brief removal from a class, etc. These frequent disciplinary actions are so minor as to require no due process protections under the Due Process Clause. They do not sufficiently impinge on any protected life, liberty, or property rights, and requiring due process for such trivial matters would unreasonably interfere with daily classroom discipline and waste limited resources.

How Much Process is Due in Student Discipline and Removals?

> *More than 10 Days = Formal Due Process*
> *10 Days or Less = Informal Due Process*
> *De Minimis in Nature = No Due Process*

© Dayton

In *Goss v. Lopez*, 419 U.S. 565 (1975), the U.S. Supreme Court held that punishments that could result in a suspension or expulsion from school (impinging on a property right to education), or significantly stigmatize the student's public reputation (impinging on a liberty interest), require due process of law prior to the imposition of these punishments.

The *Goss* Court stated due process requires "in connection with a suspension of 10 days or less, that the student be given oral or written notice of the charges against him, and if he denies them, an explanation of the evidence the authorities have and an opportunity to present his side of the story. The [Due Process] Clause requires at least these rudimentary precautions against unfair or mistaken findings of misconduct and arbitrary exclusion from school."

It should also be noted that although the Court generally requires notice and a hearing prior to the removal of students, in *Goss*, the Court recognized: "Students whose presence poses a continuing danger to persons or property or an ongoing threat of disrupting the academic process may be immediately removed from school. In such cases, the necessary notice and rudimentary hearing should follow as soon as practicable."

Generally, this hearing can be offered at a "practicable" time such as the next regular school day or later by agreement with the student and parents. For potentially dangerous students school officials should arrange for appropriate security precautions prior to the hearing. If the student disrupts the hearing, engages in violence, etc., the hearing can be discontinued, rescheduled, and any serious misconduct in the hearing could constitute a separate punishable offense.

In summary, short-term student suspensions of 10 days or less require at least informal: Notice (oral or written notice of the charges and the evidence); and hearing (prior to removal, unless the student's behavior continues to be disruptive or dangerous, in which case the student may be removed pending an appropriate hearing). Also note that disciplinary removals of special education students must also comply with the provisions of the Individuals with Disabilities Education Act (IDEA) (*see*, Chapter 8).

School officials are ultimately responsible for assuring compliance with due process of law in their schools. When state laws or local policies mandate certain due process procedures, it is difficult to defend against charges that school officials representing the state and the local school district failed to follow their own rules in these proceedings.

Generally, because the school hearing is not a formal courtroom trial, it is not necessary that school officials have extensive expertise in the rules of evidence. But great care should be taken to assure that the hearing process is fundamentally fair, and justice is the core purpose of the rules of evidence.

For example, a fundamental principle of evidence is that there should be no surprise evidence or unannounced ambush witnesses. These surprise revelations unfairly advantage one party and deny the other party a fair opportunity to prepare a response, which is of course the real purpose of the "surprise" evidence or witness, to catch the other party unprepared to fairly respond. To guard against such unfair surprises, a list of evidence to be introduced must be revealed in advance, and a list of witnesses and a summary of the issues they will testify on must be disclosed.

Irrelevant or prejudicial evidence or testimony should not be allowed in the hearing. Evidence is irrelevant if it does not prove or disprove any unresolved issue in the proceedings, or only tends to prove that the charged party is a "bad person" generally, whether or not the charges are true.

To determine whether evidence should be admitted, a tribunal should weigh the probative value of the evidence (i.e., the degree to which it proves or disproves an unresolved issue) against the prejudicial effect (i.e., the degree to which it simply prejudices the trier of fact or superfluously attacks the character of the accused).

It must always be remembered that the hearing is about whether the party actually committed the alleged violation in this instance. Irrelevant prior history, personal beliefs, or the fundamental character of the accused are not on trial. Legal relevancy is determined by weighing probative value against prejudicial effect.

Weighing Admissibility: Probative Value v. Prejudicial Effect

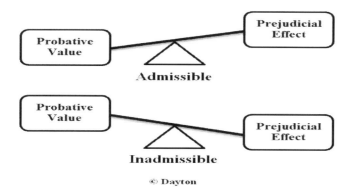

© Dayton

Although most student disciplinary proceedings are not rigidly bound by the legal rules of evidence, "hearsay" evidence (i.e., an out-of-hearing statement offered in evidence as proof of the matter asserted, including repeated rumors, second-hand statements, etc.) may be problematic if the admission of an out-of-hearing statement denies the tribunal an opportunity to assess the demeanor and honesty of the person making the statement, or denies the charged party any meaningful opportunity to cross-examine and contest the out-of-hearing statement.

Essential Questions & Answers

What do school officials have to do to comply with due process?

School officials are required to comply with both minimal constitutional standards for due process (e.g., adequate notice and hearing), and any state procedural requirements (*see*, state statutes and regulations). School districts commonly have their own operational regulations governing due process proceedings. These must at a minimum satisfy federal and state standards.

What do I do if school officials violate due process rights?

If you believe school officials have violated due process bring the violation to the attention of school officials immediately and request an appropriate remedy. If the violation is not corrected reassert your continuing objection at every reasonable opportunity. Carefully check local policy and state law for any specific requirements for appealing decisions including time limits. School officials are required to comply with established procedures, and persons appealing their decisions must also follow established procedures. Seek legal counsel when needed. If plaintiffs can prove significant due process violations, that is generally a losing case for school officials. Courts may order legal compliance, remedies, and hold schools liable for damages.

School officials transferred students and teachers to another facility based on non-punitive academic reasons. Although they were notified, they were given no opportunity for a hearing. Is this a violation of due process?

No. Generally, neither students nor teachers have a right to a specific assignment in the school system. As long as they are not deprived of any significant property or liberty rights, they may be assigned to comparable alternative assignments any time school officials decide that an alternative assignment is in the best interests of the school or the students. Although not required by the Due Process Clause, it is good practice to provide an informal opportunity to express any concerns about a proposed transfer. This helps to assure that the transfer is appropriate. Further, people are more likely to accept changes when they are notified, listened to, and treated with respect. But due process is generally not required for a non-punitive transfer.

Do students or teachers accused of wrongdoing by school officials have a right to be represented by legal counsel in due process proceedings?

They have a right to be represented by legal counsel, but not to have that legal counsel paid for by the school district, at least initially. Because public school due process hearings are civil proceedings and not criminal trials (*Gideon v. Wainwright*, 372 U.S. 335 (1963) only guaranteed state-paid legal counsel to indigent defendants in criminal proceedings), parties in civil proceedings are responsible for obtaining and paying for their own legal representation. A prevailing party may, however, be able to force school officials to reimburse their legal fees and pay other appropriate damages. Also, check on the availability of free or reduced cost legal counsel through pro bono legal services, civil liberties organizations, teachers unions, etc.

The grade our child received was lower than what we believe our child deserved. Do we have a right to appeal the grade?

School districts generally have policies allowing students to appeal a grade. If an error in grading can be proven, reasonable teachers will generally change grades. And if they refuse, school officials can order teachers to correct erroneous grades or face insubordination charges (teachers assign grades, but the grade is from the school and is ultimately controlled by the school). But otherwise judges grant broad deference to the academic judgments of educators. Students are unlikely to prevail in challenges against purely academic decisions by school officials (e.g., judges will not regrade papers; etc., as this exceeds reasonable bounds of judicial competence). Absent evidence that teachers abused their discretion; acted in bad faith; rendered decisions that were arbitrary and capricious; or issued decisions in violation of applicable laws (e.g., unlawful discrimination), judges will not interfere in purely academic judgments.

A student was found not guilty in a criminal trial. Does this also clear the student in a related school disciplinary proceeding?

No. Even though a criminal charge and a school disciplinary charge may be based on the same incident and evidence, an acquittal in the criminal proceeding does not require school officials to clear the student in a related school proceeding. Standards of proof in criminal proceedings are higher (i.e., "proof of guilt beyond a reasonable doubt") than in school civil proceedings (i.e., "proof by a preponderance of the evidence"). Based on the same set of facts and evidence criminal charges may not be proven, but there may still be sufficient evidence to prove a violation of school discipline rules under the lower civil standard of proof. The acquittal in the criminal case could also be the result of a procedural error not relevant in the school proceeding. School officials may find the student violated school rules even after an acquittal in a criminal proceeding.

Can school officials punish students for off-campus misconduct?

School officials have jurisdiction over conduct occurring on school property or at school related events. They do not, however, have general jurisdiction over off-campus conduct. To acquire jurisdiction over off-campus misconduct, school officials must establish that there is a "logical nexus" (i.e., connection) between the off-campus misconduct and a sufficient negative impact on discipline or safety in the school. Serious off-campus bullying of another student, for example, may negatively impact school discipline or safety. School officials can strengthen their case for jurisdiction over off-campus misconduct by documenting evidence of on-campus harms and disruptions resulting from the off-campus misconduct. By establishing a logical nexus between the off-campus misconduct and legitimate school discipline or safety interests, school officials may lawfully punish students for off-campus misconduct. If school officials cannot establish the necessary logical nexus between off-campus misconduct and sufficient negative impacts on legitimate school interests, the off-campus misconduct may be more appropriately dealt with by parents or law enforcement officials.

Is the use of corporal punishment in public schools legal?

Because the U.S. Supreme Court did not declare corporal punishment unconstitutional in *Ingraham v. Wright*, 430 U.S. 651 (1977), whether it is lawful in your local school depends on where you live. Most states have now banned the use of corporal punishment, and it is generally prohibited in most metro-area schools. But corporal punishment is still common in some of the more rural areas of the nation, and especially in the Southern U.S. Where corporal punishment is still used, legal challenges to the use of corporal punishment continue, as do concerns about the disproportionate use of corporal punishment based on race and gender, with minority race boys receiving the most corporal punishment.

Can school officials lie to students in order to get confessions?

Deception by government officials is generally not unlawful (e.g., falsely claiming "we have a video of you stealing the money" to encourage confession). Presumably, if the suspect was innocent, the suspect knows this is a false claim. Although commonly used against adult suspects, this technique is potentially ethically and legally problematic when used against children because it may induce false confessions. This is a special problem with younger children; very sensitive or frightened children; or children with disabilities who seek to please authority figures even when it means giving a false confession. So although not per se illegal, it should only be used in appropriate circumstances. More generally, building relationships of honesty and trust with students is preferred. Students are more likely to be honest with school officials if they believe school officials will be honest and fair.

Essential Practice Skills

Developing good skills in conducting investigations and interviewing witnesses can prove invaluable in keeping the school a safe and productive place for everyone. Most investigations begin when school officials receive a complaint, observe suspicious behavior, hear a rumor, etc., concerning misconduct, danger, or disruption. Below are useful recommendations for conducting investigations and interviewing witnesses; preparing for a successful hearing; and questioning and evidence in due process proceedings:

Investigations and interviewing witnesses

Prioritize investigations: Time and resources are always limited, so school officials must necessarily make triage decisions in allocating time and resources. Investigations affecting the safety and well-being of students and personnel must be given the highest priority. Imminent dangers must be addressed immediately.

Act quickly to secure evidence and statements: Time is the investigator's enemy. As time passes memories become weaker; evidence may be lost or destroyed; witnesses may become unavailable; hostile witnesses have more opportunities to collude; and perpetrators have more time to cover their tracks. Act quickly to secure essential documents and evidence; record initial statements from important witnesses; and secure a crime scene as soon as possible to assure safety and prevent the destruction of evidence.

Properly plan from the beginning: The formal investigation process should begin with a sound plan. The plan must address the exigencies of the specific situation: What persons or agencies should be involved in the investigation? What steps are necessary to assure a fair and effective investigation? What is the best order of events? Modifications will be necessary as the investigation evolves, but sound initial planning will save significant time and resources, and help to assure a fair, efficient, and effective investigation.

Document effectively: Cases are often won or lost based on documentation. The process and results of an investigation must be thoroughly, accurately, and professionally documented, keeping in mind that the investigation may lead to litigation.

Remain professional and objective: As an investigator, do not become emotionally involved in events or take sides in disputes. To conduct a fair investigation an investigator must remain objective until the investigation is completed.

Separate witnesses: Separate witnesses in interviews to avoid the unconscious construction of a group consensus, or giving untruthful witnesses an opportunity to "fit" their statements to those of others. The truth is far more likely to emerge from the investigator's triangulation of independent sources. Further, genuinely independent witnesses provide the most reliable corroboration.

Do not prejudice or influence witnesses: Be careful not to prejudice witnesses directly (e.g., by revealing what you really want to hear), or influence witnesses indirectly (e.g., through facial expressions or body language indicating approval/disapproval). The investigator needs candid statements and unfiltered facts, not witnesses motivated to confirm the investigator's well-intentioned but preconceived assumptions.

Focus on the facts: Focus questions on what the witnesses actually detected with their own senses (e.g., what did you see; hear; feel; smell; etc.). Do not ask witnesses to give opinions, draw conclusions, or speculate. Focus on gathering direct eye-witness accounts; physical evidence; documents; and provable events. And then the investigator draws conclusions based on the facts and not opinions and speculation.

Weigh the status and credibility of potential witnesses: Many people may have witnessed an event. Focus your interviews on the most valuable and credible potential witnesses. An ideal witness is mature, lucid, convincing, and unflappable. Very young children may not yet grasp the boundaries between fantasy and reality; a witness who was drinking, distracted, etc., at the time of the event is going to be less credible; a witness with a reputation for lying or dishonesty is less credible; as is a witness with a strong personal bias or a motive to lie. Witnesses that are psychologically or emotionally fragile are also likely to be more vulnerable during cross-examinations. The reality is, however, that your choices are always limited to only the witnesses you actually have available. Among available witnesses, focus on the most credible potential witnesses needed to testify on the most important elements in the case.

Corroborate testimony: Whenever possible attempt to corroborate important testimony. Ask potential witnesses for any confirmation of important facts (e.g., "do you know anyone who can confirm that?"; "do you have any records, receipts, pictures, saved or recorded messages, or other additional evidence confirming this?").

Guard information during a pending investigation: Tell individuals only what they need to know and no more. Once information is disclosed, it may reach hostile parties or aid perpetrators in intimidating witnesses or covering up evidence. Further, providing witnesses with details of the case may unduly influence their recollections and testimony. A witness whose understanding of events is based more on what others think and said than on personal knowledge is likely to be a weak and vulnerable witness in the hearing. While the investigation is pending, sensitive information should be shared only on a need to know basis, and investigation records and evidence should be kept in a secured area.

Appropriately respect individual privacy and confidentiality: If you have established a trust-worthy reputation in the community, and potential witnesses know you will appropriately respect their privacy and confidentiality, they are much more likely to fully cooperate in the investigation process. Always respect legal and ethical boundaries of privacy in the investigation process and keep all legally and professionally confidential information confidential. If you leak a piece of gossip acquired in the investigation, it may harm your case, the cooperating party who shared it with you, and your professional reputation for maintaining privacy and confidentiality. Further, a breach of privacy or confidentiality may expose you to potential legal and ethical sanctions.

Properly manage documents, reports, and the media: Remember that all documents and reports may be subject to open records laws or the discovery process in litigation. Everything recorded in official documents must be objective, professional, and lawful. Before releasing any potentially sensitive documents, be certain to comply with FERPA and other applicable privacy laws through redaction or other appropriate means. Members of the media should work through a single contact school official who understands relevant laws and rules concerning media access to hearings and records, and what can and cannot be communicated to the media during a pending investigation.

Preparing for a successful hearing

Good planning and preparation are the keys to a successful hearing. Below are some useful considerations in preparing for a successful hearing:

Start with the big picture and then systematically fill in the necessary details: Start with the conclusion required by the law and justice, based on the totality of the facts and circumstances (e.g. the student willfully committed an assault in clear violation of state law and the applicable discipline code; presents a continuing danger; and must be expelled from school). What testimony and evidence are necessary to convince the trier of fact to reach that conclusion? Envision the story you need to communicate to the tribunal from the beginning to the end. When the theory and vision of the case are clear in your mind, and you are confident that the fundamental arguments are persuasive, planning a convincing sequence of testimony and evidence becomes relatively easy.

In communication, less is generally more effective: Remember that the tribunal is made up of people with ordinary human limitations on their attention and memory. Your plan for the hearing must take these realities into account. Plan your case and your arguments for a presentation that is concise and focused. Be careful not to dilute the power of your case with superfluous evidence or excessive oration.

Carefully plan the sequence of events: Unless another approach is warranted, general, the sequence of witnesses and evidence follows the chronological sequence of events related to the charges and disposition (i.e., the events leading up to the incident; the incident; the harms and consequences; relevant future implications). When possible, however, there may be a strategic advantage to carefully ordering your witnesses (i.e., starting with a strong witness or evidence and finishing with a strong witness or evidence). The triers of fact are likely to form initial and lasting impressions of the case very early in the hearing, and they may also be disproportionately influenced by events near the close of the hearing.

Carefully weigh the cost-benefits of any discretionary witnesses: Some witnesses are essential, requiring you to play the hand you have been dealt. Some witnesses may be discretionary, in that they may bolster other testimony and evidence, but they are not absolutely essential to the case. For any discretionary witnesses, carefully weigh the cost-benefits of including this witness in your case (e.g., the value and impact of the witness' testimony versus risks that the witness may lack credibility; be easily impeached; open the door to unwanted issues; or otherwise unnecessarily damage the case).

Be aware of special concerns with child witnesses: Child witnesses require special consideration and planning, and the younger and less mature the child, the more care and preparation are needed. Children generally have more limited comprehension, life experiences, and vocabulary. They also often have a desire to cooperate and please adults, even if they have to alter their memories to do so. Children can be easily overwhelmed or frightened in hearings. It is important to remember that a child is not an adult, and to treat the child appropriately. In the hearing, be prepared to establish a friendly rapport with the child prior to more serious questioning. Prepare clear questions using simple words. Be certain the child understands the question (i.e., the child may be reluctant to admit he or she does not understand the question). Allow for longer pauses in questioning, giving the child sufficient time to think and respond. Very young children may need more close-ended and leading questions when testifying. Their answers may be corroborated or rehabilitated with documented consistent answers to more open-ended questions under the less stressful conditions of a previous interview with the child.

Good questions are the key to good testimony: You cannot get the right answer unless you ask the right question. Carefully plan and write down questions you need to ask of each witness. Questions should be written in a simple conversational style. Follow the overall written plan, making sure all essential questions are asked and answered in the hearing and on the record. Because the hearing is interactive it will sometimes be necessary to improvise. Do so, however, with great caution. Do not ask a question unless you already know how the witness will respond. You do not want any surprises in the hearing: In a hearing only ask a question when you already know the answer.

Plan persuasive opening and closing statements: Make a powerful case by assuring that everyone hears the essential evidence proving the charges three times: In the opening statement; in the presentation of testimony and evidence; and in the closing statement. The opening and closing statements should concisely and powerfully summarize all the essential elements of the charges and the evidence proving the charges. The opening, evidentiary, and closing statements are intentionally repetitive (i.e., the opening statement tells the tribunal what you will prove; the testimony and evidence provide the promised proof; and the closing statement summarizes what you proved). The opening and closing statements must be concise and to the point. Generally, the longer the statement; the less is remembered. Do not dilute the main message with unnecessary oration.

Questioning and evidence

Skillful investigation, interviews of witnesses, and planning will lay the essential foundation for a successful hearing. Below are considerations in conducting the hearing with effective questioning and presentations of evidence:

Introduce the witness and establish a basis for credibility: Begin by establishing the witness' identity and a basis for credibility (e.g., "please introduce yourself to the tribunal members and tell them who you are"). Follow up with close-ended questions to solidly establish the witness' credibility and the relevance of testimony (e.g., "Do you know Johnny?"; "Did you witness the event in question?"). Answering these easy yes/no questions also helps the witness to relax and get used to testifying. When the witness' credibility and basis for knowledge of the events has been established the direct examination can begin with more open-ended questions.

Conduct an effective direct-examination: The goal is to have the witness testify truthfully and persuasively. With open-ended questions guide the witness through a chronological account of the events witnessed. Stay focused on important, relevant events and testimony. Allowing the witness to ramble dilutes the testimony and may open opportunities for detrimental distractions or an unnecessary impeachment of the witness on cross-examination.

Asking open-ended questions: Open-ended questions encourage witnesses to tell the story in their own words. In general use open-ended questions on direct-examination. A helpful technique in asking open-ended, non-leading questions, is to begin the question with what, when, where, who, why, or how. Remember that although you ask the questions, only witnesses testify. The tribunal needs to hear the testimony of the witnesses, not just your conclusions confirmed with a yes or no from the witnesses. When necessary, however, be prepared to guide a straying witness back to relevant testimony with a more focused open-ended question (e.g., "please tell us exactly what you saw happen to Mary at the time of the incident").

Conduct effective cross-examinations/question hostile witnesses: The goal concerning cross-examinations and hostile witnesses is to reveal significant inaccuracies and to impeach the credibility of the witness. Close-ended questions and leading the witness are appropriate, calling for yes/no and other short answers (e.g., "Isn't it true that you personally never entered that room?"). Close-ended questions limit the hostile witness' ability to ignore the direct question, diminish or excuse damaging testimony, or introduce unwanted statements. Without badgering the witness or appearing rude to members of the tribunal, rapidly move from one question to the next to minimize open space for a hostile witness.

Asking close-ended leading questions: Close-ended leading questions only call for a yes/no type response or for a single word or short answer. Leading questions are permissible on cross-examination or when questioning a hostile witness. But you may generally also use close-ended leading questions on direct-examination to quickly get through undisputed facts or information for the record; to redirect the witness to relevant areas; to refresh the witness' memory; etc.

Impeachment of the witness: The goal is to raise significant doubts concerning the testimony or credibility of the witness. This may include, for example, comparing the witness' current testimony with prior statements and showing relevant inconsistencies (e.g., "You just testified that [quote testimony]. But didn't you previously state [quote directly from prior statement to highlight contradictions]?); comparing the witness' statement to provable facts (e.g., "you testified you witnessed the event, but here are police records proving you were arrested and jailed on a DUI charge over two hours prior to the event"); introduce evidence that the witness is biased and slanting testimony, etc. If the witness denies making a contradictory statement, be prepared to show proof that the statement was in fact made by the witness. And always directly ask if the witness made the statement. Do not ask if the witness remembers making the statement, as doing so may allow the witness to use a "memory lapse" to avoid accountability

Rehabilitation of your witness: The goal in rehabilitating your witness in the hearing is to repair damage from the cross-examination. This may merely require giving the witness an opportunity to clarify and explain important testimony that was called into question during cross-examination. Caution should be exercised, however, to assure that the scope of questioning in your rehabilitation of the witness does not exceed issues covered on direct-examination, or you may be opening the door to additional issues for the opposing party to challenge. In the planning and execution of the hearing, an ounce of prevention is worth many pounds of cure. It is best to conduct a solid and well-planned direct-examination, leaving little opportunity for damage in cross-examination, thereby minimizing chances that rehabilitation of the witness will even be necessary.

Types of questions to avoid:

Factually irrelevant questions: Questions that do not address an issue in dispute.

Legally irrelevant questions: Questions for which the prejudicial effect outweighs the probative value.

Questions calling for hearsay: Questions that call for the witness to testify about another person's out-of-hearing statements (e.g., "What did Johnny say he saw her do?").

Compound questions: Two or more questions fused together (e.g., "Did you know Johnny was at the party and did Jimmy leave?"). Compound questions are confusing, especially when answered by the witness with a single yes or no, leaving everyone to guess as to what exactly the witness meant. Further, asking a hostile witness a compound question offers the hostile witness an opportunity to choose which question to answer or claim answering a different part of the question if later confronted with perjury.

Confusing questions: Avoid questions that are too long; too complex; vaguely worded, or otherwise ambiguous.

Questions that assume facts not already in evidence: These questions contain statements of fact that have not yet been put in evidence (e.g., "Did you talk to Johnny before he attacked Mary at the party?" when it has not been established that Johnny was at the party, attacked anyone, or that Mary was attacked).

Argumentative questions: These "questions" may end with a question mark, but an argumentative question isn't really a question at all, and is instead rhetorical or gratuitously hostile (e.g., "When you came to school that day, had you already decided you were going to annoy everyone?").

Questions that have already been asked and answered: Repeating a question that has previously been clearly answered by the witness, and either wasting time or attempting to unduly call attention to an issue.

Questions that misstate the testimony or evidence: A question containing a relevant factual misstatement of testimony or the evidence.

Asking leading questions, when not appropriate: Questions that give the witness the answer. The questioner should not testify, with the witness only affirming the testimony of the questioner (e.g., to a friendly witness "Johnny was the one who did it, right?"). However, leading questions may be used on cross-examination; with a hostile witness; to aid a very young child; refresh a witness' memory; or other appropriate and limited uses.

Questions calling for conclusions: Questions that invite the witness to draw conclusions are problematic because they present the witness' speculation or personal opinion and not facts (e.g., "what was Johnny thinking at that time" requiring the witness to speculate about Johnny's thoughts).

Using non-verbal demonstrations: Remembering that a picture can be worth a thousand words, and that visual images are often remembered more vividly than words, consider incorporating non-verbal demonstrations and evidence when appropriate (e.g., "Please show the tribunal where Johnny put his hands"; presenting a picture of property damage; a scaled map of the location; etc.).

Remember that the record is officially the totality of the case: Make sure all the necessary testimony and evidence is entered into the formal record. In the appeals process, the case is considered solely on the basis of what was actually recorded in the official record. So if something is not in the record, it doesn't exist on appeal. A sure way to lose an appeal is to leave an essential element of proof out of the record of the hearing.

Summary of the essential rules of evidence

School tribunals are not judicial trials. The rules of evidence are generally more relaxed in school tribunals, and a hearing officer or the chair of the tribunal has great discretion concerning what evidence will be allowed. Nonetheless, a good working knowledge of the essential rules of evidence can be very helpful in assuring that the evidence admitted is fair and that it will likely survive challenges in the appeals process.

The rules of evidence are intended to promote fairness in the hearing process, and the paramount goal must always be a fair hearing for all parties.

Understanding and generally following the essential rules of evidence will help insure that the evidence introduced in the hearing is fair. Further, because any gross breach of the rules of evidence opens the case to the possibility of challenges and losing on appeal, assuring that the evidence introduced is fundamentally fair, as guided by the essential rules of evidence, helps to assure that the case will more likely withstand an appeal.

Moreover, understanding the essential rules of evidence will enable parties to know when to object to the admission of inappropriate evidence by the opposing party. If no objection is made to the attempted admission of inappropriate or unfair evidence and testimony, the evidence is generally admitted, and the right to appeal the admission of this evidence may be waived. And finally, understanding the essential rules of evidence can assist parties in more effectively working with legal counsel as necessary. The essential rules of evidence in brief summary are as follows:

Summary of the Essential Rules of Evidence

Evidence: Presented to prove or disprove disputed facts in a hearing.

Types of Evidence:

>*Direct evidence*: Directly proves a fact, requiring no inferences (e.g., "I saw Johnny stab Mary"). Direct evidence is almost always admissible.

>*Indirect (circumstantial) evidence*: Does not directly prove a fact but presents evidence of circumstances inferring that the fact is true as charged (e.g., "I saw Johnny with a knife running away from the area where Mary was stabbed"). Most objections to admissibility address indirect evidence and assertions that its probative value is outweighed by its prejudicial effect.

Forms of Evidence:

>*Testimonial evidence*: Sworn statements from witnesses.

>*Tangible evidence*: Real objects such as a weapon, garment, map, visual aid, etc. Tangible evidence should be: a) Identified for the record; b) Authenticated (i.e., proven genuine); c) Offered to the

opposing party for inspection; and d) Admitted into evidence with the permission of the tribunal. Concerning documents to be entered into evidence have an official copy available for review, but an electronic copy for use with an overhead projector or power-point may be helpful for simultaneous viewing by all parties in the tribunal.

Factual relevancy: Must tend to prove or disprove facts in dispute in the hearing.

Legal relevancy: Determined by weighing the probative value of the evidence against the prejudicial effect.

Competency: Concerns whether the witness is competent to testify. The witness must: a) Have direct knowledge of relevant issues (e.g., the witness directly saw, heard, etc.); and b) Be capable of truthful communication (i.e., the witness understands the duty to tell the truth and can competently communicate).

Appropriate questioning on direct-examination: Questioning of a friendly witness, generally using open-ended questions based on what, when, who, where, etc., (e.g., "Can you tell us what happened after you arrived at the party?").

Appropriate questioning on cross-examination: Questioning of a hostile witness following direct exam by the opposing party. Close-ended leading questions are allowed. Questioning is generally limited to the issues discussed on direct examination, but may include relevant issues, impeachment, etc.

Impeachment of a witness: Challenging the witness' testimony or credibility. This may be achieved through cross-examination or the presentation of contradictory evidence (e.g., prior inconsistent statements; lack of knowledge or capacity; conflicts of interest; bias; dishonesty; etc.). The basis for impeachment must be relevant to the proceedings and not simply gratuitous.

Rehabilitation of a witness: A re-direct examination to rebut the opposing party's effort to impeach the witness or give the witness an opportunity to clarify statements.

Objection: A complaint from a party in the hearing concerning the proceedings, usually an objection to the admissibility of testimonial or tangible evidence. Objections must be made in a timely manner or the right to object may be waived. A timely and continuing objection may also be necessary to preserve the issue for appeal. The objection will either be "sustained" (i.e., the tribunal expressing agreement with the objection and excluding the evidence) or "overruled" (i.e., the tribunal expressing disagreement with the objection and allowing the evidence to be admitted).

Hearsay: In-hearing testimony about another party's out-of-hearing statement offered as evidence in the hearing (e.g., "Jimmy said that he saw Johnny do it"). The fundamental concern is to protect the fairness of the proceedings, and to give the opposing party a fair opportunity to cross-examine all witnesses (i.e., the evidence is based on Jimmy's statement but Jimmy is not subject to cross-examination or an assessment of his demeanor and honesty by the tribunal). Hearsay evidence should be avoided when possible. But the tribunal generally has the discretion to allow hearsay evidence if the evidence appears trustworthy and its admission does not deny the opposing party a fair hearing. An important exception to the hearsay rule is that relevant official records by public employees are generally deemed trustworthy and admissible.

Authentication: Proof that the object offered into evidence is genuine and that it is what it is asserted to be. Official government documents are self-authenticating. Other documents may be authenticated by presenting the document for verification to a person who authored the document, saw it written, can identify the signature, responded to the document, etc. Other objects may be verified as authentic by a party in the hearing or connected to the location of the event in question. This may be achieved by having a witness identify a unique characteristic of the object (e.g., "I recognize this because it has a unique mark here"), or by establishing the chain of custody from the time and location when the object was seized to its presentation into evidence.

Privilege: A rule of law permitting a witness to withhold otherwise compelled testimony or allowing another party to prevent a witness from revealing confidential information. Possible privileges include the Fifth Amendment right not to answer incriminating questions, and confidences disclosed in the attorney-client; physician-patient; psychotherapist-patient; clergy-penitent; or marital relationship.

Burden of proof: In student discipline hearings and employment hearings initiated by school officials, the burden of proof rests with school officials who must prove the charges by a preponderance of the evidence (i.e., the evidence established that it was more probable than not that the charges are true).

Direct-Examination (asking non-leading questions): Begin with what; when; where; who; why; etc., and ask an open-ended question.

Cross-Examination/Hostile Witness (asking leading questions): Begin with didn't; isn't; wasn't . . . or end with right?; correct? true?, and ask a close-ended question.

Basic Guide to Objections

"Objection, the question is . . . "

factually irrelevant . . .	does not address an issue in dispute in the hearing
legally irrelevant . . .	the prejudicial effect outweighs the probative value
calling for hearsay . . .	asking the witness to testify about someone else's out-of-hearing statements
compound question . . .	presenting the witness with more than a single question to answer
confusing . . .	too long/complex/vaguely worded/ambiguous
assumes a fact not in evidence . . .	it has not been established that [state unestablished claim]
argumentative . . .	rhetorical/gratuitously hostile/badgering the witness
asked and answered . . .	question was already asked and the witness has answered
misstates testimony/evidence . . .	question contains a significant misstatement of the testimony/evidence
leading the witness . . .	the questioner should not testify with the witness only affirming the questioner's statements
calls for conclusions . . .	asks for speculation/personal opinions and not facts

© Dayton

Student Discipline: Hearing and Appeals Process

```
Federal Courts                          State Courts

Supreme Court  ← Certiorari ←  Supreme Court
      ↑                              ↑
Court of Appeals              Court of Appeals
      ↑                              ↑
  Trial Court                    Trial Court
       ↖                        ↗
         Appeal to State Board of Education
                      ↑
         Appeal to Local Board of Education
                      ↑
            Decision by Local Tribunal
```

© Dayton

Essential Practice Tips

1) *Uncertainty about how much process is due*: When in doubt, provide more due process rather than less. Judicial concerns over due process are never triggered by providing too much due process, only too little.

2) *School culture, safety, and discipline*: Establishing a positive school culture is essential to both avoiding serious problems and addressing problems effectively. The best way to deal with safety and discipline problems is to proactively prevent them. In discouraging crime and misconduct, an ounce of prevention is worth many pounds of cure.

3) *Investigations*: The keys to conducting successful investigations are to start with an open mind; identify relevant evidence; and follow the trial of evidence to the truth through the use of logical deductions and common sense. Throughout this process the investigator must always maintain the highest fidelity to finding the truth; acting with fairness; treating all persons with respect; and acting only in full compliance with the law and professional ethics.

4) *Teaching moments and turning points*: When students are facing serious consequences for misconduct, this may also be a powerful teaching moment and potential turning point for the student. In Dickens' A CHRISTMAS CAROL, when Ebenezer Scrooge asked the *Ghost of What is Yet to Come*: "Before I draw nearer to that stone to which you point . . . answer me one question. Are these the shadows of the things that will be, or are they shadows of things that may be, only?" In this classic story the shocking realization of the consequences of the path he was on changed Scrooge's life forever. Similarly, in the wake of an emotionally significant event, if you can help the student to understand the serious future consequences of the current path, this teaching moment could become a turning point for the student towards better choices, better conduct, and a more positive future.

5) *The suspended sentence*: In schools even punishments should be educational. Rather than approaching school discipline as a punitive tool only, look for ways to use the discipline process to educate and encourage personal growth. One powerful tool is the suspended punishment. In appropriate cases consider a suspended punishment in exchange for clear, good faith proof of positive change and personal growth. For example, a punishment may be temporarily suspended pending sincere apologies, appropriate restitution, community service, proof of positive behavioral change, etc. If the agreed change is not forthcoming within the designated

time the punishment is executed. Having the punishment hanging over one's head can be a powerful incentive for positive change and personal growth.

Essential Points:

- Due process requires adequate notice, an opportunity to be heard, and fundamental fairness.
- Due process is required when government actions may significantly impinge on a protected life, liberty, or property interest.
- Protected liberty interests in public schools include persons' interests in their good name, reputation, honor, or integrity.
- Protected property interests in public schools include students' rights to a free public education and employees' contractual rights.
- Concerning adequate notice, the "vagueness doctrine" requires that to avoid being unconstitutional vague and therefore void, government rules must be defined clearly enough so that persons of ordinary intelligence can reasonable know what is required or prohibited.
- How much process is due is based on balancing the potential loss by the individual against the burden on the government.
- More serious punishments and longer disciplinary removals require more due process:
    > Removals of more than 10 days = Formal due process is required (see state statute).
    > Removals of 10 days or less = Informal due process is required (oral or written).
    > Punishments that are *de minimis* in nature = No due process required (but may be given to help assure fairness).
- Informal due process requires basic oral or written notice of the charges, a brief summary of the evidence, and an informal opportunity to be heard.
- Formal due process procedures are defined by state statute and must be strictly followed.
- A limited in-school suspension generally does not significantly impinge on due process rights. However, extended or frequent in-school suspensions; a denial of access to the required curriculum; or a significant public stigma associated with the removal may require adequate due process.
- Neither students nor teachers have a right to a specific assignment in the school system. If they are not deprived of any significant property or liberty rights, they may be assigned to alternative

assignments any time school officials decide that an alternative assignment is in the best interests of the school or the students.

- All questioning should be respectful, professional, non-coercive, and focused on resolving only the school-related problem.
- Hearing officers or members of a tribunal should be clear concerning their duties in the hearing, the rules of the hearing, and the essential requirements of federal and state laws in these proceedings.
- Irrelevant evidence should not be allowed. Evidence is irrelevant if it does not prove or disprove any unresolved issue in the proceedings, or only tends to prove that the accused is a "bad person" generally. To determine whether evidence should be admitted weigh the probative value against the prejudicial effect.
- To acquire valid jurisdiction over off-campus misconduct, school officials must establish that there is a logical nexus between the off-campus misconduct and a sufficient negative impact on discipline or safety in the school.
- Reasonable and proportional school grading policies focused on academic evaluations are likely to survive legal challenges.

Essential Terms:

Due process: The foundation of any just legal system, requiring fundamental fairness in government actions that significantly affect persons' rights.

Exculpatory evidence: Information that tends to prove the defendant's innocence. State agents cannot hide exculpatory evidence and must share it with the defendant. The goal must be truth and justice, not "winning" a case.

Hearing: A formal proceeding to receive relevant evidence and testimony for the purpose of revealing the truth and reaching a just result.

Hearsay: An out-of-hearing statement offered in evidence as proof of the matter asserted, including repeating rumors, second-hand statements, etc.

Vagueness doctrine: Requires that government rules must be defined clearly enough so that persons of ordinary intelligence can reasonable know what is required or prohibited.

Essential Cases

Goss v. Lopez, 419 U.S. 565 (1975): A student was caught up in a mass suspension of 75 students after a lunchroom disturbance. The student claimed innocence, no evidence in the record suggested otherwise, but the student was not provided with any opportunity for a hearing. Held: "Students facing temporary suspension have interests qualifying for protection of the Due Process Clause, and due process requires, in connection with a suspension of 10 days or less, that the student be given oral or written notice of the charges against him and, if he denies them, an explanation of the evidence the authorities have and an opportunity to present his side of the story. The Clause requires at least these rudimentary precautions against unfair or mistaken findings of misconduct and arbitrary exclusion from school."

Ingraham v. Wright, 430 U.S. 651 (1977): The U.S. Supreme Court rejected arguments that the use of corporal punishment in public schools violated the Eight Amendment's prohibition against cruel and unusual punishment. Subsequently, most states banned corporal punishment by state law.

University v. Ewing, 474 U.S. 214 (1985). In upholding an academic dismissal the Court held: "When judges are asked to review the substance of a genuinely academic decision . . . they should show great respect for the faculty's professional judgment. Plainly, they may not override it unless it is such a substantial departure from accepted academic norms as to demonstrate that the person or committee responsible did not actually exercise professional judgment."

University of Missouri v. Horowitz, 435 U.S. 78 (1978): Held: Concerning challenges to grades, courts should defer to academic judgments except where allegations of misconduct are involved. Less due process is required for academic decisions than for disciplinary decisions.

A Closer Look at the Law

How do we make schools safe without turning schools into police state units in the "school to prison pipeline"? Police are going to be involved with schools. But in what ways and to what extent? Some school misconduct also constitutes a crime and must be reported to law enforcement agents consistent with state laws. But it is essential that both school officials and the law enforcement agents understand their appropriate roles in this process and that everyone stay in their proper legal and ethical lanes. This section addresses school/police legal boundaries; avoiding coercion and false confessions; protecting children in investigations and hearings; notification of parents when children are subject to criminal questioning; and avoiding errors and abuses through adherence to due process and professional ethics.

School officials are responsible for civil law matters related to the school, including student discipline and safety. Law enforcement officials are responsible for criminal law matters throughout their jurisdiction, including crimes occurring in the school. It is the role of school officials to question students about violations of school rules, discipline matters, and safety issues related to school events, none of which should directly involve criminal investigations or interrogations which are the legal domain of police.

When school officials uncover evidence of criminal violations, school officials should report criminal conduct to police and let police investigate criminal matters. Police should not be involved in ordinary school discipline matters. And school officials should not be involved in criminal investigations other than as reporters or witnesses. When either school officials or police stray out of their designated legal lane they unwisely enter areas in which they lack both legal authority and professional competence.

When law enforcement officers question students about alleged criminal conduct, constitutional protections may apply, including *Miranda* warnings. from *Miranda v. Arizona*, 384 U.S. 436 (1966). The *Miranda* warning (i.e., "You have the right to remain silent . . .") is intended to assure informed consent by the suspect, and that any subsequent confession during the custodial interrogation is voluntary and not coerced. A custodial interrogation is criminal questioning when the individual cannot leave or does not reasonably feel free to leave under the circumstances. As the U.S. Supreme Court said concerning custodial interrogations of minor children in *J.D.B. v. North Carolina*, 564 U.S. 261 (2011):

> By its very nature, custodial police interrogation entails inherently compelling pressures. Even for an adult, the physical and psychological isolation of custodial interrogation can undermine the individual's will to resist and . . . compel him to speak where he would not otherwise do so freely. Indeed, the pressure of custodial interrogation is so immense that it can induce a frighteningly high percentage of people to confess to crimes they never committed. That risk is all the more troubling--and recent studies suggest, all the more acute--when the subject of custodial interrogation is a juvenile.

A false confession is a tragedy for all parties. An innocent person may be punished; the guilty may go free; and the community remains exposed to unresolved dangers. Constitutional protections including *Miranda* and other due process safeguards are intended to limit the dangers of coercive interrogations and false confessions in custodial interrogations by police.

School officials are not required to give *Miranda* warnings for civil questioning about school issues. But to avoid false confessions and false findings of guilt, school officials must respect due process of law and practice the highest standards of professional ethics. School investigations and the prosecution of disciplinary matters conducted by school officials must never be allowed to devolve to a win/lose mindset where "winning" is the goal. The goal must always be revealing the truth and reaching a just result for all parties. All questioning must be civil, ethical, and non-coercive.

School officials must carefully oversee lawyers hired by the school as lawyers are trained as zealous advocates focused on winning cases, and not as educators whose primary duty is the welfare of the child, acting *in loco parentis*, even when the child has engaged in misconduct. Similarly, school officials must set reasonable limits when police are involved in events under school jurisdiction, assuring that treatment of students is always age appropriate and that children are protected when necessary from unlawful abuses by lawyers or law enforcement agents. Punishment comes from the sentence after a just finding of guilt; not from the process of determining guilt. School officials must always know and follow state laws, standards of professional ethics, and dutifully protect children under their care from all dangers and abuses, including abuses by lawyers or law enforcement agents.

Consistent with state law parents should generally be notified of criminal questioning of their child so that they may act to protect their child's rights and have an opportunity to seek legal counsel. Although school resource officers and probation officers of the juvenile court investigating school related issues may be permitted to reasonably question students at school without prior parental approval, law enforcement officers from other agencies investigating non-school related matters do not have the right to interview students at school simply for convenience. In such cases, the interrogation of students is generally not permitted without the consent of the parent unless the officer presents a valid court order, warrant for arrest, or the situation involves hot pursuit of a suspect linked to a felony crime.

Proper boundaries of jurisdiction and legal authority between the school and law enforcement agencies should be negotiated and respected. All parties should recognize that school administrators are not police officers and police officers are not school administrators. Law enforcement officers should not be unreasonably hindered in the conduct of their official duties. Law enforcement officers, however, should not interfere with the educational process and should recognize that school administrators are responsible for the oversight of students and school property during school hours.

School administrators are not subject to charges of interference with law enforcement for reasonably refusing access to a child or interrogation during school hours. Law enforcement personnel should be questioned as to the lawful basis for any proposed interrogation of an in-school student to assure compliance with applicable laws and policies. Arrests or interrogations of students during school hours should be discouraged in favor of off-campus and after school arrests or interrogations whenever possible.

Students must not be released from the school to any person unless identification and a lawful reason for releasing the child is confirmed. Persons impersonating police officers have kidnapped children from schools. Upon entering school property all persons, including law enforcement officers, must report to the school office immediately to state the purpose of their presence and be cleared for entry to the school unless there is an emergency or the law enforcement officer is in hot pursuit of a felony suspect. The failure of any non-school person to first report to the main office for permission to enter the school is a crime in most states.

Concerning school discipline proceedings, it is essential that school officials respect reasonable checks and balances in the school discipline process to assure fairness to all persons. The Court's due process standards were designed to help assure the protection of students' rights in schools. Too much is at stake for school officials to be guessing about what actually happened and who was responsible. The punishment process fails both standards of justice and school goals when it is arbitrary and unfair. Further, in the absence of sufficient due process checks and balances the school discipline process can be misused to punish personal enemies and vulnerable groups, or individuals may be subjected to punishment based on racial profiling and misidentification. For example, in *Goss v. Lopez*, 419 U.S. 565 (1975):

> Lopez . . . was suspended in connection with a disturbance in the lunchroom which involved some physical damage to school property. Lopez testified that at least 75 other students were suspended from his school on the same day. He also testified . . . he was not a party to the destructive conduct but was instead an innocent bystander. Because no one from the school testified with regard to this incident, there is no evidence in the record indicating the official basis for concluding otherwise. Lopez never had a hearing.

How do we know when a student is guilty of a charged offense? As the Court noted in *Goss*:

> Disciplinarians, although proceeding in utmost good faith, frequently act on the reports and advice of others; and the controlling facts and the nature of the conduct under challenge are often disputed. The risk of error is not at all trivial, and it should be guarded against if that may be done without prohibitive cost or interference with the educational process.

Most people tend to put a high degree of confidence in eyewitness accounts. But in fact eyewitness accounts are notoriously unreliable and inaccurate. This is especially true in cross-race identifications of suspects, and when events occurred quickly, at a distance, or the witness was under stress.

Due process helps to assure that school discipline policies are fair and that punishments are proportional. While this is essential, it is not sufficient: Everything a school does should have an educational purpose, including discipline policies. Discipline policies should teach students important lessons about conduct and character, with the goal of improving both. Students should learn that when they have done something wrong, they have a responsibility to tell the truth and to try to make it right, and if they do so, they will be treated fairly. Having students take responsibility for misconduct and for making it right with the people they harmed helps to resolve conflicts and teaches valuable life lessons.

Law & Professional Ethics in Practice:

"A hundred suspicions don't make a proof . . . one could never judge of a man without seeing him close, for oneself . . . what do you think, would not one tiny crime be wiped out by thousands of good deeds?"

CRIME AND PUNISHMENT, Fyodor Dostoyevsky

What constitutes a crime or conduct meriting punishment? How do we decide who will be prosecuted, and whether they are guilty? What is a just punishment? A society demonstrates its values by what it criminalizes; who is prosecuted; the nature of the trial; and how we deal with those found guilty. Although state punishment systems should be used to administer justice and deter misconduct, the reality is these same systems can be used to provide a facade of legitimacy to political agendas, government officials' personal vendettas, and to persecute vulnerable groups.

Critics of policies that increasingly criminalized school discipline and promoted active police involvement in schools have argued that these policies created a "school to prison pipeline" that disproportionately targeted minority students, resulted in unwarranted criminal records for students, and in disproportionate numbers of minority males in prisons.

Critical Legal Studies (CLS) scholars argue that the law too often serves the interests of the wealthy and the powerful at the expense of the poor and the vulnerable, legitimizing social injustice under the facade of law and perpetuating existing social hierarchy and inequalities.

The reality is that law, and school policies, are tools that may be used for good or evil. The U.S. justice system has been used to both fight against and to perpetuate social injustices. For example, the law was used to declare racial segregation unconstitutional in *Brown v. Board of Education*, 347 U.S. 483 (1954). But state and local "Jim Crow Laws" had also been used by police and school officials to enforce racial discrimination in schools and communities. Perpetuating slavery and segregation required a police state level of laws and brutal enforcement against minority race citizens, all "legal" at the time.

Similarly, concerning members of the LGTB community, in *Lawrence v. Texas*, 539 U.S. 558 (2003), the U.S. Supreme Court struck down "sodomy laws" that treated private relationships among consenting adults as felonies. State sodomy laws had been used to persecute LGTB persons with arrests, imprisonment, and denial of employment, professional licenses, child custody, and other rights. Countless teachers were fired or lived in fear of dismissal because their private relationships were criminalized by the state. The Court's decision in *Lawrence* ended criminalization of sexual orientation. And in *Obergefell v. Hodges*, 576 U.S. ___ (2015), the Court held that states could no longer discriminate based on gender in the issuance of marriage licenses. Progress. But slow and painful.

Do we still have criminal laws, school laws, or institutional practices that enforce injustice or legitimize discrimination? Do we still tolerate school practices that discriminate (even clearly unlawful ones such as school sponsored prayers; making students stand for the pledge; punishments for "taking a knee" during the anthem or other lawful protests)? Do we even recognize injustice and discrimination when it is so common and long established? As Dostoyevsky said: "Man grows used to everything, the scoundrel!" Why were legalized racial segregation; gender discrimination; LGTB discrimination; etc. tolerated in schools for so many years? Do we only recognize or care about injustice when we are its victims? What other laws, policies, and practices need to change to make schools more just and welcoming places for all persons? If we know something is wrong, how can we ignore it?

Questions for Further Exploration:

1) *Preventive discipline*: Concerning school discipline, an ounce of prevention can be worth many pounds of cure. What are the most effective means of preventing discipline problems in schools? How can you build a positive culture of trust and cooperation with students and faculty in your school? What methods of student discipline are most effective in improving student behavior? What are the laws and local rules concerning suspensions, expulsions, and corporal punishment in your state and your school? Is corporal punishment an effective disciplinary technique?

2) *"Double secret probation"*: A formal letter of reprimand was placed in a teacher's personnel file by a supervisor without prior notice or any opportunity to respond. Was this a lawful procedure? Why or why not?

3) *The hunter becomes the hunted*: A student athlete fell asleep in class. Based on this behavior, the teacher reduced the student's grade. This grade reduction caused the student to fail the class, making the student ineligible to participate in team competition. School policy prohibited the use of non-academic factors in grading. School officials asked the teacher to change the grade. The teacher refused. The teacher was fired for insubordination, and the student's grade was changed by school officials to reflect only his academic achievement, and not his conduct in class. With the grade changed he passed the class and was eligible to participate in team competition again. The dismissal of the teacher for insubordination was upheld by the State Board of Education. Was this a correct decision by the State Board of Education? Should the teacher have changed the grade? Do school administrators have the legal authority to change students' grades over the objections of the teachers who issued the grades?

4) *Open forum*: What other related issues or current events would you like to discuss?

Suggested Activities for Further Learning:

1) Review the laws governing formal due process proceedings for long-term suspensions and expulsions in your state.

2) Review your local school's student code of conduct.

3) Volunteer to serve on a student disciplinary tribunal.

4) Shadow a school administrator to observe the daily administration of student discipline in your school.

5) Talk with a juvenile court judge about the judge's work with children and how school officials and court officials can work together to help at risk children.

Chapter 7: Equal Protection of the Laws

No system of government is perfect. Further, even if a perfect system of government was possible, the individuals responsible for administering the government are imperfect. As imperfect humans, too many government officials regrettably bring the tragic human imperfections of selfishness, ignorance, and prejudice from their private lives into their public work. And while a democratic form of government has many virtues, democracy also has a serious potential flaw: In a system of governance in which the majority rules, because of selfishness, ignorance, and prejudice the majority may too often fail to respect the equal rights of minorities.

The Fourteenth Amendment to the U.S. Constitution was adopted after the U.S. Civil War to help guard against these dangers by providing rights of equal protection of the laws to all persons. The Fourteenth Amendment (1868) states:

> All persons born or naturalized in the United States, and subject to the jurisdiction thereof, are citizens of the United States and of the State wherein they reside. No State shall make or enforce any law which shall abridge the privileges or immunities of citizens of the United States; nor shall any State deprive any person of life, liberty, or property, without due process of law; nor deny to any person within its jurisdiction the equal protection of the laws.

The Fourteenth Amendment specifically prohibits discrimination by state governments, requiring states to provide due process and equal protection of the laws to all persons. Equal protection of the laws prohibits differential treatment based on factors that are legally irrelevant, and are instead the products of irrational prejudice or discrimination (e.g., differential treatment by government based on race, color, national origin, etc.). Principles of equal protection may, however, allow or even require differential treatment when there are legally relevant differences among individuals (i.e., legitimate differences may require additional resources or reasonable accommodations to participate in public funded programs).

In interpreting the Equal Protection Clause of the Fourteenth Amendment, the U.S. Supreme Court developed a multi-tiered approach for adjudicating allegations of governmental denial of equal protection of the laws. Most state courts have adopted a similar model for reviewing equal protection claims. Where differential treatment by government is established by plaintiffs, the purpose of the court's inquiry is to determine whether the differential treatment is justified by a sufficient governmental interest. The graduated levels of scrutiny reflect the Court's determination that certain categories of government action (i.e., discrimination based on race, national origin, or a fundamental right) are inherently more suspect than others (i.e., general social and economic regulations), and therefore merit heightened levels of judicial scrutiny and require greater levels of proof by government officials seeking to defend the differential treatment.

Basic Framework for Judicial Review of Equal Protection Challenges

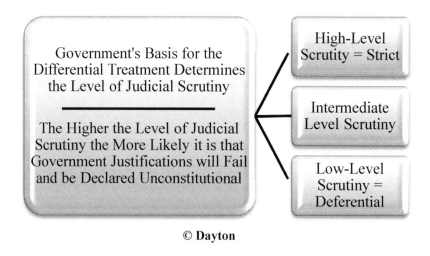

© Dayton

The Court has recognized three basic levels of judicial scrutiny based on judicial suspicion of the government's differential treatment: Low-level; intermediate; and high-level judicial scrutiny. Concerning when low-level scrutiny is appropriate, members of the legislative and administrative braches are elected to make decisions about general social and economic issues. The judicial branch is not a general overseer of all government decisions. Courts should defer to the political branches concerning general social and economic issues, and only intervene where warranted because of irrational governmental discrimination. Therefore differential treatments based on general social and economic regulations (e.g., tax rates, zoning regulations, etc.) are only subjected to the low-level scrutiny of the "rational basis test." Under the rational basis test government officials need only establish that their actions are "rationally related to a legitimate governmental interest." Whether legislative and administrative decisions on general social and economic issues are unwise is for voters to decide in subsequent elections. It is only when these actions discriminate without any rational basis that judicial intervention is warranted.

Government actions that discriminate based on gender, age, or legitimacy have been viewed as quasi-suspect by the Court and subjected to an intermediate-level of scrutiny. Differential treatment based on these quasi-suspect criteria is deemed unconstitutional under the equal protection clause unless government officials can prove that the differential treatment was "substantially related to an important government interest." Since *U.S. v. Virginia*, 518 U.S. 515 (1996) (the "VMI case" striking down a state funded military school's males-only admissions policy), however, the Court has applied a further elevated scrutiny to differential treatment based on gender, requiring that differential treatment based on gender be justified by an "exceedingly persuasive justification."

Differential treatment based on fundamental rights or suspect classifications such as race or national origin are subjected to the strictest judicial scrutiny. To qualify as a suspect classification, the Court has held that the government action must be aimed at a "discrete and insular minority" that is: 1) Politically powerless; and 2) Historically discriminated against. To be politically powerless doesn't mean the group has no political power, but instead they have no realistic opportunity to defend their rights against majoritarian power in the common legislative realm. Women, for example, have not been deemed a suspect class because voting age women outnumber voting age men, making it politically possible for women to defend their rights in the legislative realm or to even dominate the political process. Men are not a suspect class, however, because there is no substantial legislative history of discrimination against men. For this reason the Court treats gender discrimination as a quasi-suspect class, subject to an elevated standard of review, but not strict scrutiny.

Discrimination against racial and ethnic minorities, however, has been so pervasive that the Court subjects any governmental use of race, color, or ethnicity to strict scrutiny. All suspect classifications are subject to strict judicial scrutiny and must be justified by establishing that the differential treatment is "necessary to a compelling governmental interest and narrowly tailored to achieving that interest." In practice, governmental actions subjected to strict judicial scrutiny rarely survive this rigorous judicial test. Justice Marshall recognized that strict scrutiny is generally "strict in theory, but fatal in fact." Until the Court's sharply divided 5-4 decision in *Grutter v. Bollinger*, 539 U.S. 306 (2003) (upholding a prestigious law school's affirmative action admissions plan), the last time a governmental racial classification survived strict scrutiny by the Court was in *Korematsu v. U.S.*, 323 U.S. 214 (1944), the now universally condemned case in which the Court upheld forced relocations and internments of Japanese-Americans in "war relocation camps."

Summary of Judicial Standards of Review under the Equal Protection Clause

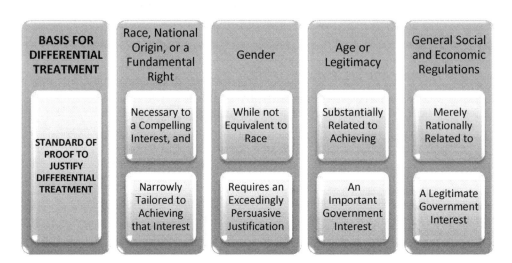

BASIS FOR DIFFERENTIAL TREATMENT	Race, National Origin, or a Fundamental Right	Gender	Age or Legitimacy	General Social and Economic Regulations
STANDARD OF PROOF TO JUSTIFY DIFFERENTIAL TREATMENT	Necessary to a Compelling Interest, and	While not Equivalent to Race	Substantially Related to Achieving	Merely Rationally Related to
	Narrowly Tailored to Achieving that Interest	Requires an Exceedingly Persuasive Justification	An Important Government Interest	A Legitimate Government Interest

© Dayton

The core teaching of the Court's cases on equal protection is that government officials cannot legally treat individuals differently for irrelevant, discriminatory reasons, such as the person's race, color, religion, sex, national origin, disability, etc., when those factors bear no appropriate relationship to a sufficient governmental justification. Absent a legitimate and sufficient reason for differential treatment, federal, state, and local governments must treat all persons equally under the laws. The Fourteenth Amendment also grants Congress the power to enforce the Fourteenth Amendment through appropriate legislation, legislation which includes, for example, the Civil Rights Act of 1964 and subsequent legislation prohibiting discrimination based on race, color, religion, sex, national origin, and disability. State laws or local policies may provide additional protections for citizens.

In summary, generally government officials must provide equal treatment to individuals in equal circumstances. Differential treatment must be justified by proving an appropriate relationship between the differential treatment and a sufficient governmental justification. Equal protection of the laws prohibits differential treatment based on factors that are legally irrelevant (e.g., race; color; national origin; etc.), and are instead the products of irrational prejudice or discrimination. But differential treatment may be allowed or even required when there are legally relevant differences among individuals.

Essential Questions &Answers

If the Equal Protection Clause requires equality why can't public schools just provide the same equal services to all children?

The Equal Protection Clause generally requires equal treatment of all persons under the laws, so the presumption is equal provision of services. But when there are legally relevant differences among children (e.g., special needs), equal protection of the laws may allow or even require differential treatment. Children with disabilities, for example, may have special needs requiring educational supports and related services beyond those generally provided to non-disabled children. Without these additional services children with disabilities may be unable to benefit from educational opportunities.

The U.S. Supreme Court declared racial segregation unlawful in Brown (1954). Why are there still schools that appear to be racially segregated?

The Constitution prohibits intentional racial discrimination using government powers (i.e., *de jure* segregation), but not racial imbalances caused by the private choices of individuals (i.e., *de facto* segregation). In short, the Constitution limits public action; not private choices. Racially and economically segregated communities result in *de facto* segregated schools. Race based student assignment remedies are now unlawful (*see, PICS v. Seattle*, 551 U.S. 701 (2007)). School officials can institute assignment policies for balancing students based on socio-economic status (SES) factors which often correlate highly with race imbalances in schools, resulting in more diverse schools. But while SES balancing is lawful it is not legally required. There must be sufficient political will to do so. Far too often there is not sufficient political will for more SES balanced/racially integrated schools in the community, leading to persistent *de facto* school segregation.

Is language discrimination in schools unlawful?

Discrimination based on language has been treated as a form of national origin discrimination, and is unlawful under both the Equal Protection Clause and Title VI of the Civil Rights Act of 1964. In *Lau v. Nichols*, 414 U.S. 563 (1974) the U.S. Supreme Court held that failure to provide necessary English language instruction to non-English speaking students denied these students a meaningful opportunity to participate in public education programs in violation of Title VI of the Civil Rights Act of 1964. At a minimum, public schools must provide an adequate English language bridge for non-English speaking students, to give these students an opportunity to benefit from public school instruction in English.

Public school board members stated they only wanted to hire "real Americans" to work in our local schools. Is this legal?

That depends on what they meant by "real Americans." The U.S. is a nation of immigrants. All U.S. citizens are real Americans. If "real Americans" is code for discrimination based on race, ethnicity, religion, or national origin, this is unlawful employment discrimination. Public school employers must fairly consider all qualified applicants.

Based on the success of separate gender private schools, the local public schools want to start separate gender education programs. Is this lawful?

No. In *U.S. v. Virginia*, 518 U.S. 515 (1996), the U.S. Supreme Court struck down publicly funded separate gender education programs. The Equal Protection Clause commands that the government and its agents must treat individuals as individuals, and not just as members of a group. The general rule of law under the Equal Protection Clause is that gender based actions in the public sphere are unconstitutional unless supported by an "exceedingly persuasive justification." Single gender education may be supported by many interesting educational theories, none of which constitute an exceedingly persuasive justification for gender based discrimination in publicly funded schools. With few exceptions (e.g., contact sports) public school programs must be open to all persons on an equal basis regardless of gender.

A public school has a policy of not allowing female students to participate in football. Is this lawful?

Female students increasingly participate in contact sports such as football. But current federal regulations do not *require* public schools to allow this participation. Football is expressly defined as a "contact sport" specifically excluded from the general requirement of non-discrimination based on gender. It could be argued that the "contact sport" exception under 45 C.F.R. § 86.41 is unconstitutional as a violation of the Equal Protection Clause, because it substitutes an individual's membership in a group (here female) for individual merits, based on male/female stereotypes and outdated paternalistic assumptions about the safety and abilities of females. But currently female exclusions are allowed in contact sports under § 86.41. Citizens may, however, lobby school officials to change their local policy

158

and allow participation. Although exclusion is allowed under § 86.41 it is not required, and public schools now commonly allow female students to participate in football and other contact sports, based on ability and not gender, which *should be* the law consistent with the Equal Protection Clause.

Local public school officials have a policy of excluding girls who get pregnant from the cheerleading team stating "as student role models they set a bad example and may encourage teen pregnancy." Is this lawful?

No. Under 45 C.F.R. § 86.40 institutions receiving federal funds "shall not apply any rule concerning a student's actual or potential parental, family, or marital status which treats students differently on the basis of sex" including pregnancy. Specifically: "A recipient shall not discriminate against any student, or exclude any student from its education program or activity, including any class or extracurricular activity, on the basis of such student's pregnancy, childbirth, false pregnancy, termination of pregnancy or recovery therefrom, unless the student requests voluntarily to participate in a separate portion of the program or activity of the recipient." School officials "may require such a student to obtain the certification of a physician that the student is physically and emotionally able to continue participation so long as such a certification is required of all students for other physical or emotional conditions requiring the attention of a physician." But otherwise pregnancy is a medical condition and not a scarlet letter offense for which only girls may be excluded from participation in public school activities. Because only females become visibly pregnant, females have historically suffered moral judgments, exclusions, and punishments that the male fathers did not. Teen pregnancy can be discouraged by school officials through appropriate nondiscriminatory educational programs. But when a student above the age of legal consent becomes pregnant, school officials often do not know, and generally have no right to know, the circumstances concerning her pregnancy. If school officials have cause to suspect child abuse, this must be reported to protect the child. But whatever the circumstance, a pregnancy resulting from a legal and consensual relationship; or rape, incest, or illegal abuse; punishing the pregnant girl by exposing her to public moral judgments, official condemnations, and excluding her from educational opportunities is inappropriate and unlawful.

Are public school officials required to provide LGTB students with protections against sexual harassment?

Yes. Despite the objections of some over the exact application of Title IX to the rights of LGTB students in public schools, public school officials have an obligation to appropriately respond to sexual harassment regardless of the sex of the parties involved. The sexual orientation or gender identity of the victim does not change the duty of school officials to protect all students from sexual harassment and bullying in schools.

Do inequities in school funding violate the Constitution?

Under the U.S. Constitution, no, but possibly yes under state constitutions. The U.S. Supreme Court held in *San Antonio v. Rodriguez*, 411 U.S. 1 (1973), that education was not a fundamental right protected under the U.S. Constitution. Since then, however, many state courts have held that funding inequities did violate provisions of state constitutions. Even when state courts order changes in state funding, however, these changes must be enacted by the state general assembly. Courts cannot legislate or appropriate funding as this is the role of the legislative branch. But this puts plaintiffs and courts in the position of trying to get help from the political forces in the general assembly that caused the funding inequities to begin with. Plaintiffs continue to challenge school funding inequities, with mixed results.

Can public schools legally charge fees, excluding students who cannot pay?

After the Court's decision *Kadrmas v. Dickinson*, 487 U.S. 450 (1988) (upholding fees for school bus transportation) it appeared that absent a complete denial of educational opportunity as in *Plyler v. Doe*, 457 U.S. 202 (1982) (holding that undocumented children could not be excluded from public schools) the legality of school fees is a question of state law, not federal law. State constitutions generally prohibit the charging of any tuition fee, at least to resident families. But what student fees may be allowed other than tuition varies among the states. State courts have struck down some student fees as unlawful under their state constitutions. Where student fees are charged, however, they are more likely to be upheld if they are not related to the required core curriculum, and are instead only for genuinely optional activities for students. Further, it is easier to defend a fee system that provides fee waivers for students and families with financial hardships. Even if children who cannot afford to pay may be lawfully excluded (i.e., "lawful but awful"), for ethical and moral reasons children should not be excluded from important opportunities in public schools because of an inability to pay. School officials should try to find funding to help support the participation of all children whenever possible. Many community members, businesses, etc., would be happy to help sponsor scholarships and otherwise support children who may not otherwise be able to participate with their peers in school activities.

Essential Practice Skills

This section addresses two important issues of practice: Sexual harassment under Title IX; and principles of cultural competence in our increasingly diverse public schools consistent with Title VI and Title VII.

No one should have to tolerate sexual harassment in order to receive an education. Institutional tolerance of sexual harassment, by employees or students, has been recognized as a form of sex discrimination. Accordingly, institutional tolerance of sexual harassment is prohibited by Title IX of the Education Amendments of 1972. In *Franklin v. Gwinnett*, 503 U.S. 60 (1992), the U.S. Supreme Court held that monetary damages are available to plaintiffs as a remedy in actions brought to enforce Title IX. Because of the serious harms associated with sexual harassment, and the potential for failing to adequately protect students (and resulting institutional damages), a working knowledge of sexual harassment law under Title IX is an essential practice skill.

Sexual harassment under Title IX

Title IX, 20 U.S.C. § 1681, governs sexual harassment of students in educational institutions receiving federal funding (Title VII governs sexual harassment of employees). To prevail in a sexual harassment suit for monetary damages under Title IX, plaintiffs must generally establish that:

> 1) School officials had "actual notice" of the sexual harassment, and;
> 2) School officials reacted with "deliberate indifference."

The Court defined "actual notice" in *Gebser v. Lago Vista*, 524 U.S. 274 (1998), finding that it required "notice to an 'appropriate person'" and that "an 'appropriate person' . . . is, at a minimum, an official of the recipient entity with authority to take corrective action to end the discrimination." The Court defined "deliberate indifference" in *Davis v. Monroe*, 526 U.S. 629 (1999), finding that "school officials will be deemed 'deliberately indifferent' . . . where the recipient's response to the harassment or lack thereof is clearly unreasonable in light of the known circumstances."

Concerning peer sexual harassment among students under Title IX, in *Davis* the Court found that: "The fact that it was a teacher who engaged in harassment in *Franklin* and *Gebser* is relevant." School officials have greater responsibility for the conduct of employees, and students are more prone to engaging in some gender-based adolescent behavior. To hold school officials liable for peer sexual harassment under Title IX the plaintiff must also prove a third element, the harassment was severe and pervasive:

Proving Peer Sexual Harassment Under Title IX

 1) Actual Notice

School officials had actual notice of the sexual harassment;

 2) Deliberate Indifference

School officials reacted with deliberate indifference; and

 3) Severe & Pervasive

Harassment was so severe, pervasive, and objectively offensive equal access was denied

© Dayton

To prevail in a Title IX case (harassment by an employee or peer) the plaintiff must prove the first two elements: 1) School officials had actual notice of the sexual harassment; and 2) School officials reacted with deliberate indifference. Peer harassment also requires element 3) The harassment was so severe, pervasive, and objectively offensive, and so undermined and detracted from the educational experience, that the student was effectively denied equal access to an institution's resources and opportunities.

It is the tolerance of sexual harassment in the school that is the basis for liability under Title IX. To avoid liability for peer harassment, school officials "must merely respond to known peer harassment in a manner that is not clearly unreasonable." Together *Franklin*, *Gebser*, and *Davis* teach the following lessons to avoid liability:

1) Have a reasonable policy in place for the prevention, reporting, and correction of sexual harassment;

2) Promptly and fairly investigate reports of alleged sexual harassment; and

3) Take reasonable remedial actions when appropriate to assure that no one is excluded from educational opportunities because of sexual harassment or other differential treatment based on gender.

© Dayton

162

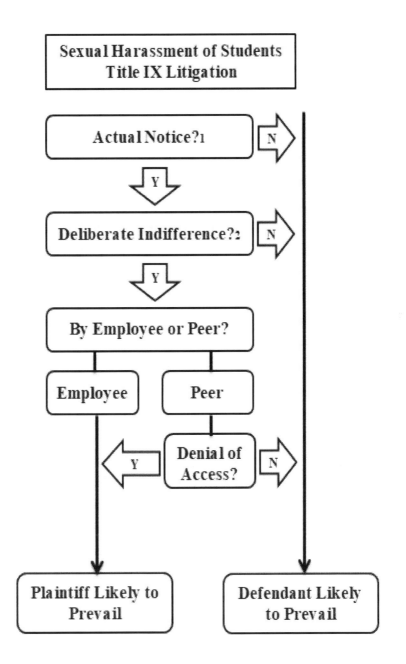

1 "Actual notice": Notice to an official with authority to take corrective action.
2 "Deliberately indifference": Response is clearly unreasonable in light of the known circumstances.

© Dayton

Essential principles of cultural competence

It is an unfortunate tragedy for all parties when easily avoidable cultural misunderstandings escalate to conflicts and litigation. It is also significant to note that whether intended or not, insensitive comments are commonly introduced as evidence of discrimination in litigation. In our increasingly diverse society it is essential that professionals develop necessary cultural competence for promoting effective cross-cultural communication and cooperation. Recommendations to improve these skills are included below:

Recognize and understand your own cultural beliefs and assumptions: We come to our interactions with others with our own cultural beliefs and assumptions. Many of these are unconscious and unexamined. Closely examine your own cultural history and beliefs, recognizing both virtues and biases. Build on the virtues and address the biases. Personally, you may or may not agree with the beliefs of others. But as a professional it is essential to model equal respect for all persons and cultures in the common school.

Learn about the cultures of others in your school and community: To effectively work with others it is essential that you understand them and their cultures. Ideally, consult with qualified persons native to the culture and familiar with your institutional policies and practices. These persons can be most helpful in identifying cultural challenges and effective institutional solutions. Also, seek out useful resources including helpful books, videos, etc., on cultural competence to learn and to teach the knowledge and skills appropriate to your circumstances.

Examine institutional policies and practices for cultural biases: Institutional policies and practices are created and administered by persons who are not culturally neutral, so the policies and practices may too often reflect cultural biases. Carefully review institutional policies and practices to assure that all persons and all cultures are treated with equal fairness and respect.

Promote a supportive and accountable culture in the school: Promote a school culture in which everyone is genuinely welcomed, valued, and respected. Support a system of communication that allows anyone to safely raise concerns about cultural issues, and to safely report any problems or abuses for fair and objective investigation and appropriate remediation. Cultural problems persist in schools when school leaders fail to recognize cultural biases or fail to hold persons accountable for acts of bias. Areas that merit special attention include:

Race: Race is a cultural construct not based in human biology. Scientists studying human genetics argue that at least from the scientific perspective race is a weak proxy for genetic diversity too crude to provide any useful information about individuals. Nonetheless, social perceptions of race continue to influence human perceptions of individuals. Racism is the belief that these cultural constructs of race define individuals. Despite legal and social progress, racism continues to be pervasive in our communities and schools. Aggressively guarding against racism in institutional policies and practices is essential to promoting social justice in our communities and schools. Understand that race (i.e., genetically inherited appearance and ancestry) and culture (i.e., learned beliefs, values, traditions, and history) are separate issues.

Religion: It is a fundamental human right to make one's own decisions about matters of faith. No one has any right to impose religious beliefs on others. Nonetheless, even many well-intentioned persons engage in religious insensitivity and bias, and some teachers, coaches, etc., are very aggressive in pushing their beliefs on other people's children. Religious coercion by public school employees is unlawful and cannot be tolerated. But more subtle biases must also be addressed. For example, even if there is a Christian majority in your community do not assume everyone is Christian or celebrates Christian holidays. Do not assume Protestant Christianity as "normal" and other faiths as somehow aberrant. In your official capacity respect all persons' sincerely held religious beliefs and traditions equally. Government employees must remain neutral concerning religion while acting in their official capacities, neither favoring or disfavoring religion or any particular religious faith.

Gender: Despite legal and social progress, gender bias is as deeply imbedded in U.S. culture as race bias, with similar false assumptions that gender defines individuals and their abilities. Except for the most general biological differences, like race, gender and gender roles are largely a social construct. Students should not be forced into "gender appropriate" choices or measured against gender stereotypes in assumed abilities and expected conduct. Co-workers must be treated as equal co-workers without gender bias in their treatment as employees. Schools hire qualified professionals and educate students, regardless of gender. Gender must not define anyone's rights or opportunities in schools.

Sexual orientation and gender identity: Sexual orientation and gender identity are not the same issues, and neither can be legitimately defined in stereotypical, absolute male/female terms. Sexual orientation is defined by an individual's innate emotional, romantic, and sexual attractions with endless variations among individuals. Gender identity is the individual's gender self-image (i.e., male; female; some continuum of both; or neither). Do not assume or expect heterosexuality or gender conformity to male/female cultural stereotypes. Respect people by respecting their expressed identity, their chosen pronouns, and family units.

National origin: Although the U.S. is a nation of immigrants, there is a sad history of discrimination against immigrants. To address this, it is unlawful to discriminate against anyone based on national origin. There are, however, significant cultural differences among the peoples of different nations. Like all cultural differences, mutual respect is the key to negotiating these differences. Do not assume members of racial minorities are recent immigrants (e.g., asking Asian-Americans "where are you from" just because they are Asian). Do not assume that all international persons currently in the U.S. desire to become American citizens. Distinguish between criticisms of a nation's policies and its people. Do not coerce international students to show allegiance to U.S. symbols through social pressure to participate in U.S. flag pledges, anthem singing, etc.

Language: Not speaking English means only that the person doesn't speak English. It does not evidence lack of effort or intelligence (remembering you probably can't speak their language either). Not being able to speak the majority language can be very isolating. Attempt to include everyone. Being included helps in learning language. Be certain translators are available when needed and that students have necessary support in transitioning into English language instruction and social settings. If welcomed by non-English speakers, invite non-English speakers to educate English speakers about their language as well, making everyone teachers and learners.

Economic status: Economic disadvantage provides sufficient challenges without adding any additional social stigma. In a culture rooted in consumerism and steeped in assumptions that personal value is defined by financial net worth; that wealthy people are hardworking and intelligent; that poor people are lazy and unintelligent; poverty can seem like a moral burden and not just a financial burden. Public schools exist, in part, to assure that all children have access to a quality education regardless of income. Be certain no child is publicly embarrassed or excluded from participation because of family income.

Disability: There is a fundamental human right for every person to have an opportunity to participate in and contribute to our common society. Disability is a natural part of the human experience and in no way diminishes this human right. Help to fight ignorance and fears related to disabilities (e.g., false beliefs in contagiousness; social stigmas related to mental illness; etc.). Be certain facilities are accessible to all persons and that everyone is welcomed and included even when mobility, vision, hearing, speech, etc., disabilities may make this more challenging. Everyone benefits from inclusion.

Age: Age does not define an individual's knowledge or abilities. Ageist "jokes" are no more appropriate than racist or sexist jokes. Asking older employees "so when are you retiring?" can make them feel unvalued and pushed out. Also, remember that parents are adults of all ages. Avoid embarrassment by not assuming an older looking person is a grandparent or the parent of a younger looking partner.

Trivializing these issues as mere "political correctness" trivializes the very real damage these biases unnecessarily do to people and institutions. Although it may seem obvious, avoid antiquated or offensive terms (e.g., "colored"; "oriental"; "retarded"; etc.) or expressions (e.g., "Jewed me down"; "I was Gypped"; "cotton pickin' minute"; "uppity"; "Indian giver"; "Chinese fire drill"; "Paddy Wagon"; "so gay"; "the Ref must be blind"; etc.) as these are, to say the least, offensive terms and expressions.

Be aware that even common American hand symbols may be offensive in an international context. For example: The American "OK" hand symbol (i.e., many Europeans and South Americans will think you are calling them "a-holes" with that gesture); the "thumbs up" symbol (i.e., perceived as "up yours" by many in Europe and the Middle East). Pointing at things is generally acceptable. But pointing at a person is considered rude and aggressive. Cultural experts generally advise the safest approach to hand gesturing is when in doubt in an international setting, use your whole hand to gesture and not any single finger.

At a minimum, all persons must comply with the law in respecting the equal rights of others. But legal mandates are just the legal and ethical floor. All professionals and all public institutions should pursue higher standards in affording universal human respect and equality to all persons.

Essential Practice Tips

1) *Equal protection of the laws*: School officials must treat everyone fairly and be diligent in assuring that group prejudice, conscious or unconscious, plays no role in the treatment of individuals. Unless there is a sufficient justification for differential treatment, all persons in similar circumstances must be treated equally by government officials.

2) *Prevention of sexual harassment*: School officials should: 1) Have a reasonable policy in place for the prevention and remediation of sexual harassment; 2) Promptly and fairly investigate reports of alleged sexual harassment; and 3) Take reasonable remedial actions when appropriate to assure that no one is excluded from educational opportunities because of sexual harassment or other differential treatment based on gender.

3) *Programs for disadvantaged students*: In allocating limited educational resources to provide special support for disadvantaged students, remedial programs based on economic disadvantage are legally far safer than programs based on race. Any use of race is subject to strict judicial scrutiny, while the use of economic status is only subject to the rational basis test. In circumstances where there is a strong correlation between economic disadvantage and race, programs based on economic status can lawfully address both concerns, without unlawfully using race as a criteria, and assure that all financially disadvantaged students, regardless of race, are helped.

4) *School related fees*: School fees are more likely to be upheld if they are not related to the required core curriculum and are instead only for genuinely optional activities for students. Further, it is easier to defend a fee system that provides appropriate waivers for students and families with financial hardships. Do not charge fees unless necessary, but when necessary, seek support from the community to fund scholarships, etc., for economically disadvantaged students so that no one is denied educational opportunities because of family economic status.

Essential Points

- Generally, government officials must provide equal treatment to all individuals in equal circumstances.
- Differential treatment must be justified by proving an appropriate relationship between the differential treatment and a sufficient governmental justification for the differential treatment.

- Equal protection of the laws prohibits differential treatment based on factors that are legally irrelevant (e.g., race; color; national origin; etc.), and are instead the products of irrational prejudice or discrimination.
- Differential treatment may be allowed or even required when there are legally relevant differences among individuals (e.g., disabilities).
- The U.S. Supreme Court has developed a multi-tiered test for reviewing equal protection claims. Where differential treatment by government is established by plaintiffs, the Court reviews whether the differential treatment is justified by a sufficient governmental interest:
  - *High-level (strict) scrutiny*: Differential treatment must be "necessary to a compelling interest" and "narrowly tailored" to achieving that interest.
  - *Intermediate-level scrutiny*: Differential treatment must be "substantially related" to achieving an "important government interest."
  - *Low-level (rational basis) scrutiny*: Government officials need only show that the differential treatment is "rationally related" to a "legitimated government interest."
- Strict scrutiny applies to differential treatment based on suspect classifications (e.g., race; color; national origin; etc.) or fundamental rights (e.g., religion), and the rational basis test applies to general social or economic regulations.
- Government officials almost always lose under strict scrutiny review, while plaintiffs nearly always lose under the rational basis test.
- In summary, the core teaching of the Court's cases on equal protection is that government officials cannot legally treat individuals differently for irrelevant, discriminatory reasons, such as the person's race, color, religion, sex, national origin, disability, etc., when those factors bear no appropriate relationship to a sufficient governmental justification.
- Discrimination based on language has been treated as a form of national origin discrimination, and is unlawful under both the Equal Protection Clause and Title VI of the Civil Rights Act of 1964. The Court's decision in *Lau v. Nichols* recognized a duty for state and local school officials to provide appropriate instruction for minority language students, but left the operational details of these programs to state and local officials.
- Concerning differential treatment based on gender, in *U.S. v. Virginia* the Court held that government officials must show "at least that the

challenged classification serves important governmental objectives and that the discriminatory means employed are substantially related to the achievement of those objectives . . . The justification must be genuine, not hypothesized or invented post hoc in response to litigation. And it must not rely on overbroad generalizations about the different talents, capacities, or preferences of males and females."

- Under Title IX students are protected from gender based discrimination and being "excluded from participation in" or "denied the benefits of" any "education program or activity receiving Federal financial assistance" on the basis of gender.
- It is the tolerance of sexual harassment in the school that is the basis for liability under Title IX. To avoid liability, school officials must respond to known harassment in a manner that is reasonable.
- Although school funding and fees are generally governed by state law, there are some federal limits. For example, state systems of funding and fees cannot result in a complete denial of educational opportunities (e.g., *Plyler v. Doe*), and federal law prohibits public disclosure of the identities of children eligible for free and reduced lunch.

Essential Terms

De facto segregation: Segregation resulting from private choices and not subject to constitutional limits or judicial authority.

De jure segregation: Segregation caused by government actions in violation of the Equal Protection Clause and subject to judicial authority.

Separate but equal: Legal doctrine from *Plessy v. Ferguson* (1896), holding that state mandated racially separate provisions of services (e.g., racially segregated public accommodations) did not violate the Equal Protection Clause (overturned by *Brown v. Board of Education* (1954)).

Unitary status: A judicial declaration that a school district has sufficiently eliminated the effects of prior *de jure* segregation to merit release from judicial supervision.

Title VI: Provision of the Civil Rights Act of 1964 (P.L. 88-352; 42 U.S.C. § 2000d et seq.), prohibiting discrimination on the basis of race, color, or national origin in programs and activities receiving federal funds.

Title VII: Provision of the Civil Rights Act of 1964 (P.L. 88–352; 42 U.S.C. § 2000e et seq.) prohibiting employment discrimination based on race, color, religion, sex, or national origin.

Title IX: Provision of the Education Amendments of 1972 (P.L. 92-318; 20 U.S.C. § 1681 et seq.) prohibiting discrimination based on sex in education programs or activities receiving federal funds.

Essential Cases

Adarand v. Pena, 515 U.S. 200 (1995): The Court declared that "any person, of whatever race, has the right to demand that any governmental actor subject to the Constitution justify any racial classification subjecting that person to unequal treatment under the strictest judicial scrutiny."

Brown v. Board of Education, 347 U.S. 483 (1954): Overruled *Plessy* and declared racial segregation of public schools unconstitutional.

Davis v. Monroe, 526 U.S. 629 (1999): Allowing damages for peer sexual harassment in public schools but holding that in cases of peer harassment the harassment must be "so severe, pervasive, and objectively offensive that it can be said to deprive the victims of access to the educational opportunities or benefits provided by the school."

Franklin v. Gwinnett, 503 U.S. 60 (1992): Monetary damages are available to plaintiffs as a remedy in actions brought to enforce Title IX.

Gebser v. Lago Vista, 524 U.S. 274 (1998): To prevail in a sexual harassment suit for monetary damages plaintiffs must establish: 1) School officials had actual notice of the sexual harassment, and; 2) School officials reacted with deliberate indifference.

Lau v. Nichols, 414 U.S. 563 (1974): Public schools must provide an adequate English language bridge for non-English speaking students to benefit from public education.

Plessy v. Ferguson, 163 U.S. 537 (1896): Upheld racial segregation in public accommodations, in this case passenger assignments on train cars, under the doctrine of "separate but equal" (overturned by *Brown* (1954)).

United States v. Virginia ("VMI case"), 518 U.S. 515 (1996): Declared state funded single sex education unconstitutional and required an "exceedingly persuasive" justification for any gender based government action.

A Closer Look at the Law

Brown v. Board of Education (1954) was a unanimous opinion by the Court. But while members of the Court were in the early stages of forming their opinions on the *Brown* case, the constitutionality of the separate but equal doctrine, and whether *Plessy* should be affirmed or reversed, a law clerk for U.S. Supreme Court Justice Jackson wrote the following memo:

A Random Thought on the Segregation Cases

One-hundred fifty years ago this Court held that it was the ultimate judge of the restrictions which the Constitution imposed on the various branches of the national and state goverment. <u>Marbury v. Madison</u>. This was presumably on the basis that there are standards to be applied other than the personal predilections of the Justices.

As applied to questions of inter-state or state-federal relations, as well as to inter-departmental disputes within the federal goverment, this doctrine of judicial review has worked well. Where theoretically co-ordinate bodies of goverment are disputing, the Court is well suited to its role as arbiter. This is because these problems involve much less emotionally charged subject matter than do those discussed below. In effect, they determine the skeletal relations of the goverments to each other without influencing the substantive business of those goverments.

As applied to relations between the individual and the state, the system has worked much less well. The Constitution, of course, deals with individual rights, particularly in the first Ten and the fourteenth Amendments. But as I read the history of this Court, it has seldom been out of hot water when attempting to interpret these individual rights. <u>Fletcher v. Peck</u>, in 1810, represented an attempt by Chief Justice Marshall to extend the protection of the contract clause to infant business. <u>Scott v. Sanford</u> was the result of Taney's effort to protect slaveholders from legislative interference.

After the Civil War, business interest came to dominate the court, and they in turn ventured into the deep water of protecting certain types of individuals against legislative interference . . . Holmes replied that the fourteenth Amendment did not enact Herbert Spencer's Social Statics . . . But eventually the Court called a halt to this reading of its own economic views into the Constitution. Apparently it recognized that where a legislature was dealing with its own citizens, it was not part of the judicial function to thwart public opinion except in extreme cases. In these cases now before the Court, the Court is, as Davis suggested, being asked to read its own sociological views into the Constitution. Urging a view palpably at variance with precedent and probably with legislative history, appellants seek to convince the Court of the moral wrongness of the treatment they are receiving. I would suggest that this is a question the Court need never reach; for regardless of the Justice's individual views on the merits of segregation, it quite clearly is not one of those extreme cases which commands intervention from one of any conviction. If this Court, because its members individually are "liberal" and dislike segregation, now chooses to strike it down, it differs from the McReynolds court only in the kinds of litigants it favors and the kinds of special claims it protects. To those who would argue that "personal" rights are more sacrosanct than "property" rights, the short answer is that the Constitution makes no such distinction. To the argument made by Thurgood Marshall that a majority may not deprive a minority of its constitutional right, the answer must be made that while this is sound in theory, in the long run it is the majority who will determine what the constitutional rights of the minority are. One hundred and fifty years of attempts on the part of this Court to protect minority rights of any kind--whether those of business, slaveholders, or Jehovah's Witnesses--have been sloughed off, and crept silently to rest. If the present Court is unable to profit by this example it must be prepared to see its work fade in time, too, as embodying only the sentiments of a transient majority of nine men. I realize that it is an unpopular and unhumanitarian position, for which I have been excoriated by "liberal" colleagues, but I think Plessy v. Ferguson was right and should be re-affirmed. If the fourteenth Amendment did not enact Spencer's Social Statics, it just as surely did not enact Myrdal's American Dilemmna.

WHR

173

* * * * * * *

The "WHR" who wrote this memo was William Hubbs Rehnquist. When he wrote this memo Mr. Rehnquist was serving as a law clerk for Justice Jackson at the U.S. Supreme Court. Mr. Rehnquist later became Chief Justice of the U.S. Supreme Court. Rehnquist was questioned about this memo in his confirmation hearings before the U.S. Senate many years after it was written. By this time *Plessy* and the doctrine of separate but equal had been soundly rejected by a unanimous Court, Congress had enacted the Civil Rights Act of 1964, and the tide of public opinion had turned decisively against segregation. *Plessy*'s "separate but equal doctrine" and segregation by law had become a shameful memory and an embarrassing political albatross around the necks of former segregationists. Nonetheless, Mr. Rehnquist's memo clearly declared "I think <u>Plessy v. Ferguson</u> was right and should be re-affirmed."

In hearings before the U.S. Senate Mr. Rehnquist claimed that the opinions expressed in his memo were not his personal opinions, but instead reflected Justice Jackson's views. Justice Jackson died in October 1954 and was not around to confirm or refute Rehnquist's claims. Only Mr. Rehnquist knew the truth about whether these were his views about equal protection of the laws, segregation, and civil rights, or Justice Jackson's. What we do know is that Justice Jackson voted with the majority in *Brown*. And although very ill, Justice Jackson traveled from his hospital bed to the Court so he could be present when the *Brown* decision was delivered.

After reviewing the "WHR" memo, if you were a member of the U.S. Senate voting on the nomination of William Hubbs Rehnquist to be Chief Justice of the U.S. Supreme Court, would you find Rehnquist's assertion that this memo represented Justice Jackson's views and not his own credible? Does this sentence written by WHR sound like Justice Jackson's view or the view of the author WHR?: "I realize that it is an unpopular and unhumanitarian position, for which I have been excoriated by 'liberal' colleagues, but I think <u>Plessy v. Ferguson</u> was right and should be re-affirmed."

The memo also raises important questions about the proper role of government, the Constitution, the Bill of Rights, the Fourteenth Amendment, and the role of the Court. Are Court opinions truly driven by legal principles or by the personal opinions of the Justices? Should the will of the political majority always prevail, or should the Court intervene to protect minority rights? Are personal rights (including the right to human equality) no different than property rights (which governments commonly regulate and limit) under the law? What role does the federal government have in protecting and promoting civil rights? What role should the Court play?

Rehnquist pointed out two clashing social views, those articulated in Herbert Spencer's SOCIAL STATICS (1851), and Gunnar Myrdal's AN AMERICAN DILEMMA: THE NEGRO PROBLEM AND MODERN DEMOCRACY (1944). In SOCIAL STATICS and subsequent works, Spencer, a British economist, articulated principles of Social Darwinism, survival of the fittest, and Lamarckian molding of individuals through social conditions. Myrdal, the author of AN AMERICAN DILEMMA, was a Swedish economist, who saw the "American Creed" (ideals of liberty, justice, and equality) as the essential common bond that kept together the great diversity of America, and allowed persons of all races, religions, and backgrounds to live and work together towards mutual progress. Myrdal saw government enforced segregation as a grave threat to the authenticity and survival of the American Creed. In his view, segregation was antithetical to the American Creed, denying liberty, justice, and equality on the basis of race. Segregation was the circular tool of racial oppression: Legally enforced segregation so limited opportunities for Black citizens that it virtually assured lower achievement, and then the resulting evidence of lower achievement was used to justify continued segregation. The remedies were changes in social attitudes and improvements in the conditions of Black citizens. Education was the essential key to both, making *Brown* a turning point in American history.

Law & Professional Ethics in Practice:

Over a half century after the Court's decision in *Brown*, what is the real legacy of *Brown*, positive and negative? What is the future of race relations in the U.S. as the U.S. transitions from a 1950s, *Brown*-era, largely Black/White social structure in much of the Nation, to an infinitely more racially diverse, and ethnically and socially complex nation? What groups will be fighting the struggles for greater equality in the future? Do courts still have a role in this process, or is the era of *Brown*-style judicial intervention over, and legal struggles replaced by social and economic struggles? Is there an ethical/moral duty to actively promote social justice or is personal fair play in a laissez-faire social/economic system sufficient?

Questions for Further Exploration:

1) *Ethnic community dynamics*: What is the ethnic and racial composition of your community? How has this changed, and what will your community look like in the future? How can ethnic and racial relationships in your community be improved? Where do significant social divisions exist in your community? Are these social divisions primarily related to race, ethnicity, or socio-economic status?

2) *Socio-economic community dynamics*: What is the socio-economic composition of your community? How has this changed, and what will your community look like in the future socially and economically? What can be done now to improve the economic future of your community?

3) *Gender issues in the community*: In the *VMI* case Justice Ginsberg, writing for the majority, noted relevant and enduring differences between the sexes, but also warned against overbroad generalizations. What are the relevant and enduring differences? What are the overbroad generalizations? Has gender equity been achieved in your community? Who faces the greatest educational challenges in your schools and community, boys or girls? What could be done to improve educational opportunities for both boys and girls in your schools and community?

4) *Open forum*: What other related issues or current events would you like to discuss?

Suggested Activities for Further Learning:

1) Read Dr. Martin Luther King Jr.'s *Letter from Birmingham Jail*. Discuss its lessons and continuing implications for the advancement of law and social justice locally, nationally, and globally.

2) Examine whether school related fees in your community may be limiting the participation of economically disadvantaged students in extra-curricular or other educational activities for which fees are charged. Could these activities be restructured to reduce costs and the need for additional fees? Could other sources of revenue (e.g., donations from businesses or individuals) help to reduce or eliminate fees and help everyone to participate on an equal basis? Develop a proposal for improving access to school activities by reducing or eliminating student fees.

Chapter 8: Disability Law

Disability is a natural part of the human experience occurring world-wide throughout the human population. It is estimated that 10% of humans have a disability, making persons with disabilities the world's largest minority group. Our common humanity requires that we respect all persons' human rights as equal members of our shared society. Impairment of physical or mental abilities in no way diminishes any person's fundamental human rights and equal place in our community.

Ignorance, fear, and prejudice, however, have always threatened to undermine the equal rights of persons with disabilities. For this reason these rights must be protected through antidiscrimination laws and the guaranteed provision of adequate social services including appropriate education. Through education and inclusion we can overcome ignorance, fear, and prejudice, helping everyone to understand that all persons have a right to be included in our common society and that inclusion benefits everyone.

With appropriate educational services children with disabilities, like all other children, can be prepared to lead productive, independent lives to the maximum extent possible. Appropriate educational services help persons with disabilities to become more independent and develop their personal strengths and talents, reducing future costs and improving everyone's quality of life. As persons with disabilities are better integrated into mainstream society, including the work force, they are able to offer their unique skills and contribute to the economy and the common good, benefiting everyone.

Historically, however, persons with disabilities have commonly been excluded, including exclusion from educational opportunities. Based on legal theories rooted in *Brown* (1954), advocates for children with disabilities successfully argued that children with disabilities were being unconstitutionally excluded from public schools through a systematic denial of equal protection and due process rights. In *Pennsylvania Association for Retarded Children (PARC) v. Pennsylvania*, 343 F. Supp. 279 (E.D. Pa. 1972), and *Mills v. Board of Education of the District of Columbia*, 348 F. Supp. 866 (D.D.C. 1972), federal courts held that children with disabilities must have access to a free public education and should be placed in regular classrooms when possible or in special classes when necessary.

In 1975 Congress passed P.L. 94-142 creating a system of special education with significant new substantive rights and procedural protections for children with disabilities. Although case law plays an important role in interpreting and clarifying disability laws, the law in this area is largely defined by federal statutes and regulations. These principally include the IDEA, § 504, and the ADA.

A Brief Overview of the IDEA, § 504, and the ADA

The Individuals with Disabilities Education Act (IDEA) is a federal conditional funding grant functioning as a contract between the federal and state governments. The federal government provides funding to support special education, the state agrees to the statutory conditions in the IDEA, and the IDEA eligible child is the third-party beneficiary of this federal-state contract. The IDEA requires the state, through local schools, to provide a Free Appropriate Public Education (FAPE) and related services for IDEA eligible students. This is a critically important mission, but also a complex and expensive undertaking with federal funding only covering a relatively small portion of the total costs of providing a FAPE, related services, and mandated due process protections and associated administrative costs.

In contrast § 504 of the Rehabilitation Act (§ 504) and the Americans with Disabilities Act (ADA) generally only require non-discrimination and the provision of reasonable accommodations, usually resulting in relatively lower costs and administrative burdens in the provision of services per eligible individual. Section 504 requires reasonable accommodations necessary to allow persons with disabilities to participate in programs receiving federal funding. The ADA extends § 504 like protections to the private sector in employment, public accommodations, transportation, and telecommunications.

Contrasting the Scope of Who is Covered and What is Provided Under the IDEA, § 504, and the ADA

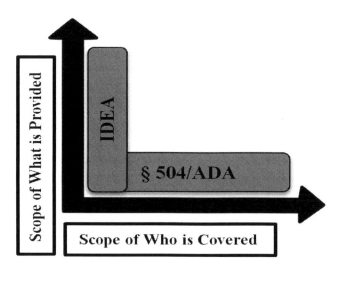

© Dayton

Through § 504 and the ADA Congress intended to cover large numbers of persons, children and adults, potentially including any person with a physical or mental disability that substantially limits a major life activity, including "caring for one's self, performing manual tasks, walking, seeing, hearing, speaking, breathing, learning, and working." Because the scope of who is potentially covered under § 504 and the ADA is so broad, the scope of what is provided is necessarily limited due to finite resources. While § 504 and the ADA cover a broad range of the population, what is provided is essentially a right to non-discrimination and to the provision of a reasonable accommodation when necessary for the participation of the otherwise qualified person with a disability in a program receiving federal funding.

In contrast, in the IDEA Congress recognized that some children would need vastly more resources to provide for their educational needs due to the severity of their disabilities. Therefore Congress limited who is covered under the IDEA to only those children who fit within 13 categories of eligibility, and who needed special education and related services because of an eligible disability. Under 20 U.S.C. § 1401 of the IDEA the term "child with a disability" means a child:

> [W]ith intellectual disabilities, hearing impairments (including deafness), speech or language impairments, visual impairments (including blindness), serious emotional disturbance (referred to in this chapter as "emotional disturbance"), orthopedic impairments, autism, traumatic brain injury, other health impairments, or specific learning disabilities; and who, by reason thereof, needs special education and related services.

Given limited resources Congress intended to prioritize the distribution of resources to those students with the greatest needs. In carefully evaluating individual cases some individuals will be eligible for services under the IDEA, others will be eligible under § 504 and/or the ADA, and others will not qualify as eligible under any of these provisions.

Congress also clearly intended to protect persons from discrimination based on disability. Discrimination is prohibited under the IDEA, § 504, and the ADA to assure fair treatment of persons with disabilities and to prevent unwarranted removals from educational institutions and opportunities. But what happens when school officials believe a removal is warranted because of misconduct? Among the most challenging areas under the IDEA is balancing essential protections against discrimination with the needs of school officials to protect order, discipline, and safety in the school.

A Summary of Discipline Options under the IDEA

Discipline procedures under the IDEA may be among the most important and the most confusing provisions for many students, parents, educators, and lawyers. Accordingly, the following summary of incrementally serious disciplinary options under the IDEA is provided:

Behavior management strategies: To attempt to modify problem behavior school officials may utilize a variety of behavior and conflict management strategies including student carrels, time-outs, detention, restrictions in privileges, etc. As long as IEP services are provided, and there is no change in placement, school officials may unilaterally implement these behavior management strategies.

Obtaining parental consent: If more serious measures are necessary school officials may first obtain parental consent for needed changes in placement or for other appropriate behavior management strategies. If parental consent is obtained, the IDEA limitations on disciplinary actions are generally not triggered.

Unilateral 10 school day removal: Provided their actions are not discriminatory school officials may unilaterally remove an IDEA eligible student for up to 10 consecutive school days for violating a code of student conduct. No services are required, and no manifestation determination is necessary.

Subsequent 10 school day or less removals: There is no absolute limit on the total number of days per year that a student may be removed for separate incidents of misconduct, so long as no single removal exceeds 10 consecutive school days and there is no pattern of removals. Factors considered in determining whether there is a pattern of removals include the length of each removal; the total amount of time the child is removed; and the proximity of the removals to one another. School officials must provide services to the extent necessary to allow the child to make progress toward meeting IEP goals and to participate in the general curriculum, although in a different setting. School officials determine which services are needed in consultation with at least one of the child's teachers. Manifestation determinations are only required when a child is subjected to a disciplinary change of placement.

Long-term suspensions and expulsions: IDEA eligible students may be long-term suspended or expelled for a violation of a code of student conduct that is not a manifestation of the student's disability. Any removal beyond 10 consecutive school days, however, constitutes a change in placement, triggering IDEA due process protections. Further, school officials must continue to provide a FAPE to these students. For removals beyond 10 consecutive school days, the child's IEP team determines what services are necessary to provide a FAPE.

45 school day removals for weapons, drugs, or inflicting serious bodily injury: School officials may unilaterally remove a student to an alternative educational placement for up to 45 school days for possession of weapons, drugs, or inflicting serious bodily injury.

45 school day removals for dangerousness: School officials may ask a hearing officer to remove a potentially dangerous student to an alternative educational placement for up to 45 school days by presenting evidence that "maintaining the current placement of such child is substantially likely to result in injury to the child or to others." Hearing officer approved further 45 school day extensions may be repeated as necessary to prevent a dangerous placement.

Court ordered remedies: In the event that the above options fail to provide appropriate remedies, school officials may obtain a court order for a removal or change of placement of a student that presents a serious danger to him or herself or others in the school.

Reporting crimes: School officials may report students suspected of committing crimes to law enforcement agents, who have a duty to enforce criminal laws, and are not bound by IDEA limitations. Neither law enforcement agents nor judges are bound by the provisions of the IDEA. The State must continue to provide a FAPE to eligible incarcerated students.

Manifestation Determinations

A critical consideration in the discipline process is determining whether the problem behavior is a manifestation of the student's disability. If a child's behavior is a manifestation of a disability, it would be unfair to punish that child for behavior that was caused by the disability and was not reasonably within the volitional control of the child. For example, children suffering from Tourette's syndrome may exhibit symptoms including involuntary movements or "tics"; vocal sounds; or obscene or inappropriate language, resulting in behaviors that could legitimately merit punishment for other students, but may be uncontrollable manifestations of a disability for a child with Tourette's syndrome.

Accordingly, the IDEA (*see*, 20 U.S.C. § 1415(k)(1)(E)), requires the IEP Team and other qualified personnel to conduct a review to determine whether an eligible child's problem behavior is a manifestation of a disability when proposed disciplinary actions constitute a change in placement:

> (i) Manifestation determination. In general: Except as provided in subparagraph (B), within 10 school days of any decision to change the placement of a child with a disability because of a violation of a code of student conduct, the local educational agency, the parent, and relevant members of the IEP Team (as determined by the parent and the local educational agency) shall review all relevant information in the student's file, including the child's IEP, any teacher observations, and any relevant information provided by the parents to determine—
>> (I) if the conduct in question was caused by, or had a direct and substantial relationship to, the child's disability; or
>> (II) if the conduct in question was the direct result of the local educational agency's failure to implement the IEP.
> (ii) Manifestation: If the local educational agency, the parent, and relevant members of the IEP Team determine that either subclause (I) or (II) of clause (i) is applicable for the child, the conduct shall be determined to be a manifestation of the child's disability.

If the behavior is a manifestation of the child's disability, the IEP Team must implement a behavioral intervention plan, and except as provided for under other relevant provisions of the IDEA (e.g., allowing for a removal for weapons, drugs, or serious bodily injury) "return the child to the placement from which the child was removed, unless the parent and the local educational agency agree to a change of placement as part of the modification of the behavioral intervention plan" (*see*, 20 U.S.C. § 1415(k)(1)(F)(iii)).

Under 34 C.F.R. § 300.530(e) manifestation determinations are only required when a child is subjected to a disciplinary change of placement. A change in placement under 34 C.F.R. § 300.536(a) occurs when:

> (1) The removal is for more than 10 consecutive school days; or

(2) The child has been subjected to a series of removals that constitute a pattern -

> (i) Because the series of removals total more than 10 school days in a school year;
>
> (ii) Because the child's behavior is substantially similar to the child's behavior in previous incidents that resulted in the series of removals; and
>
> (iii) Because of such additional factors as the length of each removal, the total amount of time the child has been removed, and the proximity of the removals to one another.

If the result of the review is a determination that the student's behavior was not a manifestation of the disability, school officials may discipline the student in the same manner that other students would be disciplined, including suspension for up to 10 consecutive school days. No special services are required during an initial 10 school day suspension. Any removal for more than 10 consecutive school days, however, constitutes a change in placement and triggers the procedural protections of the IDEA.

When a student's behavior is not a manifestation of the student's disability school officials may lawfully long-term suspend for more than 10 consecutive school days or expel the student, subject to IDEA procedural protections and state law. School officials cannot, however, terminate special education services for IDEA eligible students.

Manifestation Determination

© Dayton

Essential Questions & Answers

How are children identified for potential eligibility under the IDEA?

The IDEA's "child find" provision in 20 U.S.C. § 1412 creates an affirmative duty for school officials to identify children with disabilities. Children may be identified for IDEA eligibility testing through mass screenings of all children, or through referrals from parents, school personnel, medical personnel, or other persons.

Is parental permission required for IDEA eligibility testing?

Parental consent is not required for mass screening tests administered to all children. But before individual evaluations for IDEA eligibility may be conducted school officials generally must obtain parental consent. If parents refuse consent and denial of services may be harmful to the child, school officials may seek assistance from social service agencies to encourage parental support for testing. And if necessary, school officials may seek a court order for testing and the provision of needed services for the child.

What are the eligibility criteria under the IDEA?

Eligibility under the IDEA is based on a two-part test: 1) Whether the child has an IDEA eligible disability; and 2) Whether the child needs special education and related services because of that IDEA eligible disability. Both criteria must be satisfied for the child to be eligible for IDEA services.

What rights do eligible children acquire under the IDEA?

IDEA eligible children have rights to a Free Appropriate Public Education (FAPE) administered through an Individualized Education Program (IEP) in the Least Restrictive Environment (LRE) appropriate, along with related services and due process protections.

What constitutes an appropriate education under the IDEA?

Although what constitutes an appropriate education must ultimately be decided on a case-by-case basis, depending on the needs of the child, in *Endrew F. v. Douglas County School District*, 580 U.S. ___ (2017), the legal standard was elevated for what generally constitutes an appropriate education. The Court in *Endrew* held "that to meet its substantive obligation under the IDEA, a school must offer an individual education plan (IEP) reasonably calculated to enable a child to make progress appropriate in light of the child's circumstances." The impact of *Endrew* is that school officials can now be held accountable under the IDEA for the provision of IEP services sufficient to meet the standard articulated in *Endrew*, a higher standard than the *de minimis* standard previously allowed under *Board of Education v. Rowley*, 458 U.S. 176 (1982).

What is an IEP?

The Individualized Education Program (IEP) is the basic plan for providing special education and related services under the IDEA. The IDEA describes an IEP as a written statement for each child with a disability that is developed, reviewed, and revised in accordance with IDEA requirements. The IEP is designed by an IEP Team. The IEP Team's membership varies, but must generally include the child's parents or legal guardians; a representative of the educational agency; a special education teacher; a regular education teacher when the child is or may be participating in regular education; other appropriate persons having special knowledge about the child; and when appropriate the eligible child may participate in educational decisions concerning his or her future. There must also be someone on the IEP Team qualified to assess the instructional implications of evaluation results. The IEP drafted by the IEP Team includes statements concerning the child's present levels of academic achievement and functional performance; measurable goals; what special education and related services are to be provided; and an explanation of the extent, if any, to which the child will not participate with non-disabled children in the regular classroom. The IEP is developed based on considerations of the strengths of the child, the parents' concerns, and the results of evaluations. An IEP should also address any serious behavioral issues. The child's IEP is reviewed periodically, but not less than annually, to determine whether annual goals are being achieved.

What is the LRE requirement?

Children with disabilities must be placed in the Least Restrictive Environment (LRE) appropriate for the child. Placement decisions should be based on information from a variety of sources, these sources should be documented and carefully considered, and placement decisions should conform to LRE requirements. The IDEA mandates parental participation in placement decisions, but no single factor, including parental preferences, should be determinative in a placement decision. Children should be placed in the LRE, preferring regular classroom placements and education with non-handicapped students to the maximum extent appropriate. Further, unless the IEP requires other arrangements in order to provide a FAPE, children should be placed in the schools they would attend if non-disabled, or as close as practicable to their homes. More restrictive placements may, however, be appropriate or necessary for some children in order to assure safety and to provide the children with required services.

What are related services?

Related services are those supportive services necessary for an IDEA eligible child to benefit from special education. Under 20 U.S.C. § 1401 of the IDEA: "The term 'related services' means transportation, and such developmental, corrective, and other supportive services (including speech-language pathology and audiology services, interpreting services, psychological services, physical and occupational therapy, recreation, including therapeutic recreation, social work services, school nurse services designed to enable a child with a disability to receive a free appropriate public education as described in the individualized education program of the child, counseling services, including rehabilitation counseling, orientation and mobility services, and medical services, except that such medical services shall be for diagnostic and evaluation purposes only) as may be required to assist a child with a disability to benefit from special education, and includes the early identification and assessment of disabling conditions in children." Under *Irving Independent School District v. Tatro*, 468 U.S. 883 (1984), and the *Tatro* test, health services must be provided as related services if: 1) The supportive services are necessary for the child to benefit from special education; and 2) The services are not excluded as medical services that would require the services of a physician for other than diagnostic or evaluation purposes.

What are transition services?

Transition services facilitate the child's transition from school to post-school activities and may include instruction, related services, community experiences, and the development of employment and adult living skills. Under 20 U.S.C. § 1401 of the IDEA: "The term 'transition services' means a coordinated set of activities for a child with a disability that: A) is designed to be within a results-oriented process, that is focused on improving the academic and functional achievement of the child with a disability to facilitate the child's movement from school to post-school activities, including post-secondary education, vocational education, integrated employment (including supported employment), continuing and adult education, adult services, independent living, or community participation;

B) is based on the individual child's needs, taking into account the child's strengths, preferences, and interests; and C) includes instruction, related services, community experiences, the development of employment and other post-school adult living objectives, and, when appropriate, acquisition of daily living skills and functional vocational evaluation." Special education services terminate upon graduation with a regular high school diploma or age ineligibility.

How should school officials deal with a dangerous IDEA eligible student?

School officials should first attempt to negotiate parental cooperation. In cases where parents refuse to cooperate with an appropriate change of placement and the child poses a genuine danger, safety must remain the top priority. School officials must take prompt, appropriate, and lawful actions to assure the safety of everyone in the school. Allowing a known danger to persist could lead to consequences far more serious than a due process hearing with parents over the LRE appropriate for the child, including tragic injury, death, and resulting tort suits or criminal charges. A truly dangerous student cannot be allowed to cause self-injury or injury to others when the danger was known and the injuries could have reasonably been prevented. The IDEA does not require this result, and tort and criminal laws will not allow it. School officials should seek parental cooperation and support whenever possible, but never fail to do what is necessary to protect everyone's safety with or without parental cooperation.

What are the legal requirements under § 504 and the ADA?

Section 504 prohibits discrimination against any person who has a physical or mental disability which substantially limits one or more major life activities; has a record of disability; or is regarded as having a disability. Section 504 requires non-discrimination and reasonable accommodations. Individuals must be otherwise qualified and fundamental alterations of programs are not required. An accommodation is not reasonable, and therefore not required, if it would result in unreasonable costs, administrative burdens, or health or safety risks. Persons may be excluded from activities if participation creates serious health or safety dangers and no reasonable accommodation would effectively mitigate these dangers. Medical exclusions must be based on medical data and medical opinions, and not mere speculation or irrational phobias. The ADA extended protections similar to § 504 protections to many areas of the private sector.

What should school officials do in those close cases that occur at the border of the IDEA and § 504?

In close cases, erring on the side of the IDEA may be prudent if it assures that the child will receive needed services, avoids contentious and expensive battles with parents, and forecloses future claims for compensatory damages. This is not, however, a decision to be made without careful consideration. To legally qualify under the IDEA, the student must be able to meet the minimum statutory requirements with evidence the child: 1) Has an eligible disability; and 2) Needs special education and related services because of that disability.

Can school officials object to providing services based on costs?

Proving a cost-based defense under the IDEA is exceedingly difficult when the services are otherwise necessary under the IDEA. Before school officials may raise cost alone as a defense under the IDEA, they must establish that: 1) The school has provided a proper continuum of placements; 2) The child in question would not experience a denial of educational opportunity because of the failure to provide the expensive service; and 3) Other special education students may be denied a FAPE because of excessive expenditures on one child. In contrast to the IDEA, it is considerably easier to assert excessive expense and/or administrative burden as a defense to a requested accommodation under § 504 or the ADA. Under § 504/ADA it is an affirmative defense to a requested accommodation if the accommodation would result in unreasonable costs, administrative burdens, or health or safety risks. Further, when there is more than one reasonable accommodation possible school officials may choose which of these to provide. Because the laws concerning individuals with disabilities continue to rapidly evolve, school officials responsible for compliance with the IDEA, § 504, and the ADA should closely monitor new legislation, regulations, and judicial decisions concerning these laws to assure current compliance.

Essential Practice Skills

Like the law generally, disability law is an advocacy driven system: Parents who are knowledgeable, effective advocates for their children with disabilities tend to get superior services and support. School officials who are able to develop positive working relationships with parents are able to provide necessary services while minimizing stressful, disruptive, and expensive conflicts. Ideally, parents and school officials should work as partners in assuring that children with disabilities receive the services they need. This section addresses developing positive parental relationships and cooperation; promoting a culture of respect and inclusion for children with disabilities; and helping children receive needed services.

Developing positive parental relationships and cooperation

Although good faith cooperation is likely to yield the best results at the lowest costs for all parties, the IDEA is nonetheless largely structured as an advocacy driven, adversarial system. Parents who are the strongest advocates and who demand the most under the IDEA often get the most from the school. And when a parent-school relationship becomes adversarial, even relatively minor disagreements can become the subjects of bitter disputes between parents and school officials. Further, the system for resolving these disputes under the IDEA is litigation oriented, often aggravating rather than resolving tensions between parents and school officials. Litigation can make ongoing working relationships more difficult; delay the resolution of problems; and consume resources that are needed to support educational services.

Developing positive parent-school relationships and good faith cooperation is in everyone's best interests. Because it is easier to build functional relationships initially, rather than to try to fix broken ones later, developing a relationship of mutual trust and cooperation with parents early in the IDEA process can be invaluable in effectively meeting the needs of IDEA eligible children without undue conflict or expense. Not all relationships will be positive and functional. But with appropriate efforts at building positive working relationships, less of these relationships have to be negative and dysfunctional. To promote positive working relationships:

> *Be sensitive to parents' emotions concerning their child*: Good parents rightly want the very best possible education and future for their child. Accepting limitations resulting from a child's disability can be emotionally difficult for parents. It often takes time for parents to move through the stages of grief resulting from discovering that their child may be limited now and in the future by mental or physical disabilities. But parents are more likely to resolve these challenges and reach a positive resolution when school officials are appropriately sensitive and supportive of the emotional concerns of parents and the child throughout this process. Although educators may be responsible for large numbers of special education students, they must remember that these children are not just names and numbers, but individual, feeling humans with parents and families who love them, who want to protect them, and who want the best for

their future. Parent's emotions concerning their child are understandably strong. Failure to sufficiently recognize and respect this reality is likely to unnecessarily inflame parental anger and impede cooperation.

All of the child's teachers must understand applicable laws and regulations; what is required of them under the IDEA and § 504; and that all teachers are responsible for special education students: There are many common misconceptions among teachers concerning special education. For example, some teachers assume, wrongly, that special education and special education students are the responsibility of only those teachers certified and designated as special educators. To the contrary, the IDEA and § 504 were clearly intended to prevent unnecessary segregation of persons with disabilities from regular classrooms. Special educators have special expertise concerning disabilities. But all teachers are responsible for teaching and helping special needs students in their class. And all teachers are equally bound by the law in providing a FAPE for these children. All teachers need to understand that their compliance with the IDEA, § 504, and the ADA is mandated by law, not voluntary. Further, they have a professional responsibility to offer their best efforts in helping special needs students, and in assuring that these students, like all students, are treated fairly and respectfully in their classrooms.

Parents must understand applicable laws and what the laws actually require and provide: There are many common misconceptions among parents concerning disability laws and what these laws do and do not require and provide. Ultimately, however, what is required under the IDEA, § 504 and the ADA is what these laws actually mandate, and not what rumors or common misconceptions may suggest. If school officials can respectfully, fairly, and clearly explain to parents what the law actually requires or provides, parents are much more likely to accept the realities of the law, even if they don't like the result, than if they believe that the negative result was simply the product of an arbitrary and self-serving decision by school officials.

Help parents to fairly understand not just their child's needs, but to also recognize and respect the legitimate interests of others: IDEA eligible students are entitled to special education and related services necessary to provide a FAPE. It is the legitimate role of parents to assure that school officials are providing their child with the best educational services under the circumstances. But parents must also understand that while their child has a right to a FAPE in the LRE appropriate, school officials must also respect and protect the rights of other students and teachers in the school. Everyone has a right to a safe, orderly, and respectful learning and working environment.

Emphasize your common objective: To provide the best possible education and future for the child under the circumstances: Good parents and teachers want children to have the best possible education available under the circumstances, and an educational experience that prepares them for their best possible future. If school officials can establish a relationship of trust with parents, built on knowledge that school officials are acting in good faith with parents to pursue the best interests of the child, school officials are far more likely to succeed in developing positive parental relationships and cooperation.

Promoting a culture of respect and inclusion for children with disabilities

Despite significant progress in recent years, persons with disabilities continue to experience discrimination. Ignorance and fear are at the core of this discrimination. To reduce this discrimination, we must address its core causes. Too many people still misunderstand and dehumanize persons with disabilities based on highly irrational beliefs and unfounded fears. They may, for example, wrongly assume that a person with a severe disability is somehow not as capable of intelligence, understanding, and feelings as others; that the person may be dangerous; that the disability may be contagious, etc. In schools this ignorance and fear increases the chances that persons with disabilities will be ignored, avoided, and excluded, and become the victims of neglect, bullying, and abuse.

Promoting a positive culture of mutual respect, kindness, understanding, and inclusion in the school can help to reduce the frequency and severity of bullying and abuse and other harmful treatment of children with disabilities. Through leadership and educational efforts, school officials can help everyone in the school to see special education students as valued members of the school community, and to understand that disabilities are a natural part of the human experience. With the development of mutual understanding and respect, special education students can become valued friends and not just the targets of misguided bullying and abuse. Everyone has an important role to play in making these positive cultural changes:

School administrators: As school leaders, school administrators are responsible for creating a respectful and inclusive school culture.

School leaders must make it absolutely clear to everyone, students, teachers, staff, and community members, that the school is a place of mutual respect, and that all persons have a right to be included whenever possible and to be treated with equal respect at all times.

Teachers: Teachers are on the fronts lines in creating an inclusive and respectful classroom. The teacher sets the tone for the classroom climate, and the teacher has a responsibility for supervising student behavior in the classroom. For educational, legal, ethical, and moral reasons, it is imperative that teachers never tolerate disrespect, bullying, and abuse in the classroom.

Parents: Parents play a central role under the IDEA system, serving as the child's chief advocate and protector. It is essential that parents of children with disabilities educate themselves concerning the IDEA and other laws governing special education. Further, they must take the leading role in helping their children to become well-adjusted and strong advocates for themselves and other children with disabilities.

Children: Children with disabilities must learn to become their own best advocates actively reaching out to make new friends; in communicating their needs to others; and in standing up for themselves and their peers when necessary. Student leaders must also set a positive example for all students by respecting and including children with disabilities.

Helping children receive needed services

Children generally do not understand the physical, mental, or emotional challenges they may be facing, and they do not know what services may be available to help them. Children must rely on adults to help identify the underlying causes of their challenges, and to help them receive appropriate services. Concerning children with eligible disabilities, the IDEA's "child find" provision creates an affirmative duty for school officials to identify children with disabilities. IDEA 20 U.S.C. § 1412 mandates: "All children with disabilities residing in the State, including children with disabilities who are homeless children or are wards of the State and children with disabilities attending private schools, regardless of the severity of their disabilities, and who are in need of special education and related services, are identified, located, and evaluated and a practical method is developed and implemented to determine which children with disabilities are currently receiving needed special education and related services."

Some of these children are identified through mass screening tests including vision tests, hearing tests, and other basic tests administered to all school children. Parents, school personnel, medical personnel, or other persons who suspect a child needs IDEA services may also refer the child for an individual evaluation to determine whether the child is eligible for these services. Indicators that a child may need IDEA or other services may include challenges in these areas:

Example indicators that a child may need IDEA or other disability services

The behavioral, academic, motor, emotional, and social indicators below may be cause for further investigation into whether a child needs IDEA or other disability services.*

Behavioral:
- Frequently distracted
- Unable to stay on task
- Highly disorganized or messy
- Hyperactive or unusually inactive
- Covering eyes, squinting, or straining to see
- Loud speech or imperfect pronunciation
- Chronic illness
- Hypersensitive to touch, sound, light, etc.
- Frequently disrupts class
- Poor judgment and impulse control
- Persistently repeats the same pattern of misconduct
- Aggressive or violent
- Engages in self-injury

Academic:
- Expresses frequent confusion and frustration re: assignments
- Does well in some areas but performs poorly in others
- Unable to follow clear directions in assignments
- Difficulty reading, writing, or speaking
- Limited reasoning ability
- Impaired memory

Motor:
- Poor hand-writing
- Eye-hand coordination problems
- Lacking in age appropriate muscle development
- Trouble walking, running, jumping, etc.
- Unusual clumsiness
- Frequent accidents
- Unusual lack of physical stamina

Emotional: • Emotionally volatile
  • Situationally inappropriate emotional behavior
  • Over or under reacts to stress
  • Persistent depression
  • Frequent headaches or stomach problems

Social: • Socially isolated
  • Lacks interest in playing with other children
  • Has great difficulty playing or working with others
  • Extremely awkward or inappropriate social interactions
  • Inability to read common social cues

* *Nota bene*: This is an illustrative list only, and not an exhaustive list. This list is intended to stimulate academic discussions and raise awareness in helping children receive needed services. It is in no way intended as a substitute for IDEA child find obligations or professional evaluations of individual children.

Essential Practice Tips

1) *In close calls between the IDEA and § 504, consider the IDEA*: Erring on the side of the IDEA may be prudent if it assures that the child will receive needed services, avoids contentious and expensive battles with parents, and forecloses future claims for compensatory damages.

2) *Develop positive parental relationships and cooperation*: Developing a relationship of mutual trust and cooperation with parents early in the IDEA process can be invaluable in effectively meeting the needs of the IDEA eligible child without undue conflict or expense. Litigation can make ongoing working relationships difficult and drain away resources that are needed to support education.

3) *Dealing with a truly dangerous student*: In cases where parents refuse to cooperate with an appropriate change of placement and the child poses a genuine danger, safety must remain the highest priority. A truly dangerous student cannot be allowed to cause self-injury or injury to others when the danger was known and the injuries could have been prevented. The IDEA does not require this result, and tort and criminal laws will not allow it.

4) *Promoting a culture of respect and inclusion*: Through leadership and educational efforts, school officials can promote a positive culture of respect, kindness, understanding, and inclusion in the school, helping students to see special education students as valued friends, preventing bullying and abuse.

Essential Points

- There is a legal, ethical, and moral duty to include all persons, including persons with disabilities, when reasonable accommodations allow for inclusion. No one should be excluded from public accommodations because of discrimination or irrational fears.
- Eligibility under the IDEA is based on a two-part test:
  1) Whether the child has an IDEA eligible disability; and
  2) Whether the child needs special education and related services because of that IDEA eligible disability.
- The IDEA's "child find" provision creates an affirmative duty for school officials to identify children with disabilities. Children may be identified for IDEA testing through mass screenings of all children, or through referrals from parents, school personnel, medical personnel, or other persons.
- Parental consent is not required for mass screening tests administered to all children. Before individual evaluations for IDEA eligibility may be conducted, however, school officials generally must obtain parental consent.
- Related services are those supportive services necessary for an IDEA eligible child to benefit from special education. Under the *Tatro* test, health services must be provided as related services if:
  1) The supportive services are necessary for the child to benefit from special education; and
  2) The services are not excluded as medical services that would require the services of a physician for other than diagnostic or evaluation purposes.
- The test for determining if extended school year services are required is an assessment of:
  1) Whether the child would experience a significant regression in the absence of extended year services; and
  2) Whether sufficient educational recoupment would occur in a reasonable time when regular year services were resumed.
- The "stay put" provision requires that during the pendency of any change in placement proceedings, unless school officials and parents otherwise agree, the child shall remain in the then-current educational placement.
- A disciplinary removal that constitutes a change in placement triggers IDEA due process protections, requiring the IEP Team and other qualified personnel to conduct a review to determine whether the problem behavior is a manifestation of a disability.

- If the behavior is not a manifestation of a disability, school officials may discipline the student in the same manner that other student's would be disciplined. Any removal for more than 10 consecutive school days, however, constitutes a change in placement and triggers the procedural protections of the IDEA. If the behavior is a manifestation of the child's disability, the IEP Team must implement a behavioral intervention plan.
- A cost-based defense under the IDEA requires school officials to establish that:
  > 1) The school has provided a proper continuum of placements;
  >
  > 2) The child in question would not experience a denial of educational opportunity because of the failure to provide the expensive service; and
  >
  > 3) Other special education students may be denied a FAPE because of excessive expenditures on one child.

But school officials may choose among any appropriate option. Schools are not required to provide the most expensive services as long as the services chosen are adequate to provide a FAPE.

- Section 504 prohibits discrimination against any person who has a physical or mental disability which substantially limits one or more major life activities; has a record of disability; or is regarded as having a disability.
- Section 504 requires non-discrimination and reasonable accommodations. An accommodation is not reasonable, and therefore not required, if it would result in unreasonable costs, administrative burdens, or health or safety risks.
- Persons may be excluded from activities if participation creates serious health or safety dangers and no reasonable accommodation would effectively mitigate these dangers.
- Medical exclusions must be based on medical data and medical opinions, and not mere speculation or irrational fears.
- The ADA extended protections similar to § 504 protections to many areas of the private sector.

Essential Terms

§ 504: Section 504 of the Rehabilitation Act, 29 U.S.C § 794, prohibits discrimination against persons with disabilities and requires reasonable accommodations in programs receiving federal funding.

ADA: The Americans with Disabilities Act, 42 U.S.C. § 12101, extended § 504 like protections to many areas of the private sector.

FAPE: The right to a Free Appropriate Public Education in conformity with the mandates of the IDEA.

IDEA: The Individuals with Disabilities Education Act, 20 U.S.C. § 1401, provides children with qualifying disabilities with special education and related services through an IEP.

IEP: The Individualized Education Program, the basic plan for providing special education and related services developed, reviewed, and revised in accordance with IDEA requirements by the child's IEP Team.

LRE: An IDEA requirement that the child with a disability be placed in the Least Restrictive Environment appropriate and that the removal of the child from the regular setting occurs only when education in regular classes cannot be achieved satisfactorily.

Manifestation determination: A determination by the IEP Team and other qualified personnel concerning whether an IDEA eligible child's problem behavior is a manifestation of a disability (requiring remedial services rather than punishment).

OHI: Other Health Impaired, a non-specific IDEA category allowing eligibility for disabilities including Attention Deficit Disorder (ADD), diabetes, cancer, or many other chronic health problems, if the illness sufficiently limits strength, vitality, or alertness, and adversely affects educational performance, requiring special education and related services.

OSEP: The Office of Special Education Programs charged with "improving results for infants, toddlers, children and youth with disabilities ages birth through 21 by providing leadership and financial support to assist states and local districts." OSEP provides information on the IDEA.

OSERS: The Office of Special Education and Rehabilitative Services charged with "improving results and outcomes for people with disabilities of all ages." OSERS is the parent agency for OSEP.

Related services: Services required to assist a child with a disability to benefit from special education services, e.g., transportation, speech-language services, psychological services, school nurse services, etc.

Stay-put provision: IDEA provision, 20 U.S.C. § 1415(j), mandating "during the pendency of any proceedings conducted pursuant to this section, unless the State or local educational agency and the parents otherwise agree, the child shall remain in the then-current educational placement of the child."

Transition services: An IDEA mandate for the provision of services to facilitate the child's transition from school to post-school activities which may include instruction, related services, community experiences, and the development of employment and adult living skills.

Essential Cases

Board of Education v. Rowley, 458 U.S. 176 (1982): Addressed the definition of "appropriate" in the FAPE guarantee of substantive rights (further clarified in *Endrew*).

Endrew F. v. Douglas County School District, 580 U.S. __ (2017): Clarified and elevated the *Rowley* standard for "appropriate" in the FAPE holding "to meet its substantive obligation under the IDEA, a school must offer an individual education plan (IEP) reasonably calculated to enable a child to make progress appropriate in light of the child's circumstances."

Honig v. Doe, 484 U.S. 305 (1988): Schools must respect the "stay-put" provision, but "while the [child's] placement may not be changed [during any complaint proceeding], this does not preclude the agency from using its normal procedures for dealing with children who are endangering themselves or others. Such procedures may include the use of study carrels, timeouts, detention, or the restriction of privileges. More drastically, where a student poses an immediate threat to the safety of others, officials may temporarily suspend him or her for up to 10 schooldays" while seeking parental agreement or an emergency court order for a necessary change in placement.

Irving Independent School District v. Tatro, 468 U.S. 883 (1984): Schools must provide health services as related services under the IDEA if they are necessary for the child to benefit from special education and not excluded as medical services that would require the services of a physician for other than diagnostic or evaluation purposes.

Mills v. Board of Education, 348 F. Supp. 866 (D.D.C. 1972): The *Mills* and *PARC* cases are recognized as leading to the legislative establishment of special education programs (i.e., P.L. 94-142; later the IDEA). In *Mills*, a federal district court extended the *PARC* mandates for mentally impaired students to all school aged children with disabilities, holding that they must be provided with a free and adequate public education.

Pennsylvania Association for Retarded Children (PARC) v. Pennsylvania, 343 F. Supp. 279 (E.D. Pa. 1972): In *PARC*, a federal district court held that mentally impaired students ages 6 through 21 should be provided with access to a free public education, and should be placed in regular classrooms when possible or in special classes when necessary.

Schaffer v. Weast, 546 U.S. 45 (2005): Other factors being equal, the party bearing the initial burden of proof is less likely to prevail. In *Weast* the Court held that the party challenging an IEP bears the initial burden of proof.

Winkelman v. Parma City School District, 550 U.S. 516 (2007): The IDEA grants parents independent, enforceable rights, including an entitlement to a FAPE for their child. Parents are entitled to prosecute those rights on their own behalf and to act pro se on behalf of their children.

A Closer Look at the Law

Special education laws were necessary to address egregious neglect of children with disabilities. In his 1973 testimony before the U.S. Senate, regarding the treatment of persons with disabilities and the need for remedial legislation, Professor Oliver L. Hurley of the University of Georgia recounted a scene all too typical of the circumstances of children with disabilities prior to the passage of P.L. 94-142 (predecessor to the IDEA):

> Some years ago, during the course of a visit to the State Institution for [children with intellectual disabilities], I encountered a little girl who was lying in a crib. Wondering why she was so confined while the other children were not, I began to play with her. I found that even though I could make eye contact with her, she was unable to follow me with her eyes for more than about 12 inches. I began to try to teach her. In about 15 minutes she could follow me about a quarter of the way around the bed. I was convinced then, and still am, that with a little work the child could have been taught some useful behavior and could have been gotten out of the crib. It seems safe to say that no one with any authority was concerned about the education of that little girl. For me, this child, who showed some ability to learn typified our reactions to these difficult cases--hide them away, exclude them, forget them . . . It seems antithetical to American philosophy, as I see it, that whether or not a handicapped

child gets proper care and proper educational treatment depends on the fatness of that child's father's wallet.

Appropriate educational services can have remarkable benefits for children with disabilities, helping them to live more independent and productive lives. Since the passage of P.L. 94-142 in 1975, providing special education and related services for children with disabilities has required increasing allocations of resources to special education programs. How have escalating expenditures for special education programs affected regular education programs? How should Congress, the states, and schools balance the educational needs of children with disabilities and the fiscal realities of limited resources? Are the costs of current special education programs justified by the benefits? Are there more efficient ways of achieving equal or superior educational results?

Law & Professional Ethics in Practice:

Although special education is expensive, what are the economic costs of failing to educate children with disabilities, e.g., additional services costs; long-term unemployment; etc.? Further, how should the incalculable personal costs of denying education to these children be weighed, including the diminished quality of life for the girl discussed above by Professor Hurley, and the possibility that she might spend the rest of her natural life confined to a bed and staring at the ceiling if she does not receive appropriate educational assistance? School officials must comply with IDEA legal mandates, but what are their ethical and moral obligations to support children with disabilities who need their help beyond what is required by law?

Questions for Further Exploration:

1) *Assessing the human impacts of special education*: P.L. 94-142 was passed in 1975. How has special education changed the lives of children with disabilities, parents, educators, non-disabled students, and the community?

2) *Costs, benefits, and greater efficacy*: What are the economic benefits of the IDEA, and what are the costs? What remains to be done to help children with disabilities and to improve the effectiveness and efficiency of special education?

3) *IDEA discipline policies*: Do IDEA discipline policies strike a fair balance between the rights of special education students and the rights of everyone else?

4) *Open forum*: What other related issues or current events would you like to discuss?

Suggested Activities for Further Learning:

1) Many famous and highly successful persons have been challenged by disabilities. Nonetheless, they succeeded in spite of, or sometimes even because of their disability, when they were able to focus their special talents in a positive direction. Among those said to have been challenged by disabilities are: Moses, Sir Isaac Newton, and Thomas Jefferson (speech impairments); Leonardo Da Vinci, Albert Einstein, and Thomas Edison (dyslexia); Alexander the Great and Theodore Roosevelt (epilepsy); Michelangelo, General "Stonewall" Jackson, Sir Winston Churchill, and Howie Mandel (obsessive compulsive disorder); Stephen Hawking (cerebral palsy); Abraham Lincoln (mood disorder); Ludwig Van Beethoven (deafness); The Greek poet Homer and Stevie Wonder (blindness); Wolfgang Amadeus Mozart (hyperactivity, mood disorder, and possible Tourette's syndrome). Learn more about how throughout human history persons with disabilities have overcome personal challenges to achieve personal greatness and contribute to the progress of humanity. Share this knowledge to inspire children with disabilities to future success of their own.

2) Discuss ways to make your school more inclusive and welcoming to persons with disabilities. Identify positive ways of reaching out to persons with disabilities in your community to let them know that they are welcomed and valued members of the school community.

3) Learn more about how to prevent bullying of children with disabilities. Create a plan for what you could do to make your school culture more supportive for children with disabilities and to better protect these children from abuse.

Chapter 9: Contracts and Employment Law

A fair, effective, and efficient system of contract law is a necessary foundation for social and economic stability and progress. As a means of codifying and enforcing agreements contract law promotes predictability and mutual trust. We could not have a functional society or economic progress without enforceable contracts and reasonable certainty that most persons will respect the law and honor their contractual agreements.

Commerce functions best in a stable, predictable business environment in which everyone is subject to the same fair rules designed for the common good. Contract law forms the foundation for fair trade, and fair trade benefits everyone. Fair rules of commerce allow all persons to equitably exchange goods and services they have for goods and services they need. Contract and employment laws help to promote stability, predictability, efficiency, and fairness in procurement, hiring, conditions of employment, and the just resolution of disputes under the equal rule of law.

A contract is a legally enforceable bargain. A contract differs from an ordinary promise in that a contract can be enforced through a court of law. Everyone should strive to keep promises of course, but promises are not legally enforceable contracts. Promises carry ethical and moral obligations but only contracts carry enforceable legal obligations. To acquire the force of law as a contract a bargain must meet all the essential elements of a contract: Valid legal consideration, offer, and acceptance.

The essence of a contract is the agreement to exchange mutual benefits/detriments, or "legal consideration" (i.e., *quid pro quo,* Latin for "something for something") in which each party considers performing their part of the promised exchange (detriment) as the price of receiving the desired good or service (benefit) from the other party. The exchange of benefits/detriments must be mutual or there is no basis for a contract. A unilateral promise is not a contract. Something of value must be promised both ways or there is no valid legal consideration and no basis for a contract.

For example, a promise to give money to a school could only become a contract if legal consideration is exchanged both ways. Morally, a donor should honor a promise. But to be legally binding a donor's promise must be in exchange for something of value. If a donor declared: "I will give the school $100,000" and nothing was promised in return, there is no enforceable contract because there is no valid legal consideration, i.e. *quid pro quo*. But if the donor made a conditional promise, such as: "I will give the school $100,000 if the new athletic stadium is named after me" these bilateral benefits/detriments could serve as valid legal consideration and the foundation of a contract.

A valid contract requires not only mutual legal consideration as the foundation of the contract, but also a valid offer, and a valid acceptance of the offer to complete the contract.

Formation of a Contract

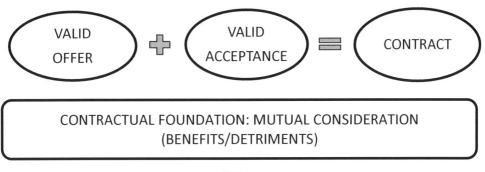

© Dayton

As noted above, on the contractual foundation of mutual legal consideration, a party must articulate a valid offer which is then accepted in a timely manner by another party through a valid acceptance. A valid offer is defined by:

1) Expression of present intent to contract; and
2) Definiteness of terms sufficient to describe the subject matter of the bargain.

Speculating about selling or buying in the future is not present intent to contract. A statement such as: "I have been thinking about selling my house" is not an expression of present intent to contract. Further, this statement does not sufficiently define the necessary terms of the contract, such as what house, how much property, the price and terms of sale, etc. Without a clear and present intent to contract and an adequate definition of the terms of the contract, there is no valid offer.

If there is an expression of present intent to contract and the terms of the bargain have been sufficiently defined, the offer remains open for the time stated. If the time is not stated, the offer remains open for a reasonable time based on the circumstances of the bargain and the common practice in the market. For example, where the timing of an offer is not expressly defined, an offer to sell a truck load of ripe bananas is necessarily a short-term offer that must be accepted quickly. The offer to sell a house, however, generally requires more extended time to reasonably secure necessary property inspections, a title search, financing, etc. In the absence of an express statement defining the timing of the offer (e.g., "this offer is valid for 30 days"), in the common law system, common practices in the market govern the reasonable time window for the offer.

To form a legally binding contract the valid offer must be met with a valid acceptance. The acceptance must:

1) Mirror the terms of the offer evidencing a "meeting of the minds"; and

2) Be communicated while the offer is still open.

A "meeting of the minds" exists when both parties reasonably share a common understanding concerning the necessary elements of the bargain. If the party responding to the offer changes a necessary element of the bargain in the asserted "acceptance" of the offer, it is generally not a valid acceptance but is instead a counter-offer which may be accepted or not by the other party.

For example, if a distributor of playground equipment offered to sell a package of playground equipment to a school for $20,000 and the School Board President responded by saying: "We accept your offer provided that you throw in an extra slide" this conditional "acceptance" is not a valid acceptance at all. This is instead a counter-offer that the distributor may or may not accept. To constitute a valid acceptance the acceptance must mirror the terms of the offer, and there must be a sufficient meeting of the minds concerning the essential terms of the bargain.

Most people generally enter into contracts intending to fulfill the contract. Contracts tend to go bad not because of insincere intentions at the time the contract was formed, but because of misunderstandings or changed circumstances that make it difficult or impossible for a party to subsequently fulfill the contract. If a contract is breached, however, the aggrieved party may seek to have the contract enforced by a court of law. The aggrieved party becomes the plaintiff in the contract case, and the party charged with breaching the contract becomes the defendant. Possible defenses available to the defendant in a contract case may include:

Mutual mistake: The defendant argues that because of a mutual mistake, there was no "meeting of the minds" between the parties, and therefore no valid contract. The formation of a contract requires a sufficient meeting of the minds in which what is in the mind of each party sufficiently mirrors the understanding of the other concerning the essential elements of the bargain. Parties may have entered into the contract based on reasonable assumptions. But because of a mutual mistake unknown to either party at the time of the bargain, their understanding of the elements of the agreement were so different there was no meeting of the minds and no valid formation of a contract. When subsequent events reveal that mutual mistake existed at the time the contract was formed, rescission of the contract may be an appropriate remedy.

Unconscionable bargain: An unconscionable bargain is one in which there was extreme unfairness in the bargaining process, and one party acted in a predatory fashion to take advantage of the other party. For example, the use of a non-negotiable form contract with extremely one-sided terms known to the party presenting the contract but not reasonably known to the other party may constitute an unconscionable bargain. Courts are charged with enforcing justice. Courts should not help predatory merchants take advantage of vulnerable consumers. Simply making a bad deal, however, is not an unconscionable bargain, and a court will not save the defendant from the consequences of making a bad deal unless the bargain was genuinely unconscionable.

Misrepresentation or fraud: The formation of a contract requires knowing, voluntary consent to the genuine terms of the contract. Misrepresentation of a material fact may void a contract, where, for example, a merchant knows what the buyer is seeking but intentionally misrepresents the goods being sold as fit for the known intended purpose. Misrepresentation occurs when the seller knows the goods are not appropriate, but intentionally misleads the buyer into believing they are. Further, fraudulently obtaining "consent" to a contract, through deception or other trickery, is no real consent at all and voids the contract.

Duress or undue influence: Contracts must be entered into knowingly and through free will. The use of threats or intimidation to obtain consent to a contract constitutes unlawful duress. And the exercise of undue influence, for example the abuse of a relationship or position of power to obtain consent to a contract, would also void the contract.

Illegal subject matter: Courts will not enforce contracts involving illegal subject matter. If the terms of the contract do not conform to the applicable law, the contract cannot be enforced in a court of law. For example, where a state statute exclusively defines the terms of employment for a public educator, a contract that is contrary to the applicable statute is unlawful and unenforceable.

Legal incapacity: Both parties to a contract must be legally competent and able to understand the purposes and consequences of the contract. A person suffering from a mental incapacity due to a disability, obvious intoxication, etc., may not understand the purposes and consequences of the contract or be capable of the necessary "meeting of the minds" required for the formation of a contract. Further, courts will generally not enforce contracts against minor children.

Statute of frauds: This legal doctrine has its origins in the 1677 English Statute of Frauds intended to limit fraudulent testimony and perjury. Contracts falling within the Statute required a written contract signed by the defendant for goods that exceeded $500 in value or for personal services that could not be performed within a year of the making of the contract. The modern significance of the Statute of Frauds is that alleged "oral contracts" are generally disfavored. For contracts important enough to seek judicial enforcement, a plaintiff should be prepared to produce a written memorandum of the agreement that identifies the parties; documents the exchange of legal consideration; adequately describes the complete subject matter of the bargain including necessary terms and conditions of the contract; and is signed by the defendant.

If the plaintiff has established the existence of a valid contract and a breach of contract by the defendant, and the defendant has failed to establish an adequate defense, the plaintiff is entitled to a legal remedy. Remedies available to the plaintiff may include the following:

Reasonable expectation damages: Generally the plaintiff is entitled to the "benefit of the bargain" and to be placed in the economic position the plaintiff would have achieved absent the breach of contract by the defendant. For example, if the plaintiff can prove that without the defendant's breach of contract the plaintiff would have profited $50,000 from the contract, $50,000 is the "benefit of the bargain" and the "reasonable expectation" is the measure of damages awarded from the defendant to the plaintiff. Courts will not, however, award damages based on unsupported speculation concerning profits. The plaintiff must be able to adequately document and prove damages caused by the defendant's breach of contract.

Liquidated damages: To avoid uncertainty and prevent costly disputes over the amount of damages, parties may make an advance agreement in contract regarding the amount of damages to be paid by the defendant if the contract is breached. These liquidated damages clauses are common in transactions in which breaches are frequent occurrences, such as contracts for the rental of property (e.g., "if the tenant breaches the 12 month lease, liquidated damages shall be equal to 2 monthly payments"). The limitation on liquidated damages clauses is that they must be reasonably related to the actual losses incurred because of the breach of contract. Liquidated damages should not be punitive to the defendant or provide an unfair windfall of profits for the plaintiff.

Specific performance: If the subject matter of the bargain was unique, like a specific property, work of art, etc., monetary damages may be inadequate as a remedy. The plaintiff may, for example, need a particular piece of land for building a business or a home, and no other piece of land offers the same location or other attributes. When appropriate, the court may order specific performance, i.e., the transfer of the unique property in exchange for the sale price as bargained for in the contract. Specific performance will not be awarded, however, when other damages provide an adequate remedy, or the contract was for personal services. Courts will not award specific performance for personal services, as doing so is unlawful, impractical, and inconsistent with public policy. Involuntary servitude is unlawful except as punishment for a crime, and even if forced work were lawful it would raise troubling enforcement problems and create unhealthy social conditions in the workplace.

Rescission of the contract: A voluntary rescission of the contract by mutual consent essentially calls off the bargain, thereby annulling the contract. A rescission can be requested by the plaintiff and judicially enforced, however, where the plaintiff can show wrongful conduct by the defendant in the contracting process.

Consequential and incidental damages: Consequential damages result from the foreseeable and provable negative consequences to the plaintiff because of the defendant's breach of contract. The claimed consequences of breach must have been reasonably known to the defendant, and therefore assumed as a potential cost of doing business. For example, a negligent failure by the defendant to deliver a critical good or service to the plaintiff at the agreed time, when that failure was reasonably known to be economically harmful to the plaintiff, especially if the contract stipulated that on time delivery was essential. Incidental damages include the costs incurred by the plaintiff in seeking substitute goods or services, or other transactional costs incurred because of the defendant's breach of contract.

Equitable relief: Courts have both legal and equitable powers. A court may issue a legal remedy, such as reasonable expectation damages, for a proven breach of contract. But if there is no legal contract, a legal remedy is unavailable. For example, where a plaintiff acting reasonably and in good faith has already performed all or a significant part of the bargain, but no legal remedy is available because the contract was technically deficient, this could result in the "unjust enrichment" of the defendant at the expense of the plaintiff. A plaintiff may have incurred the detriment, and the defendant the benefit, but no lawful contract existed. In such a case, a court may use its powers of equity to provide an equitable remedy sufficient to prevent unjust enrichment of the defendant at the plaintiff's expense: An order, for example, that the defendant compensate the plaintiff for the fair-market value of the services the plaintiff had already provided before learning of the defective contract.

It should be noted, however, that a plaintiff seeking relief for a breach of contract has a legal duty to reasonably attempt to "mitigate damages" and not unfairly run up the bill on the defendant. Allowing plaintiffs to unnecessarily run up the damages on defendants, through vindictiveness, waste, or other reasonably avoidable losses would ultimately hurt everyone and increase the costs of goods and services in the common market. Mitigation of damages includes an obligation for the plaintiff to reasonably attempt to find cover goods or services from another vender when the plaintiff learns of a pending breach of contract by the defendant.

For example, if the plaintiff contracted for the delivery of paper supplies and the defendant/vender notified the plaintiff/buyer of the pending breach of contract, the buyer must reasonably attempt to mitigate damages by finding another appropriate vender of paper supplies. If the price of cover goods from the new vender is lower there may be no damages as the buyer benefitted from the vender's breach. If the price of the cover goods is higher than the contracted price the plaintiff/buyer could sue for the difference in costs. If acceptable cover goods or services cannot be obtained, the plaintiff may sue for all appropriate damages, having satisfied the plaintiff's duty to reasonably attempt to mitigate damages.

Essential Questions & Answers

Is a "verbal contract" legally binding?

Verbal contracts are appropriate for minor matters and can be legally binding with sufficient proof. But verbal contracts for larger sums of money or personal services are generally disfavored because they can entangle courts in unnecessary factual disputes that could have been easily avoided with a simple written and signed contract, which was the reason for the Statute of Frauds. If not prohibited by the Statute of Frauds under state law, you may be able to enforce a verbal contract if you can get the defendant to acknowledge the terms and validity of the contract or otherwise prove necessary contractual elements. Generally, however, it is best to have a written contract for any matter serious enough to enforce in court.

I signed a contract without reading it. Am I still bound by all the terms of the contract?

Yes. You should always read a contract before signing it. Signing a contract assumes you have read it and that you agree to all of its terms. If there are terms you deem unacceptable, attempt to negotiate acceptable terms prior to signing the contract. In practice some contracts are "adhesion contracts" in which you have no realistic opportunity to negotiate the terms and you must agree to the boilerplate terms without modification if you want the goods or services. In these cases any ambiguities are interpreted against the party drafting the contract (as this party caused the ambiguity) but otherwise you are bound by contracts you sign, unless a valid defense can be proven, e.g., unconscionable bargain, misrepresentation, fraud, etc.

What should I do if someone refuses to honor their contract?

In any breach of contract, it is wise to select a means of resolution that makes sense under the circumstances, considering the value of the contract, the resolution options available, and the strength of your case. In important matters always seek the advice of competent legal counsel knowledgeable concerning the specific laws in your jurisdiction. But in more minor matters, it may be useful to initially explore alternative dispute resolution options. You may be able to persuade the other party to honor the contract; negotiate mutually acceptable modifications to the contract if necessary; or settle the matter informally or in small claims court to avoid legal expenses that may exceed the value of enforcing the contract.

Can minor children be held to a contract?

Both parties to a contract must be legally competent and able to understand the purposes and consequences of the contract. Courts will generally not enforce contracts against minor children as they are deemed not fully legally competent for purposes of contracting. Although minors may be held accountable for contracts concerning necessary items (e.g., food, clothing, etc.) in general contracts with minors are unenforceable.

What should I do if I have signed a contract but can't honor the contract?

Consider negotiating modifications to any terms that cannot be fulfilled or negotiating a rescission of the contract. If you breach the contract without first making good faith efforts to find a means of legal compliance or settlement, it may look like a bad faith breach of contract that would make it easier for a defendant to obtain a judgment for full damages on the contract.

What are the rules governing release from a teacher contract?

Teachers may sometimes be unable to fulfill a teaching contract because of an unforeseen change in circumstances ranging from health and family issues (e.g., long-term illness; involuntary relocations of spouses; etc.) to an offer of a superior position. The reality is that teachers will rarely be sued for a breach of an employment contract. The greater risk for a teacher who breaches a contract is in those states where a failure to honor a teaching contract or obtain release in advance may be deemed unprofessional conduct under state certification rules and negative action could be taken against the teacher's professional certificate. Teachers should notify school officials as soon as possible to negotiate a mutual rescission of the contract so that quality instructional services can be secured for students. Teachers who cooperate with school officials in assuring a smooth transition in instructional responsibilities are far more likely to get school officials to agree to a rescission of the contract and to retain good will with the school.

Can a tenured teacher be fired?

Yes. Tenure guarantees a right to due process in employment actions, not lifetime employment. If there is a legitimate cause (as defined by state law, e.g., insubordination, willful neglect of duties, incompetence, etc.) for firing a tenured teacher, a tenured teacher can be fired. Teacher tenure assures adequate notice of charges and evidence, an opportunity for a fair hearing, and promotes fair treatment generally in matters that may significantly affect a tenured teacher's employment rights, but not lifetime employment.

What constitutes unlawful sexual harassment in the workplace?

Courts recognize two types of sexual harassment in the workplace prohibited by Title VII: 1) Quid pro quo sexual harassment, and 2) Hostile environment sexual harassment. Quid pro quo sexual harassment is unwelcomed sexual requests or advances explicitly or implicitly linked to terms and conditions of employment. For example, a sexual request from a supervisor linked to continued employment, a promotion, etc. Hostile environment sexual harassment is unwelcomed sexual conduct in the workplace that would be viewed as objectively creating a hostile workplace on the basis of sex and that is so offensive that it interferes with work or conditions of employment. A hostile environment might be created, for example, if an employer tolerates or participates in sexually offensive comments or conduct in the workplace, especially when there is a persistent pattern of inappropriate behavior or any especially egregious incidents.

What constitutes unlawful pregnancy discrimination in the workplace?

Because only females become pregnant, employment sanctions based on pregnancy violate Title VII as gender based discrimination. Questions concerning marriage or pregnancy are inappropriate and unlawful in employment interviews and may be evidence of prohibited employment discrimination. The Pregnancy Discrimination Act (PDA), 42 U.S.C. § 2000e(k), defines sex discrimination to include discrimination on the basis of pregnancy or related medical conditions stating: "The terms 'because of sex' or 'on the basis of sex' include, but are not limited to, because of or on the basis of pregnancy, childbirth, or related medical conditions; and women affected by pregnancy, childbirth, or related medical conditions shall be treated the same for all employment-related purposes, including receipt of benefits under fringe benefit programs, as other persons not so affected but similar in their ability or inability to work."

What constitutes unlawful age discrimination in the workplace?

The Age Discrimination in Employment Act (ADEA), 29 U.S.C. § 621, prohibits discrimination based on age against anyone 40 or over. The ADEA applies to all employers engaged in interstate commerce with 20 or more employees, including federal and state governments. Using age as a criteria in employment is not prohibited "where age is a bona fide occupational qualification reasonably necessary to the normal operation of the particular business." In practice, however, this is a very limited exception applicable to positions such as an acting role for a child or young adult, or legitimate public safety concerns for airline pilots, bus drivers, etc.

What does the Family and Medical Leave Act require?

The Family and Medical Leave Act (FMLA), 29 U.S.C. § 2601, allows eligible employees to take unpaid family or medical leave with continued group health insurance eligibility, and a right to return to the pre-leave job under the same terms and conditions that existed pre-leave. Up to 12 work weeks per year of unpaid leave may be taken for the birth of a child, newborn care, adoption, new foster care, care for a seriously ill child, spouse, or parent, or a serious illness of the employee. The FMLA also allows for up to 26 weeks of leave to care for a close family member who is an active duty member of the military service with a serious injury or illness.

What should I do if I have been subjected to employment discrimination?

You generally have to go through Equal Employment Opportunity Commission (EEOC) administrative procedures prior to filing a lawsuit. Short timelines apply so be aware of timelines and prepare to file promptly. Details can be found at: www.eeoc.gov. Gather and preserve relevant evidence supporting the allegations of discrimination and seek the advice of a qualified attorney with expertise and experience in employment law.

Essential Practice Skills

All professionals need a working knowledge of contract law, and the laws governing employment, in order to protect their own rights and to promote legal compliance in their workplace. Entering into contracts for goods and services is a necessary part of every adult's personal life, and an important job duty for professionals involved in institutional procurement and employment decisions.

Disputes over employment are among the most common and contentious areas of litigation in educational institutions. Many employment problems can be avoided, however, by simply complying with the law and making wise decisions in the hiring and retention of personnel. Like a bad marriage, bad personnel situations are far easier to get into than out of. And the problems caused by bad hiring decisions generally don't go away until the people do. Instead, personnel problems tend to worsen and increasingly haunt and harm the institution, often resulting in significant damage to the institution and everyone in it. The harms resulting from bad hiring decisions are, however, generally avoidable.

Hiring and retention decisions are the most important decisions any institution makes. Institutions are defined by the people in them. People create the institutional culture and generate an institutional reputation that either helps or hurts the institution's present and future efforts to achieve its mission. For institutional success, it is essential that you hire and retain highly qualified and ethical persons. Just as surely as good hires help to guarantee the future success of the institution, bad hires sow the seeds for future institutional failures. One "bad apple" can do enormous damage to the culture and reputation of the institution. Bad employees drive off good people and give the institution a bad reputation. And your institutional reputation can be either your greatest asset or liability.

For these reasons, it is essential that all persons involved in the hiring and retention process fully understand the importance of making wise employment decisions. Further, they must be sufficiently versed in the law and good employment practices to assure that the institutional employment process is fair and open; that no form of invidious employment discrimination is ever tolerated in the institution; and that institutional personnel decisions are fair-minded, prudent, and lawful.

To promote these important goals this section addresses essential practice skills related to contracts and employment including tenure and due process; equal opportunity employment laws; job announcements and recruitment; pre-employment screening of applicants; pre-employment interviews; reference and background checks; employee supervision; performance evaluations; dismissals; common defenses in dismissal proceedings; and professional ethics.

Tenure and due process

Tenure carries with it a legal right to due process of law in actions significantly affecting employment including reprimand, suspension, or dismissal. To claim a right to due process of law in government employment a plaintiff must establish that there has been a sufficient impingement on a protected life, liberty, or property interest. Only liberty or property interests are relevant in the educational context. Untenured and tenured teachers hold very different types of property rights in employment. Untenured teachers are granted year-to-year contracts. The property right of an untenured teacher runs only from the start of the contract period to the end. In contrast, tenured teachers have a property right that extends indefinitely. The property right of a tenured teacher extends until the teacher leaves employment or school officials can show a valid cause for termination.

Untenured Teacher's Property Right to Employment

Tenured Teacher's Property Right to Employment

© **Dayton**

In *Board of Regents v. Roth*, 408 U.S. 564 (1972) the Court decided that when an untenured teacher has been paid the amount due under the contract, then no property right has been taken away simply by not renewing the contract. The contract promised one academic year's pay. After the teacher received what was promised under the contract, there were no further promises and no further property rights. Accordingly, there is no property right to due process based on not renewing the contract for another academic year.

Untenured teachers are also generally not entitled to an explanation for the non-renewal and a knowledgeable administrator is unlikely to volunteer one. Providing an explanation for the non-renewal may arguably create a right to due process. In *Roth* the Court recognized that: "Where a person's good name, reputation, honor, or integrity is at stake because of what the government is doing to him, notice and an opportunity to be heard are essential." If school officials give a negative reason for the non-renewal, the non-renewed teacher could argue that the statement impinged on the teacher's "good name, reputation, honor, or integrity" requiring due process.

Statements from school officials that call into question the good name, reputation, honor, or integrity of the teacher related to the non-renewal could raise a liberty interest entitling the teacher to due process. But is non-renewal itself sufficiently stigmatizing? In *Roth*, the Court stated "there is no suggestion that the State, in declining to re-employ the respondent, imposed on him a stigma or other disability that foreclosed his freedom to take advantage of other employment opportunities." The lesson from *Roth* is that because untenured teachers are only promised a year-to-year contract, an untenured teacher can simply be non-renewed at the end of the contract term, without any notification of cause or other explanation. Further, no explanation should be given by schools officials if they wish to avoid claims of infringement on a protected liberty interest.

It should be noted that if a non-renewed teacher has evidence that the non-renewal was based on an improper motivation, such as discrimination related to race, gender, religion, national origin, age, disability, etc., the teacher has a right to contest the alleged discriminatory non-renewal. But the burden of proof is with the teacher challenging the non-renewal. Unless the teacher has credible evidence of unlawful actions by school officials the suit is likely to be dismissed. In contrast, in a termination of a tenured teacher the burden of proof lies with school officials. All other things being equal, the party who bears the burden of proof is less likely to prevail. Because tenure status places the burden of proof on school officials, tenure clearly provides an advantageous employment status. But tenure only protects employment if school officials cannot meet the burden of proof.

After acquiring tenure, tenured educators can only be terminated for a valid cause that is provable by school officials. The permissible reasons for termination are specified in state statutes, and may include, for example: incompetence; insubordination; willful neglect of duties; immorality; violation of school policy, state, or federal law; or other good and sufficient causes. These statutes may also include non-punitive reasons for dismissals, including a reduction in force (RIF) due to loss of students or canceled programs. In general, any involuntary termination of a tenured educator requires extensive due process, as the right to continued employment is a substantial property interest.

Assuming that the charges are true, however, proving a charge of insubordination is a relatively simple two-step process: 1) The employee was given a lawful order; and 2) The employee refused to comply with the lawful order. Willful neglect of duties involves a similar pattern of proof. In contrast, incompetence or immorality are more subjective in nature, and while easy to prove in extreme cases, may be difficult to prove in closer cases, e.g., conduct that some may view as immoral, others may see as an exercise of poor judgment but not immoral.

Compliance with equal employment opportunity laws

Equal employment opportunity is not just good institutional practice: It is the law. The U.S. Equal Employment Opportunity Commission (EEOC) has lawful authority to address prohibited employment policies and practices. As the EEOC stated in its *Prohibited Employment Policies/Practices* rules, under the laws enforced by the EEOC:

[I]t is illegal to discriminate against someone (applicant or employee) because of that person's race, color, religion, sex (including gender identity, sexual orientation, and pregnancy), national origin, age (40 or older), disability or genetic information. It is also illegal to retaliate against a person because he or she complained about discrimination, filed a charge of discrimination, or participated in an employment discrimination investigation or lawsuit.

Discrimination violating the laws enforced by the EEOC could result in significant legal sanctions, including an order for substantial monetary damages. But even beyond those areas of discrimination now enforced by the EEOC, invidious employment discrimination based on any professionally irrelevant criteria (e.g., being overweight, appearance, etc.), should never be tolerated. Even if not in a form that is currently expressly unlawful, irrational and invidious employment discrimination, in all forms, is professionally unethical, harmful to individuals, and an unfair institutional practice. Further, in the area on employment discrimination, today's unethical practice may be tomorrow's unlawful practice. The goal of the institution must always be to hire and retain the most highly qualified and best performing individuals regardless of irrelevant personal characteristics.

Consistent with these goals, the purpose of any legitimate and lawful job announcement is to communicate the position opening to a large and diverse pool of highly qualified potential job applicants. Once applications for the position are received the process of lawfully screening applications involves an objective review of the applications based on legitimate job related qualifications in order to narrow the pool of applicants to a reasonable number of top candidates for job interviews. An aggressive, open, and lawful job announcement and recruitment process is essential to hiring the top candidates for job openings.

Job announcements and recruitment

EEOC rules prohibit any job announcement that suggests unlawful preferential treatment or discourages applications based on prohibited factors such as race, color, religion, sex, etc. In addition to having a lawful announcement, all other recruitment efforts must also be non-discriminatory. Required and preferred qualifications communicated through job announcements or other means should be based on anticipated duties.

Avoid any terms or phrases that could reasonably be misunderstood as implying an unlawful preference (e.g., phrases such as "Adams County residents preferred" when location is associated with racial or ethnic demographics; "must be available weekends" when this is not a necessary duty and it is likely to discourage applications from persons observing a weekend religious Sabbath; "salesman" implying a gender preference; "excellent communication skills" if not an actual job requirement and may appear to discriminate based on national origin or disability; "seeking energetic recent graduate" implying an age preference; etc.).

Pre-employment screening of applicants

Concerning the pre-employment screening of applicants (i.e., reviews of applications; checking references; conducting interviews; etc.), EEOC *Prohibited Employment Policies/Practices* rules state:

> As a general rule, the information obtained and requested through the pre-employment process should be limited to those essential for determining if a person is qualified for the job; whereas, information regarding race, sex, national origin, age, and religion are irrelevant in such determinations. Employers are explicitly prohibited from making pre-offer inquiries about disability. Although state and federal equal opportunity laws do not clearly forbid employers from making pre-employment inquiries that relate to, or disproportionately screen out members based on race, color, sex, national origin, religion, or age, such inquiries may be used as evidence of an employer's intent to discriminate unless the questions asked can be justified by some business purpose. Therefore, inquiries about organizations, clubs, societies, and lodges of which an applicant may be a member or any other questions, which may indicate the applicant's race, sex, national origin, disability status, age, religion, color or ancestry if answered, should generally be avoided. Similarly, employers should not ask for a photograph of an applicant. If needed for identification purposes, a photograph may be obtained after an offer of employment is made and accepted.

If the job announcement was properly drafted to include a complete and accurate description of essential job qualifications and duties, it is a relatively easy matter to extract from the job announcement a valid list of job qualifications and duties to use as objective criteria in the pre-employment screening of applicants. It is also good practice to assure that each identified job qualification and duty can be justified by a legitimate business purpose (e.g., "must be able to lift 100 pounds" was included because heavy lifting is a necessary part of the job and not intended to screen out women or persons with disabilities; "must hold a degree" was included because licensing, accreditation, etc., rules require the degree and not to screen out members of minority groups holding fewer degrees; "must be available for work on Saturday" was included because the employee will be supervising a Saturday program and not to exclude persons who observe a Saturday Sabbath; etc.).

Pre-employment interviews

Pre-employment interviews can be stressful and socially awkward for applicants and interviewers. When faced with social stress, an awkward silence, etc., even a well-intentioned interviewer may be tempted to try to fill the silence with a question that is not well thought out. Unplanned questions can, however, potentially stray into impermissible areas of inquiry or otherwise be misperceived as involving employment discrimination. To avoid potentially falling into the abyss of suspected employment discrimination, avoid irrelevant personal questions.

Avoid Irrelevant Personal Questions in Job Interviews

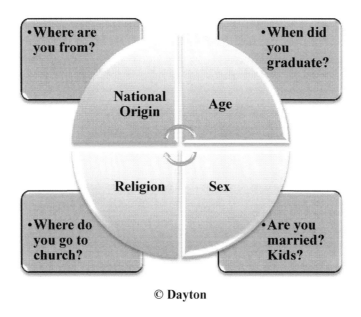

© Dayton

To survive a legal challenge, interview questions should be related to actual job requirements, i.e., employment inquiries should be logically connected to Bona Fide Occupational Qualifications (BFOQs). A useful test for determining the legal relevancy of an interview questions is: Can you clearly explain what your question has to do with a BFOQ if challenged? If not, do not ask the question.

218

Relevancy Test for Potential Interview Questions

| Interview Questions | Should be Logically Connected to | Lawful BFOQs |

All applicants should be asked the same general questions and given the same fair opportunity to respond and demonstrate qualifications. Be certain to inquire of all applicants whether any reasonable accommodations (i.e., under § 504 or the ADA) are needed for the interview, along with an express assurance of non-discrimination for all persons consistent with applicable federal and state laws.

Reference and background checks

Employers have a duty to reasonably inquire into the relevant qualifications, conduct, and character of potential employees. If employers fail in this duty, and third parties are injured because of the new employee's discoverable lack of qualifications, a violent criminal history, sexual offenses, etc., the employer has negligently introduced an avoidable danger into the institution and may be held liable for resulting damages.

Employer inquiries may include reference checks, verification of educational and work history, criminal background checks, etc., to verify information received through the application and interview, and to assure that the individual is qualified and presents no known danger to others in the workplace. It is good practice to generally inform applicants that references and background checks will be conducted, and to request that job candidates sign a waiver form authorizing necessary background checks. Criminal background checks may be required by state law. In making an initial contact with a previous employer or other reference person:

1) Identify who you are, your title, and the institution you are with;
2) Generally explain the nature of your inquiry;
3) Confirm the identity of the person you are contacting, their title, and institution; and
4) Verify the identity of the person you are inquiring about (i.e., you want to make sure you are both discussing the right person).

In questioning prior employers about potential employees for your institution, as with employment interviews, questions should be related to BFOQs for the new position and relevant job performance in the prior position. Questions may include, for example: The applicant's prior job title; dates of employment; duties; work performance; attendance; the quality of working relationships with supervisors, subordinates, colleagues, and students; and other legitimate job related questions.

As an employer, you will also likely receive similar calls from other potential employers concerning your current or former employees. In responding to inquiries about current or former employees, responses should be based on employment related facts and good faith efforts to respond to BFOQs. Do not respond to discriminatory, unethical, or otherwise improper questions from potential employers. Do not say anything to the potential employer that you would not say directly to the employee or others. Do not defame the employee or others, breach their privacy, or make malicious statements intended to interfere with contract or employment. Keep all communications factual and professional. Note that depending on state law it is possible that your phone conversations may be lawfully recorded by the other party even without your knowledge and consent.

State law or professional ethics may require you to disclose certain material facts that may make a job candidate unfit for employment. Public policy should certainly prohibit what was known among personnel directors as "passing the trash" (e.g., agreeing to give a known child abuser a positive recommendation in exchange for a resignation, thereby quietly solving their institution's problem, but allowing the abuser to find unsuspecting new targets in the new institution). You must warn others about known dangers. When doing so, however, only communicate facts sufficient to satisfy your legal and professional duty (e.g., "Mr. Jones, resigned in March of this year after being arrested for child abuse, all of which is public record. We have no further comment"). You must provide a sufficient warning. But you do not want to open the door to a defamation suit by going beyond provable facts to rumor and speculation you cannot prove if challenged.

If you discover clear evidence that a potential employee is unfit for the position or presents a significant risk to students or others, this person cannot be hired. Applicants will often omit negative but relevant information from their applications. Evidence of dishonesty alone, however, may make the individual unfit for employment. It is possible for anyone to make a good faith misstatement, omission, or harmless error. But clear evidence that an employee intentionally misrepresented a material fact on an employment application, or lied during a job interview, may be grounds for termination of employment even after hiring.

In the age of the Internet and extensive online public records it is very difficult to keep a secret. If an employee has a negative event in his or her employment history, it is better for the employee to be honest about the event; to provide an explanation for the event; evidence of remediation or rehabilitation; and to explain why it does not make him or her unfit for the current position.

Employee supervision

As noted above, employers are required to exercise due diligence in assuring that employees have adequate skills, certification, and character prior to assuming their duties. Employers must conduct all necessary reference and background checks to assure that they are protecting others in the institution from reasonably discoverable dangers. Further, employers are required to provide adequate post-employment training and supervision to assure that employees continue to safely perform their duties and do not engage in unlawful work-related activities.

Under the legal doctrine of *respondeat superior* (i.e., the superior must answer) employers may be held liable for wrongful acts of employees when those acts occur within the scope of employment. To protect the interests of the institution and to assure workplace safety, employers have the right and responsibility to supervise work performed by employees.

Performance evaluations

An effective system of performance evaluations is essential to any successful institution. The quality of individual work performance collectively defines the quality of the institution. To support institutional success, evaluations must effectively document work performance for accountability, reward, remediation, or dismissal of employees as warranted.

Work performance evaluations are significant events for employers and employees. The consequences of evaluations can be enormous for both parties. Evaluations affect retention, promotion, and tenure decisions, and may also be used as the evidentiary basis for performance pay, reassignments, or reduction in force decisions by the institution.

Most states have enacted statutes addressing teacher evaluations. But many of these statutes simply require an evaluation system; authorize local school officials to require evaluations; or otherwise leave considerable discretion to local school officials. Depending on state law, performance evaluations of school employees may be governed more or less by state law or local policy. Union agreements may also affect aspects of the evaluation process in many states.

What is consistent among all U.S. public educational institutions, however, is that because an evaluation may significantly affect the individual's employment rights and professional reputation, evaluation policies must be in accordance with the requirements of the Due Process Clause. Evaluation systems must provide adequate notice; an opportunity to be heard; and policies and practices that are fundamentally fair.

Where lawful state or local evaluation policies have been established, school officials should strictly comply with established policies or risk charges of arbitrariness and violations of due process in the evaluation process. Generally, judges tend to be highly deferential to professional judgments by school officials. But judges have been firm in enforcing requirements of established policy and procedures in the evaluation process where non-compliance significantly affected an employee's protected rights. If there is no harm to the employee judges may accept substantial compliance with established procedures as minimally sufficient in deference to good faith efforts by school officials. But reliance on judicial deference to save the institution from legal non-compliance is, to say the least, unwise.

There is really no legitimate excuse for failure to follow current state laws and established institutional policies. Further, if an administrator makes a procedural error serious enough to result in litigation, even if the educational institution does not lose the case or incur significant monetary damages, this level of negligence and incompetence will likely be remembered by the administrator's supervisors in future decisions concerning retention and promotion. A clear message emerges from the case law and experiences in practice: Read your state's statutes and your local policies governing employment and evaluations and comply with established procedures.

Administrators and other supervisors are hired in part for their ability to be fair and exercise good judgment, in realization that a certain degree of subjectivity is inevitable in the evaluation process. Human behavior and the totality of the employment circumstance cannot be accurately and fairly distilled to only simple, objective measures without missing important individual factors and the genuine context of the employee's work and performance. To maximize objectivity and fairness in the evaluation process, however, formal evaluations should generally focus on criteria that are:1) Related to essential job duties; and 2) Observable or measurable.

Persons being evaluated should have advance notice of the criteria for the evaluation, and a fair opportunity to demonstrate successful job performance under the established criteria (i.e., fair notice and an opportunity to be heard consistent with due process). Following the evaluation, the employee should receive timely notification of the results of the evaluation, including any noted deficiencies.

When remediation is still possible, it is good practice to start with positive observations (i.e., so that the employee knows that the evaluator is attempting to be fair and supportive) and then move to the areas needing improvement. In addressing deficiencies the supervisor should:

> 1) Clearly identify the observed deficiencies, providing a summary of the criteria and evidence for reaching these conclusions;
> 2) Precisely explain what is necessary to correct the deficiencies;
> 3) Give the employee a fair opportunity to be heard in response; and
> 4) Allow a fair opportunity to remedy deficiencies prior to the next evaluation.

A failure to remedy identified deficiencies after sufficient notice and a fair opportunity to do so may constitute neglect of duties or incompetence. A willful refusal to correct identified deficiencies may constitute insubordination.

The evaluation process must be an open and honest process, with good faith efforts by the supervisor to help the employee improve performance, and good faith efforts by the employee to comply with the lawful orders of the supervisor. The evaluating supervisor is responsible for both coaching for success when possible and documenting failure when necessary. But there should be no pretenses or duplicity about the evaluator's true role, and all aspects of the process should be fair and open. Honesty is essential to building trust between the supervisor and the employee. Secrecy or duplicity in the process may unfairly blind-side the employee, and also jeopardize employment actions based on any unfair evaluation practices.

When negative employment actions are necessary, negative employment actions should be proportional and progressive. Consequences should be proportional to the employee's conduct and employment status. If necessary changes do not occur, however, the consequences should appropriately escalate in seriousness toward dismissal when necessary. For example, if employee conduct is serious enough to warrant sanctions but does not constituent an immediate peril to anyone, the employee may first be given a verbal warning; then a written notice and warning for a subsequent occurrence; followed by a suspension or other appropriate employment sanction as warned in the prior written notice; and then final dismissal if the problem is not satisfactorily remedied. This series of progressive employment consequences is fair to all parties; giving employees fair opportunities to attempt to correct any deficiencies; and documenting the good faith efforts of the employer to notify, warn, and remediate employee deficiencies prior to the ultimate termination of employment.

Progressive Employment Consequences

Very serious misconduct or actions that pose a present danger in the workplace may require immediate removal and the initiation of formal dismissal proceedings.

The employer should thoroughly document the process of proportional and progressive consequences, proving that the employee had clear notice and an opportunity to conform conduct to acceptable standards but did not do so. This proportional and progressive approach, and the resulting paper trail, helps to document that any impacts on protected liberty or property rights were consistent with procedural and substantive due process, and that the process was fair and proportional even when the final result was dismissal.

Dismissals

Dismissal proceedings succeed or fail based on the fundamental fairness of the process and the quality of the documentation. No amount of documentation, however, should cover up an unfair dismissal rooted in retaliation, discrimination, or other improper motives. A fair evaluation process and thorough documentation, however, are the keys to success in necessary dismissals where the employee is being properly removed from the institution for good and sufficient cause.

Hourly staff, non-certificated support personnel, and other at-will employees generally have no long-term contract or any reasonable expectation of continued employment. They can generally be dismissed at any time. Untenured teachers are offered year-to-year contracts until they acquire tenure. They can be let go simply by not renewing their contracts. Only tenured educators have a right to continued employment beyond the current contract term. Tenured teachers can only be dismissed based on a valid cause, and they are entitled to adequate due process of law.

Common defenses in dismissal proceedings

Common employee defenses in dismissal proceedings may include allegations of violations of due process; failure to comply with institutional policies; insufficient evidence; discrimination; evaluator bias; and retaliation. In responding to all of these defenses, due process and solid documentation are the keys to a successful dismissal hearing and prevailing in any subsequent appeals. Strong documentation can help prove that it was the employee who failed, not the institution. But poor documentation by supervisors may end up proving the opposite: Institutional failure.

To guard against charges of bias, when possible use multiple sources of evidence from multiple persons (e.g., consistent evaluations by different evaluators; corroborating evidence and testimony; peer evaluations; documented complaints from parents and students; etc.). To guard against charges of retaliation, be certain the claims are not true. Never be a party to employment retaliation and assure that dismissals are the product of good faith, lawful efforts to protect the legitimate interests of students and the institution. Personal grudges must never be enforced by public institutions.

Professional ethics

Professionals hold themselves out to their communities as persons with special knowledge, skills, and experience worthy of public trust. Public trust in professionals is further reinforced by the awarding of professional degrees, the receipt of state licenses, and admission to membership in respected state and national professional organizations. The admission to professional practice also implies an acceptable record of honesty and good character in the conduct of duties. Based on these professional representations and credentials, persons needing special expertise rely on professionals for necessary services and guidance in health care, law, education, etc.

To help assure that the persons holding themselves out as professionals are worthy of this public trust, universities, state licensing boards, and professional organizations establish applicable codes of conduct and professional ethics. Professional codes of ethics help to clarify standards for professional conduct; codify professional responsibilities; provide guidance for ethical decision-making in practice; and serve as a basis for policing the profession and sanctioning unprofessional conduct when necessary.

Professional conduct is guided by a hierarchy of laws, ethics, and morality, with legal compliance forming the essential foundation, standards of professional ethics establishing higher professional norms, and moral ideals setting the highest aspirational goals in professional practice.

The Relationship between Law, Ethics, and Morality

Standard	Function	Applicability	Enforcement
Moral Ideals	Aspirational	Personal Choice	Conscience and Association
Professional Ethics	Normative	Condition of Membership	Sanction or Expulsion
Legal Compliance	Protective	Mandatory	Civil and Criminal Penalties

© Dayton

In order to protect the public from abuse, exploitation, and the dangers of malpractice, all professionals must comply with applicable laws or be subject to civil and criminal penalties. These penalties serve to deter and punish the worst types of professional misconduct. But they are insufficient to support the higher professional norms essential to good practice. Conduct that is legal may still be unethical or immoral, i.e., "lawful but awful."

Professional codes of ethics impose higher standards than general civil and criminal laws. Compliance with applicable ethical codes is a condition of holding a professional license, certificate, or membership in a professional association. Breach of the code makes the individual subject to professional sanctions including formal reprimand, probation, suspension, expulsion from the professional association, or revocation of the right to legally practice in the profession.

Moral ideals should impose even higher standards of care by professionals. But while moral ideals that exceed legal and professional standards may be desirable, unless moral conduct falls below established legal or ethical standards, these higher ideals are based on voluntary personal decisions to pursue higher moral duties. Immoral conduct so extreme that it violates civil or criminal laws, or breaches the ethical code, is subject to appropriate sanctions. Otherwise, individual moral opinions are subject only to the individual's conscience; the personal judgments of peers and the

226

community; and individual decisions concerning who to hire for professional services and who to associate with in practice. Professional codes of ethics should, however, be broad enough and strong enough to address immorality that exceeds mere differences of opinion and presents any credible risk of harm to clients or the community.

Each profession has a code of ethics uniquely tailored to the profession, but these codes generally have common foundational elements. An overview of general principles of professional ethics is provided below, but all professionals should also review the specific code of ethics applicable to their profession in their jurisdiction.

Essential Elements of Professional Ethics

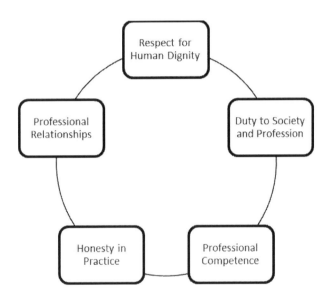

© **Dayton**

Respect for human dignity: Professionals respect the inalienable human dignity of all persons regardless of race, color, creed, gender, gender identity, sexual orientation, national origin, social status, economic status, or any other professionally irrelevant personal circumstances of the individual. All persons are treated with appropriate human dignity, equal respect, and non-discrimination in the provision of professional services. The professional further respects the individual human right to free-will and informed choice, protects individual and family dignity and privacy, and respects appropriate privacy and confidentiality in communications and records.

Professional relationships: Professionals conduct all relationships with colleagues and clients/students in a professional manner. This includes good faith efforts to maintain a culture of mutual respect with colleagues, and refraining from any exploitation or abuse, especially where there is an imbalance in power or experience among colleagues. Because there is always an imbalance in power or experience among professionals and clients/students, there is a special duty to protect the interests of clients/students; to warn or protect them from known dangers; to exercise due diligence in advancing their best interests; and to refrain from any exploitation or abuse. This duty is especially strong when the clients/students are children or are otherwise diminished in their capacities to independently protect their own interests.

Honesty in practice: Professionals have a fiduciary duty to manage finances, business relationships, and property in their care appropriately. Financial, personal, and other relevant conflicts of interests must be avoided or disclosed. To protect public trust the professional has a duty to recuse him or herself when an actual conflict or the appearance of a conflict of interests reasonably requires recusal. There should be appropriate transparency in all business operations; records must be honest and accurate; and all evaluations and advice must be honest, objective, and directed towards the best interests of the client/student.

Professional competence: The professional owes nothing less than professional best efforts to clients/students and colleagues. The professional has an obligation to assure personal mental and physical fitness for duty, refraining from the use of alcohol or other substances that could impair judgment or performance while on duty. The professional should diligently perform duties in a timely and responsible manner; fairly assign and accept work-load burdens; maintain current and adequate knowledge and skills; and comply with all applicable requirements of the law.

Duty to society and the profession: Professionals have a right to fair payment for services provided, but the privilege of professional practice carries with it a corresponding duty to society and the profession. Professionals should actively work to protect and advance the public good, including regular engagement in appropriate pro bono service. Professionals should further strive to advance knowledge and practice in their profession. In order to protect society and the profession from the harms of misconduct, there is an affirmative duty to report any abuse, exploitation, corruption, or other unethical conduct to the appropriate governing board.

Professional codes of ethics can provide a fair and effective means of establishing and enforcing higher professional standards. Enforcement systems must provide adequate due process including public notice of the standards; sufficient clarity of requirements; fair hearings; adequate opportunity for appeals; and professional sanctions that are just and proportional to the offenses. Codes of ethics should also respect appropriate boundaries between the individual's professional responsibilities and private life.

Essential Practice Tips

1) *Contracts and tenure*: Take great care in who is offered a contract and even more care in who is granted tenure. Serious personnel problems are far easier to prevent than they are to fix. In addition to objective job qualifications also appropriately assess the professional ethics and collegiality of potential employees. Do not grant tenure to employees who clearly failed tests of professional ethics and collegiality during the probationary period prior to tenure. Personnel problems rarely get better after tenure. A positive, professional culture is essential to everyone's success. One rotten apple can spoil the barrel for everyone. Do not tenure a rotten apple.

2) *Employment discrimination*: Never be a party to employment discrimination in any form. Take care to assure that all employment decisions are made fairly and on the basis of valid employment criteria, and that even unconscious bias is guarded against. Actively seek a diverse pool of applicants; make employment decisions based only on lawful criteria; and hire the most qualified candidate regardless of race, color, religion, sex, sexual orientation, gender identity, national origin, disability, age, family status, or other criteria unrelated to legitimate employment qualifications.

3) *Professional ethics*: Compliance with the law is necessary, but it is not sufficient. Professionals hold themselves to the higher callings of professional ethics and personal morality. You will never regret doing the right thing, even when it is difficult at the time. There is no honor in prevailing dishonorably. Always do the right thing, and then win or lose you will have won personal honor and self-respect. And by having a reputation for personal integrity you will win the respect of your colleagues as well. In all cases, do what is right and treat others as you would wish to be treated. Do not allow the negative emotions of anger, fear, etc., to deter you from doing what you know is right, always choosing what is legally, ethically, and morally right over what is merely expedient at the time.

4) *Alternative dispute resolution*: In most cases, neither party in a dispute wants to see the dispute escalate to litigation. As Sun Tzu said in THE ART OF WAR: Build your enemy a golden bridge to retreat on, as the greatest victory comes from achieving your goals without the costs of battle. With some careful thought and planning, you may be able to achieve your necessary goals in a win-win scenario, thereby building rather than harming working relationships. Negotiation and mediation skills can be invaluable assets. Nonetheless, throughout the process, document and prepare to prevail in litigation if necessary. The preparation of a solid legal case will also strengthen your hand in negotiations.

Essential Points

- Generally, non-certificated personnel are at-will employees with no reasonable expectation of continued employment and can be dismissed at any time. Untenured educators have property rights in their yearly contracts, but can be non-renewed at the end of the contract term. Only tenured educators have an ongoing property right to continued employment beyond the current contract term.
- Untenured teachers are generally not entitled to any explanation for a non-renewal. Further, providing an explanation for the non-renewal may create a right to due process including notice and a hearing.
- Tenured educators can only be dismissed for a valid cause specified in the applicable state statute, for example: incompetence; insubordination; willful neglect of duties; immorality; violation of school policy, state law, or federal law; reduction in force; or any other good and sufficient cause allowable under state law.
- The Establishment, Due Process, and Equal Protection Clauses broadly prohibit discrimination by government agencies based on religion, race, gender, or national origin. Title VII extended these prohibitions to the private sector. Government agencies, including public schools, are prohibited from discriminating in employment by both Title VII and the Constitution.
- Employment discrimination under Title VII generally falls into two categories: Disparate treatment or disparate impact claims. To establish a prima facie case of disparate treatment discrimination in employment the plaintiff must prove:
  - The plaintiff is a member of a protected class under Title VII;
  - The plaintiff suffered harm in employment;
  - The defendant illegally discriminated; and
  - The discrimination caused the harm in employment.

- Disparate impact claims arise when the employment practice or policy is facially neutral, but has a significant negative impact based on race, color, religion, sex, or national origin. The plaintiff's burden of proof in disparate impact claims is defined by 42 U.S.C. § 2000e-2(k).
- Employment discrimination based on age (40+), and discrimination based on pregnancy or related medical conditions are prohibited.
- Under appropriate circumstances, religion, sex, or national origin may be BFOQs and permissible employment criteria under Title VII. Race and color are never BFOQs.
- To prevail in a Title VII sexual harassment case the plaintiff must establish either:
  - Quid pro quo sexual harassment; or
  - Hostile environment sexual harassment.
- If the plaintiff meets this initial burden of proof, it must be determined whether the plaintiff suffered any tangible injury (e.g., discharge, demotion, undesirable reassignment, etc.) as a result of the sexual harassment. If there was tangible injury, liability is imputed to the employer. If there was no tangible injury, the employer may raise as an affirmative defense that:
  - The employer exercised reasonable care to prevent and correct any sexual harassment; and
  - The employee unreasonably failed to exercise an opportunity to report the sexual harassment.
- Professional conduct is guided by a hierarchy of laws, ethics, and morality, with legal compliance forming the essential foundation, standards of professional ethics establishing higher professional norms, and moral ideals setting the highest aspirational goals in professional practice.
- Public educators have a right to privacy and liberty in their private lives, provided that their private lives do not interfere with the performance of their professional duties. To acquire valid jurisdiction over activities in teachers' private lives for purposes of employment sanctions, school officials must establish that there is a logical nexus between the challenged off-campus conduct and a resulting negative impact on the teacher's ability to perform professional duties. Otherwise, private lives should remain private.
- In the performance evaluation process, established state and local policies and due process must be strictly followed.

- School officials must know and comply with the laws governing open records and open meetings in their state. Failure to comply with these laws may result in civil liability or criminal penalties.
- The National Labor Relations Act protects the rights of all private sector employees to form unions and engage in collective bargaining. State laws govern rights to collective bargaining for state employees. Even where there is no legal right to collective bargaining, public educators retain their right to freedom of association and may join professional and political organizations.
- Alternative Dispute Resolution (ADR) may be a useful alternative to litigation. Options in ADR include informal resolutions; mediation; negotiations; and arbitration.

Essential Terms

Alternative dispute resolution (ADR): The use of arbitration, mediation, or negotiation as an alternative to litigation.

Arbitration: Parties agree to resolve a dispute based on presenting their cases to a neutral third party for resolution. Parties may agree in advance that the arbiter's decision will be binding.

Bona fide occupational qualification (BFOQ): Title VII 42 U.S.C. § 2000e-2(e)(1), recognizes that under some limited circumstances employment discrimination based on religion, sex, or national origin may serve a legitimate employment purpose "in those certain instances where religion, sex, or national origin is a bona fide occupational qualification reasonably necessary to the normal operation of that particular business or enterprise." Race and color are never BFOQs.

Mediation: Informal means of promoting conflict resolution. The mediator attempts to help the parties find common ground and voluntarily resolve disputes.

Mitigation of damages: A plaintiff cannot unreasonably run up the bill on a defendant and must reasonably attempt to find cover goods or services when the plaintiff learns of a pending breach of contract by the defendant.

Negotiation: Parties may represent themselves or trained negotiators may represent parties in bilateral efforts to resolve a dispute.

Quid pro quo: Latin for "this for that" used to describe the necessary exchange of benefits/detriments essential to forming a legal contract.

Essential Cases

Adarand Constructors v. Pena, 515 U.S. 200 (1995): Holding that "any person, of whatever race, has the right to demand that any governmental actor subject to the Constitution justify any racial classification subjecting that person to unequal treatment under the strictest judicial scrutiny" and stating: "More than good motives should be required when government seeks to allocate its resources by way of an explicit racial classification system."

Board of Regents v. Roth, 408 U.S. 564 (1972): Holding that when an untenured teacher has been paid the amount due under the contract no property right has been taken simply by not renewing the contract and there is no right to further notice or a hearing. However, statements from school officials that call into question the good name, reputation, honor or integrity of the teacher related to the non-renewal could raise a liberty interest entitling the teacher to due process: "Where a person's good name, reputation, honor, or integrity is at stake because of what the government is doing to him, notice and an opportunity to be heard are essential."

Clark County v. Breeden, 532 U.S. 268 (2001): Defining the legal line for hostile environment sexual harassment under Title VII by stating "whether an environment is sufficiently hostile or abusive must be judged by looking at all the circumstances, including the frequency of the discriminatory conduct; its severity; whether it is physically threatening or humiliating, or a mere offensive utterance; and whether it unreasonably interferes with an employee's work performance."

McDonnell Douglas Corp. v. Green, 411 U.S. 792 (1973): "Establishing a prima facie case of racial discrimination . . . may be done by showing (i) that he belongs to a racial minority; (ii) that he applied and was qualified for a job for which the employer was seeking applicants; (iii) that, despite his qualifications, he was rejected; and (iv) that, after his rejection, the position remained open and the employer continued to seek applicants from persons of complainant's qualifications."

Meritor Savings Bank v. Vinson, 477 U.S. 57 (1986): Holding that: "Without question, when a supervisor sexually harasses a subordinate because of the subordinate's sex, that supervisor 'discriminates' on the basis of sex" but: "For sexual harassment to be actionable, it must be sufficiently severe or pervasive to alter the conditions of the victim's employment and create an abusive working environment" and that the "gravamen of any sexual harassment claim is that the alleged sexual advances were unwelcome."

Washington v. Davis, 426 U.S. 229 (1976): Government actions are not unconstitutional merely because they happen to have a racially disproportionate impact. A test that is racially neutral on its face; administered without discriminatory intent; and reasonably related to a legitimate state interest is constitutional.

A Closer Look at the Law

Bullies grow up and become workplace bullies. These are often troubled people who are venting their personal demons in the workplace. When they are allowed to maraud unchecked they can do enormous damage to people and institutions. *See*, e.g., John Dayton, *Law and Policy Remedies for Workplace Bullying in Higher Education*, Vol. 1 of the EDUCATION LAW & POLICY REVIEW, available free at www.edlawcon.org:

> Even among people who should certainly know better than to tolerate such abuse, personnel misconduct in the form of workplace bullying remains a serious but largely neglected problem. A problem so serious it can devastate academic programs and the people in them. If allowed to maraud unchecked, workplace bullies can poison the office culture; shut down progress and productivity; drive off the most promising and productive people; and make the workplace increasingly toxic for everyone who remains in the bully dominated environment. A toxic workplace can even turn deadly when stress begins to take its all too predictable toll on victims' mental and physical health, or interpersonal stress leads to acts of violence.

This article examines the problem of workplace bullying, reviews possible legal and practical remedies; and makes suggestions for law and policy reforms to more effectively address this very serious but too often tolerated problem. Importantly, it also details self-help steps readers may use to protect themselves and their schools from workplace bullies. *See also*, Robert I. Sutton, THE NO ASSHOLE RULE: BUILDING A CIVILIZED WORKPLACE AND SURVIVING ONE THAT ISN'T (2010).

Law & Professional Ethics in Practice:

Professional codes of ethics can provide a fair and effective means of establishing and enforcing professional ethical standards. The rules and their application must, however, respect appropriate boundaries between the individual's professional responsibilities and private life. But where is the appropriate boundary between teachers' professional responsibilities and their private lives? Clearly, this boundary has changed over time.

Rules for Teachers: Sacramento, California (1915)

1. You will not marry during the term of your contract.

2. You are not to keep company with men.

3. You must be home between the hours of 8 PM and 6 AM unless at a school function.

4. You may not loiter downtown in any of the ice cream stores.

5. You may not travel beyond the city limits unless you have permission of the chairman of the school board.

6. You may not ride in carriages or automobiles with any man except your father or brother.

7. You may not smoke cigarettes.

8. You may not dress in bright colors.

9. You may under no circumstances dye your hair.

10. You must wear at least 2 petticoats.

11. Your dresses may not be any shorter than 2 inches above the ankles.

12. To keep the classroom neat and clean you must sweep the floor once a day, scrub the floor with hot soapy water once a week, clean the blackboards once a day and start the fire at 7 AM to have the school warm by 8 AM when the scholars arrive.

Many of the standards included in this 1915 code of conduct for teachers are recognized as unconstitutional today. Adult citizens, including teachers, have a right to marry; to privately associate with other adults; they are subject to no home curfews or arbitrary limitations on travel; and they have a right to live their private lives as they see fit, provided that their private lives do not interfere with the performance of their professional duties.

Nonetheless, teachers remain role models for students, giving some continued validity to concerns about teachers' private conduct where the conduct can be shown to have a substantial negative impact on teachers' abilities to perform professional duties. An arrest and conviction for any serious crime could serve as a valid basis for the professional termination of a teacher, as could other conduct that established serious moral turpitude, dishonesty, or any credible danger to students or others in the school.

But what about private conduct that is simply disfavored by many community members but otherwise lawful? Clearly, sexual misconduct that constituted a crime and merited official designation as a registered sex offender would serve as a solid lawful basis for dismissal. But what if the teacher is simply engaging in lawful, private sexual conduct that many in the community may disapprove of for personal or religious reasons, such as professional nude dancing; nude modeling; performance in adult films; sexual promiscuity; adultery; "swinging", or other alternative life-styles? Should any of these otherwise lawful, private behaviors be subject to investigation and employment action by school officials based on community disapproval even though otherwise lawful?

Is it ever acceptable for a teacher to "date" a student? What if the student is: 18 years old?; age 21?; not a student in the teacher's school?; the relationship is romantic but not physical?; the relationship is personally very close but not physical or romantic?; the teacher is 21 and the student is 21? While some circumstances seem less disturbing than others, many would argue that the core concerns in prohibiting these teacher-student relationships do not fundamentally change with the facts because they are based on the inherent status differences between teachers and students; the risk of exploitation of students by teachers; the sexualizing and corrupting of the teacher-student relationship; the appearance of impropriety; and the risk of institutional liability for sexual harassment by employees.

Even if there is a legal right to engage in the relationship, that does not mean there is also a right to remain a publicly employed teacher if the conduct results in a sufficient negative impact on the teacher's professional ability to serve as a teacher. Consenting adults have a right to continue their relationships without state interference. But the state may not have to continue their employment. Even if the conduct is not prohibited by law, an inappropriate relationship with a student violates professional ethics and morality standards concerning the teacher-student relationship.

Drinking while on duty or alcohol related crimes could serve as a lawful basis for termination of employment. But if the local community disapproves of alcohol generally (as is the case in some parts of the rural U.S. South) does this mean that off-duty local teachers can be prohibited from drinking beer or wine in their community? What is the proper balance between teachers' rights to live a private life free from governmental snooping and sanctions by school officials, and legitimate community concerns about the fitness of teachers as role models for their children?

Questions for Further Exploration:

1) *The bad apple*: Why are bad teachers allowed to receive tenure? Why are truly incompetent teachers allowed to remain in the classroom? How would you deal with a tenured teacher who is competent but highly disruptive and destructive to the school culture and faculty morale?

2) *Employment law protections*: Are current federal employment discrimination laws adequate, or are additional protections needed? What additional protections may be needed (e.g., additional protections against discrimination based on sexual orientation; gender identity; obesity; physical appearance; etc.)? Do current federal or state laws provide adequate protections in these areas? Does your school district provide needed protections through local policy?

3) *Workplace bullying*: U.S. states are increasingly enacting laws to better protect students from bullying, recognizing the destructive nature of these behaviors, and extending protections from physical bullying to the arguably more harmful and destructive emotional abuse associated with bullying. Many nations in Europe now also prohibit bullying in the workplace through employment laws. Is workplace bullying a significant problem for individuals and institutions? Should U.S. employment laws address workplace bullying?

4) *Open forum*: What other related issues or current events would you like to discuss?

Suggested Activities for Further Learning:

1) Review your state's laws governing tenure, dismissal, open records and open meetings, and other relevant statutes governing employment and personnel issues in your state.

2) Learn to recognize incidents of workplace bullying, emotional abuse, and "academic mobbing" in schools, and discuss what you can do to improve the workplace culture for everyone.

3) Read, ROGER FISHER AND WILLIAM L. URY, GETTING TO YES: NEGOTIATING AGREEMENT WITHOUT GIVING IN (2011). Practice mock negotiations to develop personally and professionally useful negotiations skills.

Chapter 10: Tort Law and other Liability Issues

Tort law is civil law recognizing a plaintiff's legal right to just compensation for damages caused by a defendant. A just system of tort law is a necessary foundation for any civil society. We do not personally know most of the persons we encounter in commerce (e.g., food safety; repairs; etc.) or in public (e.g., driving, etc.). But tort law helps to support public trust that most persons will conduct themselves reasonably in their business activities and daily conduct, and avoid acts that may injure others.

Tort law provides a lawful means of obtaining just compensation for damages caused by a defendant, and acts as a general deterrent against future injurious conduct. The law of torts and contracts are similar, but the tort "contract" is an implied social contract to act reasonably in interactions with others. The civil society "offers" all citizens an opportunity to participate, and everyone "accepts" this general social contract by participating in society. If you have a legal duty to others, then there is also the implied social contractual obligation of acting reasonably in fulfilling that duty.

Individuals may also assume higher duties of care by choosing to participate in activities that have a higher potential to harm others if reasonable care is not exercised. For example, all members of the common society have a general duty to refrain from harming others. But if you choose to operate potentially dangerous power equipment around other people, special care is required, and there is a higher duty to protect others around you from foreseeable harms. Licensed and certificated professionals also accept a higher duty of care by holding themselves out to the community as having special knowledge and skills worthy of public trust.

A tort is a civil wrong, as opposed to a criminal wrong, where a party has suffered harm because of the injurious conduct of another party. A single wrongful act, however, could serve as the basis for both a prosecution under criminal law, and a civil suit under tort law. For example, if a defendant attacked and injured a victim, the defendant could be prosecuted under criminal laws for assault and battery and face criminal fines and imprisonment. And the victim/plaintiff could file a civil suit under tort law seeking monetary damages for harms caused by the intentional tort of assault and battery. The criminal charge would require the prosecutor to prove the defendant's guilt beyond a reasonable doubt, while the civil law tort suit would only require proof of the plaintiff's tort claim by a preponderance of the evidence. Because the criminal charge requires a higher burden of proof, under the same set of facts the defendant could be found not guilty in the criminal case yet still be held liable for monetary damages to the plaintiff in the tort law suit.

This section addresses tort law negligence claims; possible defenses to negligence claims, including assumption of risk, plaintiff's negligence, and sovereign immunity; constitutional torts and 42 U.S.C. § 1983; educational malpractice; duty to warn; defamation; intentional torts including assault and battery, false imprisonment, invasion of privacy, and intentional infliction of emotional distress.

Tort Law Negligence Claims

Most tort cases concerning schools involve negligence claims. Negligence is the failure to use ordinary care. A legal cause of action arises when negligence results in harm to other people or property. School officials may be either the plaintiff or the defendant in these cases. But generally, a plaintiff student, parent, or community member is seeking monetary damages for some harm that was allegedly caused by the negligence of defendant school officials or those under their supervision.

Part of the explanation for school officials' frequent defendant status is the financial "deep pocket" of larger educational institutions. Schools are often the largest institutions in the community, with relatively substantial insurance coverage and other financial resources to pay monetary damages. If school employees have arguably been negligent, the school district is an attractive legal target, while persons with no resources may be functionally "judgment proof" lacking a means of paying damage claims.

Plaintiffs will generally name as defendants every school official in the chain from the individual who is alleged to have directly caused the harm, through all intervening supervisors, and up to the heads of the educational institution with control of the "deep pocket" resources and responsibility for policy decisions and general governance of the school. While individual liability is possible under some circumstances, the goal is usually not to obtain damages from individuals, but to obtain compensation for damages from the larger funds available to the educational institution. Even large educational institutions, however, do not have unlimited capacity to pay damage claims. And every dollar paid out in tort liability or increased insurance premiums is one less dollar to fund education, making liability prevention a high priority for educational institutions.

To prevail in a negligence claim the plaintiff must prove by a preponderance of the evidence that a legal duty to the plaintiff existed; the defendant breached that duty; the breach of duty caused the plaintiff's injuries; and there are compensable damages. The plaintiff must prove all four elements of a negligence claim to prevail:1) Duty; 2) Breach of Duty; 3) Causation (both factual and legal cause); and 4) Damages.

Establishing the defendant's duty to the plaintiff

Under the U.S. system of tort law the only general duties are to refrain from harming others and to act as a reasonable person under the circumstances. There is, however, no general duty to act affirmatively or render aid to others absent the creation of a legal duty by the defendant's actions or through a special relationship with the plaintiff. While there may be an ethical or moral duty to help others in need of help, these are not legally enforceable duties under tort law.

For example, if you were to see someone laying on their back in the parking lot calling for help, while most people would agree that you should help people in need if you can, there is no legal duty to help. Unless, of course, the reason the person is laying in the parking lot is because you ran over him or otherwise caused his injury. No general duty to render aid exists, but you may acquire a duty to help if you caused the injury; if you offered to help and the plaintiff reasonably relied on that offer of help; or if you somehow made the person's situation worse. But absent actions on your part that cause a legal duty to attach there is no general duty to render aid to persons with whom you have no special relationship.

There is, however, a special duty to help someone with whom you do have a special relationship. For example, parents have a duty to their children; teachers have a duty to students; doctors have a duty to patients; etc. The duties of parents include providing their children with necessary food, shelter, clothing, medical care, education, protection, and adequate parental supervision. Teachers acting *in loco parentis* have a general duty to instruct, reasonably supervise, and protect children from known or reasonably foreseeable dangers while the children are under the teacher's care. School officials also have a duty to reasonably supervise employees and students, keep school property safe, and to protect against or warn of any known or reasonably foreseeable dangers to students, faculty, staff, and visitors on school property.

Those who do choose to voluntarily render aid even when there is no legal duty to do so are generally protected from liability under state "Good Samaritan" laws. Although laws vary among jurisdictions, these laws generally provide immunity from liability where persons voluntarily render aid to others in need of help, the rescuer acted in good faith, and acted reasonably under the circumstances. A few states require witnesses to accidents to render minimal emergency assistance, such as calling for help. But most states leave these matters to the conscience of the individual. Assistance is encouraged with good faith immunity. But most states have not established any general legal duty to render aid to others.

Proving the defendant's breach of duty

Once a duty of care exists for the defendant, the duty is to act as a reasonable person under the circumstances. The defendant's actions are measured against what would be expected from a hypothetical "reasonable person" acting under the circumstances that prevailed at the time of the alleged breach of duty. The reasonable person is a legal fiction created as a standard for measuring whether the defendant met or breached the duty of care.

The Hypothetical Reasonable Person Standard:
Did the Defendant Breach the Duty?

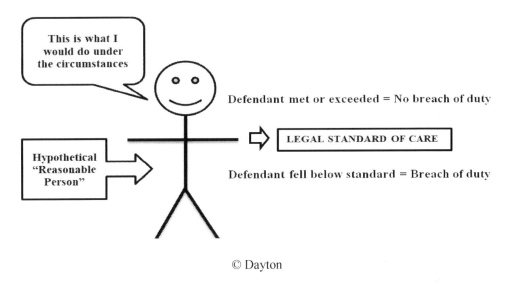

© Dayton

The hypothetical reasonable person is deemed to be an ordinary person in every way, with ordinary intelligence, knowledge, skills, judgment, etc. If the defendant's actions met or exceeded the level of care by the ordinary reasonable person under the circumstances, the defendant did not breach the duty of care and the plaintiff will fail in proving the case.

Whether the defendant breached the duty of care must be considered based on the totality of circumstances at the time. When the accident occurred was it raining, icy, or dark? Reasonable people use greater care under adverse conditions. Did the defendant have advance notice of a potential problem? Had a similar incident occurred previously? Reasonable people take sensible precautions to prevent foreseeable dangers. Was the activity in question one that required special care, training, or safety equipment? As the circumstances change, so does the reasonable person's actions. Greater care is required under circumstances that present greater potential dangers to others.

Although defendants are generally measured against the objective standard of a reasonable person under the circumstances, in some cases the special abilities of the defendant may also be relevant. Persons with greater training and skills may be held to a higher standard of care, especially if they hold themselves out to the community as having special knowledge and skills in a relevant area. For example, a plaintiff can reasonably expect greater medical knowledge and skills from medical personnel, and greater knowledge and skills related to education and children from professional educators.

In general, while some persons are held to a higher standard because of special abilities, allowing lowered standards of care is disfavored by courts. Nonetheless, persons with disabilities may sometimes be allowed a lowered legal standard if the disability prevented them from doing what someone without the disability could have done under the circumstances. Children may also be held to a lower standard of accountability than adults. In these cases the disability or minority age is viewed as one of the circumstances under which the reasonable person standard is assessed (e.g., what would the reasonable disabled person, or child, have done under those circumstances?). Children and persons with disabilities must necessarily engage in regular daily activities like everyone else, and holding them to a standard they cannot possibly meet in doing so may be unjust under some circumstances.

However, the disability or minority age is also a condition that requires extra care in other circumstances. Persons with disabilities or children must not voluntarily engage in potentially dangerous activities that exceed their known limitations, or they may be held to the same legal standard as all other persons engaged in those inherently dangerous activities. For example, children or persons with disabilities that prevent them from safely driving should not drive, as any unqualified driver presents an unnecessary danger to everyone on the road. For public safety reasons, persons unqualified to participate in potentially dangerous activities cannot be granted a lowered standard of care. As with all inherently dangerous activities, all drivers must be qualified and fully accountable or they must not drive.

Courts will also generally balance the foreseeable risks to plaintiffs against the reasonableness and social value of the defendant's actions. We cannot live in a risk free world, but some risks are more reasonable and have greater societal value than others. Operating heavy equipment is always potentially dangerous, but it is necessary for farming, construction, etc. Choosing to operate heavy equipment while heavily intoxicated, however, greatly increases the danger to others and has no added societal value.

To prove a breach of duty the plaintiff must prove by a preponderance of the evidence that the defendant failed to use ordinary care and do what a reasonable person would have done under the circumstances. The conduct of the defendant is measured against the conduct expected from a reasonable person. If the defendant meets or exceeds the standard of the reasonable person, the plaintiff will fail in proving the case.

Proving the breach of duty was the cause of injury

To prove a negligence claim, proof of two separate and distinct types of causation are required. The defendant's actions must have been: 1) The actual cause (cause in fact) of the plaintiff's injuries; and 2) The proximate (legal cause) of the plaintiff's injuries. These two different elements of causation require independent proof and both elements must be established to prove a claim of negligence.

Cause in fact is established if the plaintiff can prove that the defendant is the factual cause of the plaintiff's injury. For example, if the defendant carelessly dropped a rock and the rock hit the plaintiff, the defendant clearly appears to be the cause in fact of the injury. But the defendant may still be found to be the cause in fact of the injury even if the defendant dropped a rock, the rock hit a board, and the board hit a shelf that then hit the plaintiff. As long as the plaintiff can prove by a preponderance of the evidence that the defendant's failure to exercise reasonable care was either a direct or a substantial cause in the chain of events leading to the injury, and that but for the defendant's actions the injury would not have occurred, the plaintiff has established the defendant's actions as the cause in fact of the injury.

It is not sufficient, however, to prove only cause in fact. The plaintiff must also prove that the defendant's actions were the proximate or legal cause of the injury. The principle question in proving legal cause is whether it was foreseeable that the defendant's actions would cause the plaintiff's injuries. Everyone is expected to act reasonably under the circumstances. But it is unfair to punish defendants just for bad luck or freak accidents that were not foreseeable to a reasonable person. The requirement of establishing legal cause involves a policy decision by the court concerning how far the defendant's potential liability should fairly extend under the circumstances. The plaintiff must prove that it was foreseeable that the defendant's actions could have caused the injury, and that the possible dangers were foreseeable to a degree sufficient to justify liability by the defendant.

It is important to note that negligence is not strict liability. A defendant charged with negligence is only responsible for harms caused by the defendant either directly or as a substantial causative factor, and only when it was reasonably foreseeable that the defendant's actions could have caused the harm under the circumstances. Defendants are not responsible for harms caused by others, or for bizarre unpredictable events that could not have been reasonably foreseen under the circumstances.

Proving compensable damages

Negligence claims require proof of actual damages. These may include present and appropriately calculated future property loss, wage loss, medical expenses, compensation for pain and suffering, etc. Claims must be proven by a preponderance of the evidence, and must not be based on mere speculation about future possibilities. A student athlete may, for example, recover for the losses associated with an injury resulting from a coach's negligence. But whether years later the student athlete would have received a valuable athletic scholarship and made millions of dollars as a professional athlete likely involves speculation that exceeds reasonable bounds of just compensation and liability for the defendant. The speculated events may or may not have happened depending on countless future variables. Mere speculation about future possibilities is not proof of compensable damages.

In some cases punitive damages may also be available. Punitive damages are not related to actual damages, but are instead intended to punish the defendant for outrageous misconduct. Punitive damages are not available in suits involving mere negligence by the defendant. These damages will only be awarded if the plaintiff can prove that the defendant acted recklessly or intentionally in causing serious harm to the plaintiff. Because these damages are intended to punish, punitive damages may be scaled to the financial resources of the defendant, with wealthier defendants being assessed higher punitive damages as lesser damages may be insufficient to punish and deter future misconduct.

As with contract law, there is also a requirement in negligence cases for the plaintiff to reasonably attempt to mitigate damages. If the plaintiff failed to reasonably attempt to mitigate damages, the plaintiff cannot recover for damages resulting from the failure to mitigate. For example, a defendant may be held liable for the costs of a personal injury caused by the defendant's negligent conduct. But the defendant would not be liable for additional injuries caused by an infection resulting from the plaintiff's unreasonable refusal to submit to medical treatment or follow medical advice.

In summary, to establish a prima facie case of negligence the plaintiff must prove:

1) The defendant had a duty to the plaintiff;
2) The defendant breached that duty;
3) The breach was both the cause in fact and legal cause of damages; and
4) There are provable, compensable damages.

Possible Defenses to Negligence Claims

After the plaintiff has established a prima facie case of negligence, the defendant may attempt to rebut the plaintiff's case, attacking the plaintiff's arguments on duty, breach, causation, and damages. The defendant need only successfully rebut one of the essential elements of the plaintiff's case. To prevail, the plaintiff bears the burden of proving all four elements of negligence (i.e., duty; breach; causation; and damages) by a preponderance of the evidence. When applicable, the defendant may also offer the following further defenses or arguments for reductions in potential liability:

Assumption of risk

We do not live in a risk-free world. Engaging in activities means assuming responsibility for the natural consequences of those activities. Reasonable people weigh the potential risks and benefits before deciding whether to participate in an activity. Contact sports, swimming, skiing, sailing, ocean fishing, sky diving, racing, etc., are potentially hazardous, yet people want to participate in and watch these events. If owners, managers, and administrators were held liability for all foreseeable harms associated with these activities, as potential defendants they would be unlikely to offer these opportunities to anyone, or the costs of participating in or watching these events would become prohibitively high.

Assumption of risk allows potential defendants to shift some of the responsibility for personal safety to persons who choose to participate. This legal doctrine holds that when a plaintiff recognized and understood potential risks associated with the activity, yet voluntarily chose to participate anyway, the plaintiff assumed the reasonable risks associated with participation.

The defendant is still responsible for his or her own negligence, and must act reasonably in providing equipment that is safe, proper safety instructions, warnings of known dangers, etc. But based on assumption of risk by the plaintiff, the defendant is not liable for harms that were reasonably foreseeable as the natural consequences of voluntary participation. For example, a football player may injure a leg in the game or suffer other injuries that are the natural consequences of voluntary participation in a contact sport. The defendant is not liable for reasonable risks voluntarily assumed by the plaintiff.

The risk is not voluntarily assumed, however, when the plaintiff had no reasonable alternative to participation. For example, students assigned to play football as part of a required physical education class are not voluntarily assuming risks in the same way as students who voluntarily play football on an extracurricular team. Accordingly, the level of contact and risk should be adjusted appropriately for the students involved (e.g., "flag football" instead of full contact tackle football). However, all participants, assigned or voluntary, are expected to follow reasonable safety instructions and rules that were adequately explained to them by teachers and coaches. A student does assume the risks associated with a knowing and intentional disregard for safety rules, or other willful misconduct beyond the control of the teacher or coach.

Defendants will find it difficult, however, to argue assumption of risk by younger children. Younger children's age and inexperience generally makes them less able to recognize and understand risks and consequences. Adult defendants charged with the care and protection of young children cannot shift the consequences of foreseeable harm by claiming assumption of risk when the child was too young to fully understand the risk. Extra care is always required in protecting young children from dangers they do not fully understand. Younger children should not be allowed to participate in inherently dangerous activities until they are old enough to recognize and understand the risks, and they are capable of safely participating. It may also be difficult to shift the consequences of foreseeable harm to adults when the defendant knew the adults were inexperienced or otherwise unable to fully recognize and understand the risks involved in participation in a potentially dangerous activity.

The use of waiver forms and other documents intended to shield defendants from liability through assumption of risk may have some utility, but they also have some limitations. Having a parent sign a permission form for a student field trip provides notice to the parent of student participation, and gives school officials evidence that the parent knew about and consented to the child's participation in activities that may involve some reasonably foreseeable risks. These forms do not, however, act as total waivers of liability and responsibility for defendants. Regardless of what the form may say, no waiver form can lawfully waive the defendant's responsibility to use reasonable care in supervising and protecting children from known or reasonably foreseeable harms. Nor do these waiver forms shield defendants from any harms inflicted recklessly, knowingly, or intentionally by the defendant.

It is contrary to public policy to allow defendants to waive their responsibilities to act reasonably through fine print exculpatory clauses in waiver forms, especially where parties are in unequal bargaining positions or the notice is constructive and not actual. For example, printing "by accepting this ticket for admission you agree to waive all claims for liability" in fine print on the back of an admission ticket does not constitute a knowing, voluntary assumption of risk by the recipient. Nor will it allow culpable defendants to escape their legal duty to not harm others and to act as reasonable persons under the circumstances. Waiver forms may be useful in providing notice of participation by children and warnings of reasonable risks, but they are not a license for unreasonable, irresponsible, or wrongful conduct by the defendant.

Plaintiff's negligence

Legal doctrines that may bar or limit recovery from the defendant because of the plaintiff's own negligence include "contributory negligence," "comparative negligence," and the rule of "avoidable consequences." Everyone is expected to use ordinary care in their daily activities, including plaintiffs. Plaintiffs who could have reasonably avoided an injury, but through their own negligent or reckless conduct contributed to their own injury, may be barred from recovering damages from the defendant under the legal doctrine of "contributory negligence." For example, a custodian may have negligently left an electrical cord lying across the hallway. But a plaintiff who trips on the cord and is injured because he was engaged in foolish antics, running backwards, and not looking where he was going may be barred from recovering damages for the injury because his own negligence significantly contributed to the injury.

Even if the plaintiff's negligence is not a total bar to recovering damages from the defendant, it may serve to reduce the extent of the defendant's liability through "comparative negligence." Comparative negligence allows the defendant to offset damages in proportion to negligence attributable to the plaintiff. For example, if it is found that damages totaled $100,000 but that 30% of the injury could be attributed to the plaintiff's own negligence, liability for the defendant is reduced to $70,000. Many jurisdictions bar any recovery, however, if the plaintiff's negligence equaled or exceeded that of the defendant, the so-called "49% rule" as the limit on plaintiff negligence in which any damages may still be recovered from the defendant who must be 51% or more responsible for the injury.

Plaintiffs who failed to reasonably attempt to mitigate damages may be barred from recovery for any reasonably avoidable further damages under the doctrine of "avoidable consequences." The plaintiff may be able to recover damages for injuries caused by the defendant, but the plaintiff must take reasonable actions to mitigate and avoid further damages. Failure to do so may bar recovery for any avoidable consequences of the injury. A plaintiff must make reasonable efforts to attempt to mitigate damages including protecting damaged property from unnecessary further damage, seeking prompt medical care for injuries, etc.

Sovereign immunity

The English Magna Carta proclaimed that King John was King of England, Lord of Ireland, etc., by the grace of God. Because the King was deemed to be acting under Divine authority, it was held that to question the King or the King's government in a court of law was the legal equivalent of questioning God, and therefore prohibited by law. Under the doctrine of sovereign immunity "the King can do no wrong." Although U.S. law rejected the theory of Divine rights of Kings, with the formation of the new U.S. government the English common law doctrine of sovereign immunity was incorporated into U.S. law to provide government agencies with protections from liability.

More recently, however, while some significant remnants of sovereign immunity remain, absolute sovereign immunity has been modified or abandoned in most jurisdictions. Judges clearly do not believe that federal, state, and local governments are chosen and acting under Divine authority. Instead, elements of sovereign immunity are retained to protect limited government resources for the purposes for which they were allocated.

What would happen, for example, to a small rural school district if a plaintiff's tort liability award exceeded the school district's annual operating budget? Closing down the district's schools and not educating children for that year is not an option. Modern sovereign immunity laws attempt to allow reasonable compensation to injured plaintiffs through available insurance, etc., without exposing school districts to absolute financial ruin from massive tort liability judgments.

The U.S. Constitution still provides states with some protections from suits in federal court. Suing state government in federal court may offer some strategic advantages, but also raises some additional challenges under the Eleventh Amendment. In *Hans v. Louisiana*, 134 U.S. 1 (1890), the U.S. Supreme Court found that the Eleventh Amendment prohibited a citizen from suing the state in federal court without the consent of the state. In *Ex parte Young*, 209 U.S. 123 (1908), however, the United States Supreme Court held that when state officials act unconstitutionally, suits in federal court may proceed regardless of immunity.

Constitutional Torts and 42 U.S.C. § 1983

Tort law is generally governed by state law. But plaintiffs may also sue state officials for a "deprivation of any rights, privileges, or immunities" protected by the U.S. Constitution and federal laws, a "constitutional tort" under 42 U.S.C. § 1983. In the wake of the U.S. Civil War, Congress enacted legislation to help secure the rights of all citizens, and in particular citizens subjected to a pattern of deprivations of rights because of their former status as slaves. The Thirteenth Amendment (1865) abolished slavery, and the Fourteenth Amendment (1868) guaranteed equal protection of the laws to all persons. Both amendments also granted Congress powers to enforce these provisions through appropriate legislation.

Without real consequences, however, these protections were nothing but words on paper to state and local officials determined to continue patterns of discrimination. In the face of such persistent discrimination by state and local officials Congress determined that citizens needed a lawful means of enforcing rights of federal citizenship, and enacted 42 U.S.C. § 1983 (1871) pursuant to legislative powers granted by the Thirteenth and Fourteenth Amendments. This statute continues to provide a legal basis for holding state officials accountable for deprivations of rights of federal citizenship through monetary damages awarded to plaintiffs.

Under 42 U.S.C. § 1983 plaintiffs may seek damages from both the school district and individual school officials. Individual school officials are only denied qualified immunity and held personally liable for damages, however, when they have personally disregarded well-established law. In *Wood v. Strickland*, 420 U.S. 308 (1975) the U.S. Supreme Court affirmed that ignorance of the law does not excuse school officials from a duty to comply with the law. School officials are not required to guess what a court will decide the law is in the future when the law is unsettled. But school officials are expected to know and comply with laws that were well-established at the time of the events the plaintiff is challenging. School officials who violate well-established law may be held personally liable for damages. In addition to monetary damages federal courts may also order injunctive relief, for example, ordering an expelled student or a dismissed teacher reinstated by school officials.

Educational Malpractice

Those who hold themselves out to the community as having special knowledge and skills may be held to a higher standard of care when persons reasonably relied on their promise of professional expertise. Therefore all professionals, doctors, nurses, lawyers, counselors, etc., must at least conform to the minimal level of knowledge and skill that is recognized in their profession.

Tort suits against professionals for failure to meet professional standards in practice are called malpractice suits. Malpractice suits require proving the same four elements required in negligence suits (i.e., duty; breach; causation; and damages) except that whether there is a duty and whether the defendant breached that duty are judged by standards applicable to professionals engaged in professional practice. Bad results for the plaintiff, however, do not prove malpractice. Professionals cannot always guarantee good outcomes, and they are only required to provide professional services that meet or exceed reasonable standards of competence recognized in the profession.

Suits for educational malpractice have generally been unsuccessful, especially concerning the "Johnny can't read cases" in which plaintiffs graduated from high school but were unable to read at a high school level. There is a general duty for educators to use professional level skills in educating students in their classes. But whether they breached that duty can be difficult to prove. Education is far more of an art than a science. There are many schools of thought on educational methods, making it difficult for plaintiffs to clearly define duty and breach of duty in educational malpractice cases.

But even if a plaintiff could establish a breach of duty in a "Johnny can't read" case, showing causation would likely prove fatal to the plaintiff's claim. Defendants need only introduce evidence that the vast majority of students who graduated in Johnny's class were taught to read by the school, and that Johnny was among the few who failed to learn. Who then caused Johnny's failure when most students in the school successfully learned to read? The defendants can argue that Johnny's own negligence caused his failure to learn through a pattern of willful inattention to instruction; lack of effort; failure to ask for help; misbehavior resulting in removals; etc. Plaintiffs' cases are further complicated if the student moved among several school districts, allowing the defendants to further minimize their control and responsibility in Johnny's education.

Successful educational malpractice suits are more likely in specialized areas such as special education and counseling. In the area of special education, the Individualized Education Program (IEP) clearly documents the school district's duties, making it much easier to prove a breach of duty, and that the breach was a cause of injury. While it is more likely that a court would order remedial services than monetary damages for a special education student, remedial services can be very costly to a school district.

Duty to Warn

Property owners, product manufacturers, and professionals may have a duty to warn of specific known dangers. Counselors and other school officials, for example, should take care to adequately address situations where there is clear evidence that a student poses a serious danger to the student or others, appropriately addressing and warning persons in danger of known threats.

In *Tarasoff v. Regents*, 551 P.2d 334 (Cal. 1976), the Supreme Court of California recognized a duty for mental health care professionals to warn when there is clear evidence of an intent to harm an identified person, so that at a minimum targets of threats may take appropriate actions to protect themselves or their children. In *Tarasoff*, despite clear evidence of a specific threat, university mental health care professionals failed to warn a targeted victim of the threat from a patient under their care. The patient ultimately killed the targeted victim as threatened. The court in *Tarasoff* stated: "We conclude that the public policy favoring protection of the confidential character of patient-psychotherapist communications must yield to the extent to which disclosure is essential to avert danger to others. The protective privilege ends where the public peril begins."

Many states have codified the *Tarasoff* principle into state laws. These statutes require counselors and other mental health care professionals to warn of specific dangers to identified persons, whether these are warnings to parents if a minor child threatens to harm him or herself, or warnings of threats to targeted third parties, e.g., specific individuals or groups.

Defamation

To defame someone is to unlawfully harm that person's public reputation. Slander is spoken defamation and libel is written defamation, but both are governed under the same laws of defamation. The English Common Law origins of defamation law are complex and archaic. Defamation law is further complicated under U.S. law because of broad protections for free speech under the U.S. and state constitutions, and different state standards of law concerning whether the plaintiff is deemed a private or public figure for purposes of defamation. U.S. citizens have a First Amendment right, sometimes further strengthened by a state constitutional right, to express their opinions concerning other people, and especially concerning public officials and other public figures.

It is not enough for a defamation plaintiff to merely prove that the defendant said something negative about the plaintiff. The plaintiff must generally show that the statement was untrue and that there was at least negligence by the defendant concerning the truth when the plaintiff is deemed a private figure. Those plaintiffs who are deemed to be public figures will find it much more difficult to prove a case of defamation because proof of reckless disregard for the truth or malice by the defendant is generally required. U.S. defamation law seeks to balance the individual's right to be free from untrue damaging public statements, with the rights of others to free speech and the public expression of their opinions, especially concerning public figures.

Nonetheless, while there is a broadly protected right to freedom of speech in the U.S., defamation is not protected speech. To establish a prima facie case of defamation, the plaintiff must show that the defendant's alleged defamatory declarations:

1) Contained untrue statements of fact concerning the plaintiff;
2) The statements were communicated to one or more persons other than the plaintiff;
3) The statements caused foreseeable prejudice towards the plaintiff; and
4) There are provable damages to the plaintiff.

As noted above the plaintiff's burden of proof also depends on whether the plaintiff is deemed a public or a private figure. Public officials are generally deemed public figures in defamation suits. According to the U.S. Supreme Court, in *Rosenblatt v. Baer*, 383 U.S. 75 (1966), public officials are those government officials that reasonably appear to the public to have substantial control over governmental affairs. In *Hutchinson v. Proxmire*, 443 U.S. 111 (1979), however, the U.S. Supreme Court noted that the public figure designation does not extend to all public employees. State courts have tended to hold that elected or higher-level appointed public school officials are public figures, including elected school board members, elected or appointed superintendents, and college presidents and deans, and that lower-level appointed school officials such as faculty and staff retain their citizen status as private figures even when they work for public institutions.

Mid-level appointed officials, such as school-level principals, have been a much closer call for courts, with some state courts holding that school principals are public figures and others holding that principals are not public figures under state law. A particular plaintiff's public status may also influence a court's decision concerning whether that individual is deemed a public or a private figure for purposes of defamation. For example, even if principals were generally deemed private figures under applicable state law, a principal that was a former celebrity; a prominent state, national or international figure; an elected official; or otherwise sought and achieved broad public recognition, might still be held to be a public figure in that unique case regardless of the general rule under state law. It is expected that citizens will make statements about public figures, and one of the prices of broad public recognition is that public figures must tolerate more critical comments and opinions from the public than private figures.

Accordingly, to prove a case of defamation plaintiffs that are public figures must meet a higher burden of proof. In *New York Times v. Sullivan*, 376 U.S. 254 (1964) the U.S. Supreme Court required that to prove defamation as a public figure the plaintiff must prove "that the statement was made with actual malice . . . that is with knowledge that it was false or with reckless disregard of whether it was false or not." In contrast plaintiffs that are private figures need only establish by a "preponderance of the evidence that the defendant failed to use ordinary care to determine the truth or falsity" of the statement concerning the plaintiff.

A defamation plaintiff must prove all elements of a defamation claim by a preponderance of the evidence under the applicable standard for a public or private figure. A plaintiff who proves a defamation claim may seek monetary damages from the defendant, attorney's fees, and an injunction against the defendant to prevent further harms. In cases involving especially malicious behavior by the defendant punitive damages may also be awarded.

In nearly all jurisdictions, however, truth is an absolute defense to a claim of defamation. Defamation law only protects plaintiffs from untrue statements concerning their character and reputation. True statements of fact are not defamation. The defendant's expression of personal opinion is also not subject to claims of defamation. A defendant's statement that "I do not believe the principal is a nice person" is a statement of personal opinion. But even though it may be cast as a personal opinion, a declarative public statement by the defendant stating "I believe that teacher, Ms. Smith, is a child molester" is not merely a statement of opinion, but is reasonably understood as based on some underlying facts within the knowledge of the defendant and may be subject to a defamation claim. It is important to remember, however, that good faith reports of suspected child abuse made in compliance with state laws requiring these reports are not defamation. Even if the reports turn out to be unfounded, if the statements were made in good faith and were not communicated beyond official routes of required reporting, good faith reports are protected under state law.

Intentional Torts

Intentional torts are distinguished from the tort of negligence in that the plaintiff must prove intent to cause harm, and not merely negligence in performing a duty. Because of the element of intent, many intentional torts are also crimes. Claims of intentional torts in educational institutions may include assault and battery; false imprisonment; invasion of privacy; and intentional infliction of emotional distress.

Assault and battery

Assault and battery are often discussed together, because an assault may be followed by a battery if a defendant carries through with a threat.

Nonetheless, these two intentional torts are separate and distinct causes of legal action, and depending on the facts, the plaintiff may claim either or both of these intentional torts. An assault occurs when the defendant acts with the intent of causing apprehension of bodily harm or offense by the plaintiff, while battery is the actual and intentional infliction of harmful or offensive bodily contact.

Proving a prima facie case of assault requires the plaintiff to establish by a preponderance of the evidence that there was an action by the defendant intended to cause apprehension and that it did in fact cause apprehension. For example, a defendant may have pulled out a knife and said "I am going to cut you." If the plaintiff can prove that the defendant's actions were taken with the intent to cause apprehension, and in fact did cause apprehension, the plaintiff has proven a prima facie case of assault and may argue for appropriate damages.

Damages for assault may include compensation for emotional stress caused by the assault, physical injuries resulting from the distress, and other provable damages. Punitive damages may be appropriate where the defendant's actions were sufficiently malicious or outrageous. Defenses may include attempting to rebut any necessary element of the prima facie case of assault, claiming consent to the interaction (e.g., the interaction was part of a game, a play, etc., or otherwise consented to by the plaintiff), or an appropriate exercise of disciplinary authority (e.g., a teacher threatened physical punishment but the threat was of lawful corporal punishment).

Proving a prima facie case of battery requires the plaintiff to establish by a preponderance of the evidence that there was an action by the defendant intended to inflict harmful or offensive bodily contact and that it did in fact result in this bodily contact. For example, a defendant may have punched the plaintiff, or a defendant may have approached the plaintiff with the intent to touch the plaintiff in an offensive way (e.g., sexual contact or an affront to personal dignity such as ripping clothing, etc.) and in fact did so. The plaintiff has proven a prima facie case and may argue for appropriate damages.

Damages for battery may include compensation for physical injuries, damages to personal property, emotional distress, punitive damages, and other provable damages. Defenses may include attempting to rebut any necessary element of the prima facie case of battery; arguing the defendant's act was not intentional (e.g., caused by mistaken identity, accident, involuntary movement (e.g., reflex, seizure, etc.)); arguing the plaintiff consented to the contact; or the touching was an exercise of self-defense, defense of others, or lawful disciplinary authority. Use of force in defense must not exceed what is reasonably necessary for defense, and the use of force must end when the threat ends. Retaliation is not self-defense.

False imprisonment

False imprisonment occurs when a plaintiff has been unlawfully confined by the defendant without consent. Proving a prima facie case of false imprisonment requires the plaintiff to establish by a preponderance of the evidence that there was an action by the defendant intended to cause the confinement and that it did in fact cause unlawful confinement without the consent of the plaintiff.

Confinement may be caused by physical barriers; physical force; verbal orders or intimidation; or removing of the ability of the plaintiff to physically leave. For example, if the plaintiff can prove that the defendant unlawfully seized the plaintiff's car keys with the intent of confining the plaintiff to the area, and the plaintiff was in fact unable to leave without her car keys, the plaintiff has proven a prima facie case and may argue for appropriate damages.

Damages for false imprisonment may include compensation for any physical injuries resulting from the confinement, damages to personal property, emotional distress, punitive damages, and other provable damages. Defenses may include attempting to rebut any necessary element of the prima facie case of false imprisonment, e.g., presenting evidence that the plaintiff consented to the confinement or failed to leave through a known and reasonable means of leaving, or arguing the defendant's acts were lawful, necessary discipline, self-defense or in defense of others.

Temporary restraint or seclusion of students may be necessary in some cases to protect safety. Nonetheless, when restraint, seclusion, or any use of force is necessary, school officials should be certain not to exceed what is required and lawful under the circumstances; to document the need for their actions and what occurred; and to seek and implement the least severe options sufficient for protecting safety in the school.

Restraint or seclusion of students is potentially dangerous and may be regulated by federal or state laws. Restraint or seclusion should only be used in response to an imminent danger and where less restrictive interventions would prove ineffective in protecting against the imminent danger.

School officials should assure that any school policies concerning the restraint or seclusion of children are in compliance with applicable laws which may prohibit the use of mechanical restraints (e.g., handcuffs, ties, shackles, etc.); chemical restraints (e.g., non-prescribed drugs or other chemicals to alter behavior); physical restraints that restrict breathing; or any other aversive interventions that may endanger health or safety.

If a student is temporarily restrained or secluded for valid safety purposes, the health and safety of the student must be closely monitored. Further, the restrictive conditions should be ended as soon as practicable through disciplinary removal; change in placement; transfer of the student to law enforcement officials; or other appropriate expedited resolutions of the safety risk.

Invasion of privacy

Everyone has a general right to be left alone and to not be subjected to unreasonable intrusions on their personal privacy. And everyone has a general duty not to invade the privacy of others in unreasonable and unlawful ways. In the U.S., legal causes of action for invasion of privacy have been recognized in four general areas:

1) Invasion into the plaintiff's private life;
2) Public disclosure of the plaintiff's private facts;
3) Misappropriation of the plaintiff's name or likeness; and
4) Presenting the plaintiff in a false and offensive light.

Like most tort actions, establishing a prima facie case of invasion of privacy generally tracks the basic elements of negligence and most other torts: Duty, breach, causation, and damages. There is a general duty to respect other persons' reasonable expectations of privacy. That duty is breached if the defendant's actions in invading the personal privacy of the plaintiff were serious and unreasonable. The defendant's actions must have caused foreseeable harm to the plaintiff. And there must be provable damages which may include serious emotional distress and mental suffering resulting from the invasion of privacy.

An invasion of the plaintiff's private life may occur, for example, if school officials remotely activated cameras on school computers loaned to faculty or students for home use. Publicly disclosing private information acquired through this invasion of privacy, or any other public disclosure of private information, might also constitute a public disclosure of private facts. The unauthorized use of an individual's name or likeness for commercial purposes would constitute a misappropriation of the plaintiff's name or likeness. Further, an unauthorized use of the plaintiff's name or likeness may also constitute presenting the plaintiff in a false light if it wrongfully portrays the plaintiff to the public in a manner that would be highly offensive to the reasonable person (e.g., photo of the person eating candy but falsely claiming the "pills" were illegal drugs).

Truth is generally not a defense to a claim of invasion of privacy because in these cases the plaintiff had a right to keep the truth private. But false statements about the plaintiff related to a breach of privacy may also be grounds for a defamation suit. The plaintiff's lawful consent to the breach of privacy generally is a valid defense to a claim of invasion of privacy. In some cases, there may also be First Amendment defenses available, especially to members of the press reporting on matters of legitimate public concern.

Intentional infliction of emotional distress

It is an unfortunate reality that some troubled individuals are motivated by jealousy, hatred, personal insecurities, a desire for power and control, etc., to intentionally inflict emotional distress on others. And it is not true that "sticks and stones may break my bones, but words will never hurt me." Words can do serious emotional, psychological, and even physical harm to the person targeted for harassment. The tort of intentional infliction of emotional distress provides a remedy for wrongful emotional abuse intentionally inflicted on the plaintiff by the defendant.

With increased awareness of the connection between mental stress and physical health, and broader knowledge of the serious human and institutional consequences of harassment and bullying, U.S. courts are increasingly recognizing the validity of claims of intentional infliction of emotional distress. Nonetheless, the burden of proof for the plaintiff is still very high under U.S. law. The plaintiff must prove that the defendant engaged in extreme and outrageous acts intended to cause foreseeable harm to the plaintiff. Damages may include compensation for the pain and suffering of emotional distress; consequential damages such as lost wages; counseling expenses; medical costs; and punitive damages where the defendant's actions were truly outrageous in nature.

Essential Questions &Answers

Isn't tort law just a scam for lawyers to get rich on injury claims?

Tort law is a necessary legal system for any society in order to provide a peaceful means of settling disputes over injuries and for deterring future harms. No system is perfect. Most everyone has heard horror stories of extreme tort claims and also seen kitschy advertisements for questionable legal representation. Nonetheless, most tort lawyers are professionals acting under the ABA Code of Ethics and helping to protect the rights of persons who have been harmed. Any unethical conduct should be reported to the state bar association. Yes, there are some abuses of the system, but your chances of falling victim to an unjust tort claim can be greatly reduced if you understand the tort law system and use common sense and prudent preventive measures to avoid unnecessary risks, injuries, and liability.

Do I have to be represented by a lawyer in a tort case?

No. Whether to hire a lawyer is a decision that should be made based on a careful assessment of your circumstances. In some cases, such as minor property damage, you may be able to informally reach a reasonable settlement with the responsible individual, or a settlement with an insurance company, expediting the resolution of the case and saving everyone the costs of formal litigation. In more serious matters, and especially in cases involving serious personal injuries and large potential damages for medical costs, lost income, pain and suffering, etc., it is generally wise to seek qualified legal counsel to assure that your rights are fully protected. Even lawyers retain legal counsel in cases involving substantial damages.

I don't want to settle a claim and then find out there were unanticipated and expensive long-term impacts from an injury. How long can I wait before filing a tort suit?

In general, property damages are relatively easy to calculate shortly after an incident because the extent of the damages is usually obvious and unlikely to increase. Damages for personal injuries, however, may be far more difficult to gauge quickly, because some injuries may be hidden, fail to heal, worsen, or cause additional complications. For this reason, defendants may want to push for a quick settlement in a personal injury case, but plaintiffs may wish to wait and see what the actual injuries and damages are longer term. If plaintiffs wait too long, however, their claim may be barred by the statute of limitations. The statute of limitations on tort claims in most states is two years, but this varies among states. Check your state's laws concerning the timely filing of a tort suit or consult with qualified legal counsel.

Will I have to go to court to resolve a tort claim?

Generally, no. Most cases, and especially smaller claims, can be settled informally. This is especially true when the defendant's fault and liability are clear, and the amount of damages is relatively low and easily calculated. The cases that tend to go to court are cases where the defendant contests fault and liability or rejects the amount of claimed damages. To be taken seriously in settlement negotiations, however, the plaintiff must demonstrate to the defendant that there is a strong case, and be prepared to go to court if necessary. Reasonable defendants agree to reasonable settlements, if they believe they are unlikely to prevail in court and that they may face greater liability and costs resulting from a trial.

What types of tort suits are most common in schools?

Vehicle related accidents. Buses are generally a very safe form of transportation, but accidents happen, and when a bus collides with a much smaller vehicle, or a person, the damage and injuries can be extensive. Every precaution should be taken to assure that drivers are well qualified and trained, and that students do not distract drivers. Personal injuries on school property are also common, from simple slip and falls, to lab accidents, to serious sports injuries. Prevention is key. Safety hazards must be addressed as soon as possible. And all school personnel must be properly trained, certified, and supervised to assure that they are taking appropriate precautions to protect everyone's safety.

If an accident happens, should I admit fault?

No. Even if you think it may be your fault, in a common sense way, you do not know at the moment whether you are legally at fault. Determining legal fault and liability can be complex. There may be factors that caused or contributed to the accident that you are currently unaware of, e.g., the plaintiff's contributory negligence, etc. It is appropriate to express genuine concern for the victim of an accident, and to reasonably render aid when necessary. But if you admit fault, you may be stuck with your admission of fault. You can be kind and supportive without immediately assigning blame, at least until all of the facts are known and you have consulted with legal counsel concerning your true legal fault and liability.

How can I best protect myself and my family from tort liability?

Concerning tort law, an ounce of prevention can be worth many pounds of cure. It is always best to prevent accidents. Use common sense in your daily conduct. Never engage in distracted or intoxicated driving. Inspect your property to identify and repair safety risks. And carry adequate insurance to cover potential liability.

How can I find out about the laws governing torts in my state?

Although the general principles of tort law are the same nationally, the details, e.g., statutes of limitations, rules governing damages, attorneys' fees, etc., are controlled by state law. Search "tort law" or "negligence law", etc., and the name of your state. Start with a good quality state law overview from a reliable source, and this will help you to identify the specific issues and state statutes you need to find to understand the law in your state.

Essential Practice Skills

Prevention is the key to avoiding tort liability. More important, prevention is the key to avoiding dangers and injuries. To promote safety and security in our schools this section provides essential practice skills related to school safety and security; personnel safety and security; adequate child supervision; harassment, assaults, and abductions; safety intervention and self-defense; safe facilities; safe grounds, parking areas, and transportation; safe play areas; accident and injury prevention; environmental safety; and emergency planning and response.

School safety and security

The core lesson of tort law is that you must do what a reasonable person would do under the circumstances. Reasonable persons recognize potential safety and security dangers in advance, and take reasonable, commonsense precautions to promote safety, avoid foreseeable risks, and prevent unnecessary losses. Addressing potential problems before they become emergencies or disasters is the key to good school safety and security management and liability prevention.

Concerning school safety and security, an ounce of prevention is worth many pounds of cure. If it is not already in operation, school officials should consider establishing a School Safety and Security Task Force made up of, for example: School administrators, teachers (including teachers with expertise in higher risk areas, e.g., athletics; labs; vocational education; etc.), law enforcement and safety personnel, a school nurse or other medical personnel, transportation personnel, buildings and grounds personnel, student and community representatives as appropriate, and a competent attorney. The general charge of the Task Force is to anticipate and proactively address emerging dangers and oversee ongoing safety and security efforts. Although prevention efforts do require the investment of time and resources, prevention is far superior to unnecessary damages, injuries, deaths, and liability.

It is hoped that the overviews and examples in this section will encourage readers to think further about safety and security concerns in their schools; review applicable state laws and local policies; and discuss with colleagues, safety personnel, students, and community members how everyone can work together to improve safety and security in their schools.

The school safety and security measures suggested below are illustrative only, and it is essential that you consider not only these general examples, but also any unique concerns in your area and circumstances. Be certain you comply with applicable laws and policies, and seek professional advice when needed. These materials should, however, be helpful in getting you started towards a safer and more secure school for everyone.

Further information on school safety and security can be obtained through your state and federal department of education websites and through other public and private sector resources. A search of these and other related websites should produce many useful resources.

Personnel safety and security

Because resources are always limited, school officials must be good stewards of school resources and take care not to expose the school to unnecessary liability. Regardless of costs or concerns about liability, however, the safety of personnel, and especially children, must always remain the top priority for school officials. All safety and security efforts must be planned in accordance with safety as the non-negotiable priority. With wise planning, however, safety and security efforts can prevent harm and liability, protecting both people and limited resources.

Adequate child supervision

School officials have a duty to reasonably protect the health and safety of children in their care. Adequate child supervision is a legal duty and a community expectation. It is per se negligence to leave children unsupervised. A responsible adult must be in charge at all times, supervising children from the moment school officials take physical custody until physical custody is transferred back to the parent.

If children are not supervised and an assault or injury occurs because of inadequate supervision, school officials may be held liable for negligent supervision and dismissed for neglect of duties. Adequate supervision includes protecting children from foreseeable dangers and reasonably rendering aid when necessary. Although there is a far greater duty to supervise and protect children in their care, school officials have a general duty to guard all persons on school property from foreseeable dangers.

Choking hazards

A serious and foreseeable danger for children (and others) is choking, which is a leading cause of injury and death among young children. Choking hazards are serious but often overlooked dangers until tragedy strikes. School administrators, classroom teachers, students, parents, school nurses, and cafeteria personnel must work together to reduce risks associated with choking in schools. Younger children are at higher risk of choking, but choking is a serious danger for all persons. Younger children may choke on a toy or other small object. But food is the most common cause of choking for everyone. Allergic reactions resulting in anaphylactic shock can also cause choking when the airway becomes blocked from severe allergy-related inflammation. A blocked airway is a critical emergency with only minutes to respond before permanent injury or death occurs.

Take action:

• Avoid serving younger children round, firm, or sticky foods such as grapes, hotdogs, meat or cheese chunks, gumballs, caramels, etc., or serve these foods cut in safer-sized pieces appropriately portioned for younger children to safely eat.
• Prohibit running and other strenuous physical activities while eating as exerted breathing while eating greatly increases the risks of choking for all persons.
• Do not allow any risky antics, pranks, or games that increase the risk of choking.
• Require parents and students to notify school officials of student allergies.
• Instruct students in how to take age-appropriate actions to protect themselves from choking hazards and allergens, and what to do in an emergency.
• School personnel should be trained in administering first-aid to a choking victim, including as appropriate, techniques for very small children and children with special needs.
• All school personnel should be trained in recognizing the symptoms of a serious allergic reaction, and in administering first-aid under the school's emergency plan for anaphylactic shock victims.
• Consistent with applicable laws, epinephrine should be stored in strategic locations and available for emergency use when needed.

Harassment, assaults, and abductions

Despite media reports of school violence, schools remain relatively safe places for children. It is a sad reality that some children are safer in the classroom than in their own homes. It is always possible that an armed intruder could attack a school, and reasonable precautions must be in place to protect against these attacks to the degree possible. But this is not the most common risk facing most children in schools. The sections below address awareness and prevention measures for harassment, assaults, and abductions as these are core concerns in protecting the health and well-being of children.

Harassment

The most common risk to the health and well-being of most children in schools likely comes from the daily psychological violence of bullying and harassment from peers and sometimes teachers who may allow or even participate in the abuse. Bullying and harassment can cause severe suffering for its victims leading to psychological and emotional damage; stress related physical illnesses; impaired school performance; increased absenteeism; increased risks of suicide; and revenge motivated violence.

Perpetrators of bullying and harassment can be either students or teachers, and victims may be either students or teachers. If not addressed, bullying and harassment can cause serious harm to its victims or trigger retaliation through spontaneous physical violence. More rarely and alarmingly, relentless bullying and harassment may provoke planned attacks on schools involving weapons and the potential for significant casualties.

Many acts of violence could be prevented by addressing interpersonal conflicts and improving the social culture of the school, supplanting destructive bullying and harassment with mutual respect and a collective focus on achievement. It is also important to note that the same types of school climate and culture changes that make schools safer places for everyone are also likely to improve teaching, learning, and student achievement: Safe schools are also good schools. As incidents of harassment and violence decline, the well-being and achievement of students will increase.

Assaults

Guard against threats of assaults from external persons by securing the building and establishing safe routes to school for students who walk to school. Safe routes should be planned considering both avoiding potential dangers and getting the children to school efficiently. The first priority must be planning a route that avoids any serious known dangers. But if the designated route is too indirect, some children will likely travel the more direct route anyway because it is easier and faster, making them both more isolated and at risk. Also, the longer children are on the street, the longer they are exposed to general dangers. The planned route must be safe, but it must also be realistic and efficient.

As needed, law enforcement agents, school officials, and community volunteers can be posted along the safe route to assure that children are supervised and safe. It may also be useful to designate safe houses along the route with trusted persons children know they can go to for help and safety in an emergency. Also explain to students that there is safety in numbers, that whenever possible they should travel together with other children, and that everyone must make sure no one gets left behind in a dangerous situation.

Guard against threats of assaults by internal persons by removing known dangerous individuals from the school. Criminal acts should be dealt with as crimes and perpetrators removed from the school or incarcerated. If the dangerous behavior is a manifestation of a disability, a student who is not able to confirm conduct and who presents a serious danger to others must be placed in a more restrictive environment until the student can safely return to a less restrictive setting.

Provide adequate supervision of all personnel and students at all times. Encourage everyone to stay together in dangerous areas and situations. Instruct them in what to do in the event of a safety emergency. And as necessary, instruct personnel and students in how to protect themselves from assaults.

Abductions

To guard against risks of abductions, children should only be released to the custody of parent authorized and school approved and confirmed safe, sober, adult pick-up persons. When there is any doubt, always confirm the identity and valid authorization of the adult seeking to take the child from the school before releasing the child. The time necessary for a little extra caution by school staff and a brief delay for pick-up persons is a small price to pay to protect children from potential abductions (*see also* under Safe Grounds, *infra*).

Take action:

• Secure the exterior and interior areas of the building with a thorough security audit and necessary remediation including establishing a general plan adequate for the level of security necessary in the area; securing all routes of entry (e.g., doors; windows; basement/rooftop entry; etc.); adequate lighting; removal of brush and other physical and visual obstructions; a security system; video surveillance; posting school resource officers and other school personnel in strategic locations, etc.

• Identify "safe routes" and "safe houses/persons" along the safe routes for students walking to school in high risk areas.

• Consistent with state law establish a system requiring all visitors to report to a central location for security clearance prior to entering the school. School personnel should be instructed to politely question any unknown persons they find in the school or any persons outside of designated event areas.

• Any suspicious person should be reported to school administrators or law enforcement officers to either confirm that the person has a legitimate cause to be present and poses no danger, or to remove the person from school property or into police custody.

• To deter child abductions, do not rely only on the child identifying the adult (e.g., "that's my Daddy"), as unauthorized non-custodial parents are among the most likely persons to abduct a child.

• Even if an unknown person is wearing a uniform or showing official credentials, confirm the person's identity and valid legal authority with a call to an official phone number of the authorizing agency (i.e., not just the number provided by the unknown person). For a well-planned abduction uniforms and false credentials can be purchased or fabricated, and an accomplice's phone number can be provided for a fraudulent confirmation.

• Take extra precautions on field trips beyond the secured boundaries of the school. Students must be adequately supervised at all times and strictly prohibited from talking with strangers or leaving the group. Adequate numbers of teachers and parent/chaperones must be present to safely supervise children. Parent/chaperones must be trustworthy persons who have been cleared through a criminal background check consistent with state law and school policy.

• Encourage everyone to take responsibility for school safety and security. Promote a culture of responsibility in which it is not acceptable to ignore violence or abuse, and everyone understands it is their duty to call for help when violence occurs and to report abuse. This will only work, however, if the reporters of violence and abuse see that school officials will take prompt, consistent, and effective action when needed and that the reporters are protected from retaliation.

Many safety programs are now available for schools, and some are better than others. The programs with the greatest likelihood of success are those that help school officials to clearly identify the core causes of violence and address those causes in a systematic, comprehensive way. A single video or lecture is unlikely to have any long-term impact. Unless a program can help to improve the culture and climate of the school and community, making violence and abuse socially unacceptable, it is unlikely to succeed in reducing violence and abuse longer term. For all programs, and especially for-profit programs, *caveat emptor* (i.e., let the buyer beware). There are increasingly many good free or low-cost programs available for reducing violence and abuse. Programs, however, are like diets: They don't work unless they change long-term behaviors, replacing harmful daily behaviors with healthier daily behaviors for long-term progress.

In general adopt a practical, persistent, preventive approach to addressing violence and abuse. If a few students are disproportionately responsible for conflict and violence in the school, for example, lawfully remove these students to more restrictive and appropriate educational settings. Do this first to protect safety and order in the school. But also so that these students can focus on learning better social and academic skills, the skills they need for a better future. Determine what factors (e.g., social; economic, cultural; environmental; etc.) are stimulating violence and abuse and work to move everyone toward healthier behaviors. Provide everyone with education in respecting diversity and healthy conflict resolution skills to build a culture of mutual respect and non-violence in the school. When necessary, however, provide instruction in safety intervention and self-defense to minimize risks of injury to all persons.

Safety intervention and self-defense

The goal of safety intervention and self-defense is to keep others and yourself safe, not to "win" battles that could have reasonably been avoided. As the ancient philosopher and strategist Sun Tzu said, the greatest victory comes from the battle that was never fought. You want to achieve your goal of keeping everyone in the school safe without violence and the resulting risks to safety. The first rule of safety intervention and self-defense, therefore, is to always avoid unnecessary conflicts likely to lead to violence.

High risk areas, people, and situations should be avoided whenever possible. Remember also that an area that may be safe during the day or during school hours may not be safe at night or when other people are not present. When high risk areas, people, and situations cannot be avoided, try to choose the most favorable time and circumstances possible to deal with potential threats, and be as prepared as possible to safely deal with foreseeable dangers. When faced with a potential threat of violence:

Leave the area: Trust your instincts. If a situation doesn't seem right, just leave. If needed, try to lead others who may be in danger out of the area with you. No explanation to potential attackers is required. Don't provoke aggressors. Keep calm, keep moving, and keep interaction and eye contact with potential aggressors to a minimum. Before attacking, assailants often attempt to "shark bump" potential victims with seemingly benign requests (e.g., "can I borrow a cigarette?") or more aggressive verbal provocations to single out the victim and gauge fear and vulnerability. Engaging potential assailants in unnecessary interactions may increase the risk of becoming the target of an attack. What if you can't just leave an area with no explanation, such as your office during a meeting turned ugly? If you encounter a threat of violence and under the circumstances you can't just get up and leave with no explanation, attempt to politely excuse yourself (e.g., "please excuse me; I will be right back" but you are not really coming back of course). Proceed to a safe location and send a school resource officer to your office to safely escort the person out of the building or into police custody as appropriate. What if your exit is blocked and the assailant will not let you leave?

Try to de-escalate the conflict: If you cannot leave the next best option may be to try to de-escalate the anger/conflict. Who was right in an argument is not the priority at this point. Do not further provoke a potentially violent person. Try to delay any violent confrontation while calling for backup (e.g., covertly text message the school resource officer for help; have a pre-arranged emergency verbal code to use to signal the office secretary to surreptitiously call for emergency help (e.g., "Ms. Smith, I need some coffee please" (her name is not really Ms. Smith and you don't really need any coffee); try to get the angry potential attacker to sit down, wait for the "coffee", calmly dialogue or at least monologue his or her list of demands while you wait for security personnel to arrive). Before a crisis occurs think through possible strategies that would work best in your circumstances and have an emergency plan ready for addressing potential violence.

If you are attacked: Try to get away and to get others to safety. If you cannot get away, defend yourself and others until help arrives. If you must defend yourself:

• Continue to call for help. If you cannot stop the attacker by yourself, you need others to help you as soon as possible.

• Never go willingly into an isolated area with a potential attacker or abductor. If necessary it is better to resist and fight the person where you are and where help from others is still possible.

• Try to stay on your feet or get back on your feet. When you are on the ground your options for escape and self-defense become much more limited.

• Always try to avoid violence, and to end the violence as soon as you safely can. But do what is necessary to defend yourself and others, including using available objects as barriers, shields, or weapons to stop the attacker.

• If you experience a mortal threat from an attack and cannot escape, fight back as hard as you can when protecting your life and the lives of others requires violent resistance.

• When using self-defense, however, be certain it is only self-defense. Do not allow yourself to become emotionally out of control and become the aggressor, even in response to an attack. You want to have the violent person arrested. You do not want to be arrested also. When in doubt, however, do what is necessary to defend yourself and others from a violent aggressor, using force that is reasonable necessary to defend yourself and other innocent persons.

• Do not pursue a fleeing attacker. Secure the premises so the attacker cannot return to harm others, and call 911 for emergency medical personnel if needed and for police to pursue the attacker. Then focus on providing first-aid and security for any victims while awaiting the arrival of emergency personnel.

• Understand that having a well thought out and practiced plan for dealing with violent persons in advance of an emergency situation may make the difference between safety and tragedy.

• Learn more about "Active Shooter Preparedness" at www.dhs.gov/active-shooter-preparedness.

Safe facilities

To enhance safety and avoid liability, buildings and grounds should be regularly inspected, identifying and correcting security risks and safety hazards. Periodic checks for school security risks should include inspections of all possible routes of entrance including doors, windows, and basement/roof entries, examining whether unauthorized persons could gain access through these areas. Inspectors should attempt to see these areas through the eyes of a potential intruder who may break windows, force weak locks, remove grates or covers, or break weak walls to gain entry.

Among the questions inspectors should ask is what level of security is necessary in this circumstance; are security fences, lighting, cameras, or alarm systems needed; what affordable building or landscaping modifications could enhance security; how can the most security sensitive areas within the school be protected even if an intruder enters the building; how can students and personnel be protected from an intruder; are room numbers clearly marked and is an accurate map available for emergency personnel; do systems to keep intruders from getting in interfere with the ability of persons to get out in the event of an emergency; and are security measures compatible with daily uses of the school? Inconvenient systems will be unused or circumvented (e.g., not turning on the security system; propping open doors, etc.).

Mobile classrooms and other outbuildings must be included in inspections and planning. Assure that persons in these units are also safe, and that they have an emergency means of communicating with security personnel in the main building if needed. Be certain to plan for students and personnel with special needs as well.

Buildings and grounds should also be inspected to identify and correct safety hazards such as tripping hazards (e.g., objects in walkways, weather heaved or broken side-walks, exposed drain pipes, cords, cables, rodent holes, tree roots, etc.); fire and electrical safety; sharp or protruding objects; heavy objects that could fall; defective chairs, desks, and other equipment; and dangerous animals (e.g., feral dogs, rabid animals, poisonous snakes, spiders, hornets, fire ants, etc.). Athletic areas should be inspected to assure safety for students and to reduce the risk of injury to players and spectators from flying baseballs, unsafe seating areas, etc.

To guard against theft, vandalism, and inappropriate or unlawful uses, unsupervised areas of the school should be secured during school events open to outside visitors. Through postings and/or verbal notices, visitors should be instructed to remain in authorized event areas only. For larger events a school resource officer or other law enforcement officer should be present. Additional law enforcement officers are needed for events with larger crowds or with hard to manage crowds (e.g., events more likely to attract intoxicated persons). For smaller, lower risk events, faculty and staff supervising the event should have an established emergency procedure for contacting law enforcement officers and school officials when necessary.

Take action:

• Conduct periodic, thorough security and safety inspections of all buildings and grounds supplemented with daily inspections of areas as needed.
• Logically and clearly number all rooms and areas. Provide security personnel with copies of the most current maps of buildings and grounds. Have a current copy available in the building, in the central office, and an electronic copy available remotely.
• Using a current map of the building and school grounds, divide areas (inside and outside the building as necessary) into zones properly sized for adequate supervision by an individual; assign an individual to monitor each zone; and hold the individual responsible for supervising/patrolling that zone as needed during high risk times (e.g., during athletic events; dances; recess; class changes; etc.).
• Trim or remove any brush that could be used as cover by an attacker or others engaged in misconduct on school property.
• Confirm that fences are in good repair and have not been compromised with breaks or areas dug out under the fence (to deter intruders, feral dogs, etc.).
• Check illumination systems at night. Be certain the coverage of lighting is adequate. Reposition lights as needed and replace non-working lights.
• Test security systems as recommended by the monitoring company.
• Make sure that video monitoring systems are functioning properly; that security cameras have not been moved, covered, or damaged to create blind spots; that the recording system is working; and that live video of high risk areas is properly monitored.

Safe grounds, parking areas, and transportation

Although students spend relatively short periods of time outside of the school building in comparison to time in the classroom, nonetheless, most injuries on school property occur outside of the school. The majority of injuries to younger students happen on the playground, and older students are most often injured on athletic fields. Safety issues for playgrounds and athletic fields are addressed in more detail in the subsequent sections. This section addresses safety and security issues on school grounds generally, including parking areas, and transportation safety.

Serious and even fatal injuries can occur anywhere. Many serious or fatal injuries, however, are associated with the areas where traffic passes, enters, exits, and travels through school grounds. A busy road adjacent to the school creates an ever-present risk for children crossing that road and vehicles entering or exiting school grounds. If traffic is traveling at a higher speed the risk is greatly increased. Designated "school zones" commonly have reduced speed limits. But the lower speed limits only reduce risks of accidents and injuries when drivers actually slow down and pay greater attention to children and vehicles entering and exiting the school grounds.

Schools located near high traffic areas also have special security risks. The more people that view the school area, the more likely someone will see the school and children as potential targets. School officials may want to consider fencing or landscaping barriers between the school and busy roads to limit the view of the school from high traffic areas and to reduce distracting noises, exhaust fumes, etc., from the road.

Schools near interstates may also be at greater risks for abductions. The interstate brings countless numbers of strangers into the area. An abductor could quickly spot the school, abduct a child, make an escape on the interstate, and otherwise have no known link to the community making these individuals and their victims very difficult to locate once they have left the area. In response to this danger the U.S. Congress passed P.L. 108-21 including the "AMBER Alert" national communication network.

An AMBER Alert is designed to enlist the help of the entire extended community in locating an abductor and the victim as soon as possible, so that law enforcement agents can rescue the child. The alert is broadcast through mass media, electronic traffic alert signs, cell phone networks, etc. The system recognizes that delay can be deadly, but also that unwarranted over-use of the system diminishes its efficacy. To balance these concerns the criteria for issuing an AMBER Alert are:

> • There is reasonable belief by law enforcement that an abduction has occurred.
> • The law enforcement agency believes that the child is in imminent danger of serious bodily injury or death.
> • There is enough descriptive information about the victim and the abduction for law enforcement to issue an AMBER Alert to assist in the recovery of the child.
> • The abduction is of a child aged 17 years or younger.

• The child's name and other critical data elements, including the Child Abduction flag, have been entered into the National Crime Information Center (NCIC) system. *See*, www.amberalert.gov.

If a child has been abducted, time is of the essence. An alert must be issued as soon as possible to maximize the chances of safely recovering the child. Call law enforcement officials immediately. Share as much information about the child (e.g., age; description; clothing worn; distinguishing features; etc., and forward a recent photo); the abductor (physical description; clothing worn; distinguishing features; and forward any recorded security video, etc.); and the vehicle (make; model; year; color; license number; distinguishing features; recorded video; etc.). School personnel must know what to do before there is an emergency. Surprise and shock must not prevent them from attempting to stop the abduction, getting as much information as possible if they cannot stop the abduction, and knowing who to contact immediately to issue a proper alert without delay when minutes and even seconds may matter. The longer the child is missing, the less likely it is that the child will be returned safely.

School bus stops are also areas that may attract potential abductors. Parents should be instructed to supervise their children until the child is safely on the bus. Children should be instructed to stay in a group with other children whenever possible; not to talk to strangers (e.g., take candy, gifts, help "look for a lost puppy" etc.); never to accept a ride from a stranger; to go with the other children to a safe house or safe person if a suspicious stranger appears; to tell the bus driver, teachers, principals, parents, police, etc., about any suspicious behavior; and if someone tries to abduct them they should scream for help and fight to get away so that anyone in hearing or sight range can clearly see what is happening and help or call for help.

Parking areas create special dangers for serious or fatal injuries. All students are at risk. But younger students are harder to see in parking areas and they are less likely to pay attention to traffic. Further, because of their fragile bodies and small size relative to vehicles, being hit by a vehicle is far more likely to result in serious injuries or death for a smaller child. But older students also pose unique risks in traffic areas and parking lots. Older students tend to take greater risks as pedestrians crossing busy roads. And as new drivers they have very little experience and limited comprehension of the finality of serious injury and death, leading them to take greater risks as drivers. For all of these reasons, potential dangers in parking lots and traffic lanes near schools must be taken very seriously, appropriate precautions must be taken, and adequate supervision must be provided.

For children riding school buses, school buses are generally a very safe mode of transportation. Children are far safer traveling in a school bus than in other vehicles. The greatest danger to children from school buses is being run over by the bus when attempting to board or depart. Drivers illegally passing stopped buses also create a serious danger for children. The youngest and smallest children are at the greatest risk. Bus drivers and other drivers are less likely to see small children, and small children are more likely to act unpredictably and not be aware of the danger from the bus or an oncoming vehicle.

School bus drivers have a very difficult job. They are first and foremost responsible for safely driving the bus, which requires them to keep their eyes on the road at all times, and to be aware of the movement of traffic around them as well. If this was not a sufficient burden, bus drivers are responsible for the safety and discipline of students while they are riding on the bus. Anything school officials, parents, drivers, and students can do to improve student conduct on the bus also improves student safety on the bus.

Take action:

- Informed by both an aerial view map and a ground level personal tour of the site, consider (in consultation with other professionals as needed) what structural and landscaping changes can be made to school grounds, parking areas, and traffic lanes to improve safety and security on and around school property.
- Work together with local government planners and law enforcement agents to reduce the volume of traffic and the speed of vehicles in the school zone.
- Provide training to all school personnel in how to prevent and respond to abductions.
- Instruct parents and children in how to promote safety and security at bus stops.
- Design the parking lot area to maximize the safe flow of traffic and pedestrians.
- Have adequate staff on duty to supervise the school parking lot area.
- Strictly enforce safety and speed rules in the school parking lot area.
- Clearly mark all parking lot lanes, walking lanes, and bus drop-off/pick-up areas.
- Clearly mark the areas children are required to stand in and wait until the bus has come to a complete stop, the door has been opened, and they are signaled to board.
- Be aware that a crowd of children surging forward toward an oncoming bus can push a child in front, off the curb and into danger. If necessary, assign seats to avoid any temptation for children to rush forward to get a favored seat when the bus is coming.

• Regularly remind bus drivers that they must be 100% certain where the child leaving a bus is located before putting the bus in motion, and to be certain the child's clothing, backpack, etc., is not caught on the door or any other part of the bus.

• Instruct children to never hang an arm, head, etc., out of a bus window because of possible impact with tree branches, passing vehicles, street signs, flying objects, etc.

• Warn children and parents that fighting, yelling, or anything that distracts the bus driver creates a serious danger for everyone on the bus. Warn everyone that in order to protect the safety of all riders conduct violations on the bus will be swiftly and severely punished. Encourage constructive peer pressure to improve student behavior on the bus.

• Install video cameras on the bus to monitor student behavior. Make certain all students know they are being video recorded to deter misconduct. If students engage in serious misconduct punishment must be swift and certain to maintain the deterrent effect.

• Consistent with state and local laws, install video cameras monitoring traffic around the bus to deter and punish drivers who pass a bus when children are boarding or departing the bus, or otherwise risk the safety of children.

• Consider having a second adult on the bus to help with discipline, safety, and security (e.g., escorting children across a busy street or safely into a secure building in high crime areas). If there are severe discipline, safety, or security issues, assign a security guard to ride until the problem is resolved.

• Train bus drivers in essential behavior management and discipline skills.

• Train bus drivers in emergency procedures, and make sure they know who to call in the event of a safety emergency.

• Never assume that children will watch for vehicles. Drivers must watch for children. Drivers must be regularly reminded to do so through posted signs, periodic reminders, and warnings from parking lot supervisors.

Safe play areas

Play areas and playground equipment merit special attention as frequent and sometimes severe injuries occur in these areas. The U.S. Consumer Product Safety Commission found that more than 200,000 U.S. children receive emergency room treatment each year as a result of playground injuries. A third of these injuries are classified as severe, and at least 15 children die each year due to playground injuries, mostly caused by falls to hard surfaces, strangulation by entanglement, or head-entrapment.

Playground safety is an important area of concern with rapidly evolving standards. The general rule of tort law is that one must do what a reasonable person would do under the circumstances. As the circumstances change, so does what is reasonable under those circumstances. In decades past a major factor in the design of playground equipment was durability. This resulted in playground areas dominated by steel structures embedded in concrete. In retrospect these ultra-durable playgrounds presented unnecessary safety risks for children. These structures would fail current safety requirements, creating potential tort liability for foreseeable injuries.

Child safety and tort law concerns drove dramatic advancements in playground safety standards. To protect safety and avoid liability play areas and equipment must comply with current safety standards. Outdated and unsafe equipment should be removed and the play area should be regularly inspected to assure proper maintenance of equipment and to guard against preventable safety hazards. In reviewing the play area for safety, it may be helpful to inspect the area not only from the height, view, and mindset of an adult, but also to examine the area from the height and perspective of a child at play, identifying otherwise hidden dangers and likely triggers for child behaviors that could result in injuries.

While outdated and unrepaired equipment may pose special risks, injuries are not confined to a few aging playgrounds. Safety problems are shockingly widespread. Most playground injuries and deaths could be prevented with safer equipment and play area designs, regular safety inspections, and proper adult supervision of children.

Take action:

- Be certain there is adequate supervision of children in play areas as inadequate supervision is a major contributing factor to child injuries and liability.
- Make certain that supervising teachers understand that while the children are given free-time during play periods, this is not free-time for teachers. Teachers are on duty and special vigilance is necessary to prevent child injuries.
- Make a list of clear, simple, but effective safety rules for children to follow during playtime. Make sure the children are taught the rules; that they understand the rules are necessary for their safety; and make sure the rules are consistently enforced.
- Do not tolerate harassment. Harassment causes serious harm to its victims and may provoke violence. Bullying; sexual harassment;

racial, ethnic, or religious harassment, etc., have no place in a healthy play environment and cannot be tolerated by teachers.

• Students planning to engage in misconduct will likely seek unobserved areas. Be certain there are no blind spots in the play area and supervisors are positioned to observe all areas adequately. Patrols of the grounds should be regular but not overly predictable.

• Conduct a safety and security inspection of your play area. Playground safety standards published by the U.S. Consumer Product Safety Commission in its *Public Playground Safety Handbook* are available free online. Do a field inspection of the play area to assure that:

__ Play equipment meets current safety standards.
__ Ground surfaces have adequate depths and widths of impact safety materials.
__ Play equipment and ground safety materials are non-toxic.
__ Swings are made of soft materials and safely located.
__ Play equipment is safely spaced.
__ Elevated areas have adequate guard rails to prevent falling.
__ Hardware is properly tightened and not protruding.
__ There are no sharp edges, splinters, broken glass, etc., in the area.
__ There are no dangerous dogs, wild animals, snakes, spiders, etc., in the area.
__ There are no tripping, strangling, trapping, or pinching hazards.
__ Only authorized persons have access to the play area.
__ Children are adequately supervised.

Accident and injury prevention

Accidents and injuries involving older students are most likely to occur in athletic instruction, training, and competition, calling for special precautions in these activities. To help prevent accidents and injuries school officials must assure that physical education teachers, coaches, and other athletic instructors are qualified to safely supervise activities; safety equipment is appropriate and checked regularly for wear or defects; activities are safe and appropriate for the ages and abilities of students; proper safety instruction is documented; medical safety for each student's participation in strenuous athletic training is documented; and students are adequately supervised at all times.

Safety equipment and activities must comply with current standards of practice accepted in the sport for children the ages, sizes, and abilities of those participating. It cannot be assumed that activities appropriate for high school students are necessarily safe for younger children also. Before engaging in physical activities students must be instructed in all necessary safety rules related to the sport (e.g., precautions in using a baseball bat; swinging a golf club; etc.). Coaches and students should regularly review safety rules and practice emergency safety procedures so they know exactly what to do in the event of a serious injury or emergency.

It is important to include all interested students in school athletics if the students are able to safely participate, including students with special needs whenever possible. Remember, however, that individual students have different levels of physical health and fitness. Coaches and instructors should not push students beyond their individual safe physical limits, especially under hot and humid weather conditions. Unreasonably dangerous activities should be prohibited for everyone (e.g., javelin throwing; activities that risk serious head and neck injuries; etc.).

Coaches and other instructors should be trained in first-aid. Necessary first-aid equipment should be stored and available near the area it will most likely be needed. For everyone's protection treat all body fluids as potentially infectious at all times. Wear gloves to protect yourself and others. For each individual treated, use new and clean disposable gloves, bandages, wipes, and towels. Properly dispose of all potentially infectious waste and thoroughly clean all contaminated areas with an appropriate disinfectant solution.

Locker rooms, weight rooms, and shower areas must be adequately supervised. Access to these areas should be restricted unless authorized and under adult supervision. Students should be instructed that running, roughhousing, and other activities that risk slipping and falling or other injuries are strictly prohibited. Further, students should be instructed that they have an affirmative duty to immediately report any abuse, hazing, misconduct, injuries, or breaches of safety protocols to the supervising coach or instructor.

Science labs, vocational training classes, and other instruction involving chemicals, tools, and hands-on work also have higher rates of accidents and injuries than traditional paper and pencil classroom instruction. The above precautions generally apply in these higher risk settings also. Be certain that instructors are qualified to safely supervise the activities; equipment is appropriate and regularly checked for safety, defects, or wear; assigned activities are safe and appropriate for the ages and abilities of students; instruction in safety procedures is documented; and students are adequately supervised to assure safe participation in instructional activities.

Take action:

• Be certain that persons teaching in higher risk settings (e.g., activities involving contact sports; chemicals; power tools; etc.), are properly trained and certified.

• Require all teachers to provide adequate supervision, consistently observe applicable safety protocols, and regularly inspect equipment and work areas for safety.

• Assure that students are instructed in safety practices and what to do in the event of an emergency before beginning any potentially hazardous educational activities.

• Consider using safety contracts that require older students to affirm that they have been taught the necessary rules of safety, understand the rules (summarized in the safety contract), and that they will comply with all applicable safety protocols.

• Stress to all teachers that while there may be greater dangers in some learning environments, safety hazards exist in every classroom (e.g., cords and other tripping hazards; broken glass or other sharp objects or edges; dangers from misconduct; etc.) and that all teachers must regularly inspect their classroom for safety and security risks and provide adequate supervision of students at all times.

Environmental safety

Students and school personnel spend much of their waking hours at the school. For good or ill the school environment has a significant impact on their health and safety. For this reason school officials must do all they can reasonably do to protect students and personnel from known dangers related to environmental toxins, infectious diseases, etc. School officials must comply with federal and state laws concerning hazardous materials (e.g., asbestos, lead, mercury, etc.), storage and use of chemicals, mold control, and any other significant environmental, biological, or other known hazards.

The primary law governing workplace safety is the Occupational Safety and Health Act (OSH Act), 29 U.S.C. § 651. This federal Act is administered by the U.S. Occupational Safety and Health Administration (OSHA). Section 654 (a) (1) of the OSH Act established a general duty for employers to protect employees from known hazards, stating: "Each employer shall furnish to each of his employees employment and a place of employment which are free from recognized hazards."

In some states, state laws supplement OSHA safety standards, creating additional safety protections for workers. In all states employees have a "right to know" concerning recognized hazards in the workplace, so that they may take reasonable precautions to protect themselves and others from known dangers such as the presence of potentially harmful levels of chemicals, radiation, bio-hazards, etc.

Modern life would be impossible without chemicals. But even very useful chemicals may create unnecessary health and safety risks when improperly or excessively applied. Children are especially susceptible to environmental toxins, including cleaning chemicals and pesticides.

Cleaning chemicals can release harmful vapors that may cause irritation to eyes, noses, and throats; trigger asthma attacks and allergic reactions; and cause long-term health problems resulting from prolonged and repeated exposures. Whenever possible, chemicals should be applied when children are not present, and custodial staff must assure the use of proper ventilation and appropriate safety gear (i.e., respirators; goggles; gloves; etc.).

Many pesticides use neurotoxins to kill pests. While these chemicals may be effective in killing pests, over time repeated exposures may also do serious harm to humans, increasing risks of neurological disorders, cancer, and other serious health problems. Concerning the dangers of pesticides in schools, the U.S. Environmental Protection Agency (EPA) recommends the use of Integrated Pest Management (IPM) in schools. State laws may require the use of IPM in schools.

In using IPM, school officials working with the custodial staff first attempt to use non-toxic means of controlling pests, including sanitation, traps, and other non-toxic methods. If these non-toxic methods prove ineffective, they next use the least-toxic means of controlling pests. If the use of more toxic chemicals is ever necessary these are only used sparingly and at the times most remote from when students and personnel will be present in order to limit human exposure to toxins as much as possible.

School custodial staff should be trained in the safe use of necessary pesticides and herbicides; only use these products when necessary and consistent with federal and state laws; and always wear appropriate protective gear during application. Where toxic chemicals have been applied warning signs must be posted in the area consistent with state laws.

Most infectious diseases can be prevented through regular attention to basic hygiene. Hand washing is an essential and inexpensive first line of defense. To protect themselves and others from preventable infections, children should be instructed in proper methods of hand washing and taught that hand washing is essential before eating, after bathroom use, and after contact with any bodily fluid (e.g., mucous, saliva, blood, etc.).

Regular hand washing by all students and personnel should be encouraged by making hand washing facilities available in classrooms, cafeterias, and work areas when possible. If this is not possible hand sanitizer should be available. Students should be cautioned not to drink or eat from shared containers, share personal hygiene items, or engage in any activities that result in an exchange of blood or other bodily fluids.

Cafeteria and custodial staff can help keep everyone healthy through careful attention to hygiene in food preparation and storage, and by regularly and thoroughly cleaning commonly used surfaces (e.g., tabletops, desktops, computer keyboards, hand rails, door handles, water fountains, sinks, and bathrooms). Athletic surfaces (e.g., weight training benches; wrestling, gymnastics, and yoga mats; etc.), must be regularly cleaned and sanitized. And all open wounds must be properly treated and dressed before students engage in contact sports or contact with commonly used athletic surfaces.

Universal biological safety precautions must always be used, treating all body fluids as potentially infectious. Disposable protective gloves should be worn, and bio-hazardous materials (e.g., used needles, body fluids, contaminated bandages, etc.) must be safely disposed of in accordance with federal and state laws. Consistent with § 504 and the ADA, persons who pose a significant risk of transmitting a serious communicable disease should be supported with reasonable accommodations in continuing their studies or work from home or a medical facility until they can safely return to the school.

Take action:

• Begin to replace chemical-based cleaning supplies, etc., with less toxic or natural alternatives.
• Work with custodial personnel to find ways to reduce their exposure, and everyone else's, to any toxic chemicals that are still used on the buildings or grounds.
• Use Integrated Pest Management (IPM) techniques to address pest problems.
• Educate all students and personnel about the necessity to use good hygiene, including regular hand washing.
• Make it easy for everyone to practice good hygiene by making hand washing facilities or hand sanitizer available when and where these are needed.
• Be certain that all commonly used surfaces are regularly cleaned and sanitized by custodial personnel.
• Assure that good hygiene and food safety are practiced in the school cafeteria.
• Offer healthy foods in the school cafeteria to support good health and strong immunity.
• Properly dispose of all used needles, body fluids, contaminated bandages, and other bio-hazardous materials.

• Conduct an environmental review of your school. To help in improving the health of the school environment, the U.S. Environmental Protection Agency (EPA) provides comprehensive information on environmental safety in schools through its "Healthy Schools, Healthy Kids" program at: www.epa.gov/schools.

Emergency planning and response

Consistent with federal and state laws and local ordinances, school officials must have an emergency management plan ready to respond to the dangers most likely in their areas including fires; storms; earthquakes; floods; chemical and bio-hazards; attacks by school shooters, etc. The U.S. Department of Education's Readiness and Emergency Management for Schools (REMS) Technical Assistance (TA) Center describes four phases of emergency management:

> *Prevention-Mitigation*: Identifying all potential hazards and vulnerabilities and reducing the potential damage they can cause;
> *Preparedness*: Collaborating with community partners to develop plans and protocols to prepare for the possibility that the identified hazards, vulnerabilities or emergencies will occur;
> *Response*: Working closely with first responders and community partners to effectively contain and resolve an emergency in, or around, a school or campus; and
> *Recovery*: Teaming with community partners to assist students and staff in the healing process, and restore a healthy and safe learning environment following an emergency event.

Additional information is available through the U.S. Department of Education website, www.rems.ed.gov, and further assistance can be obtained through state and local safety officials.

After the Columbine tragedy special concern has been given to preventing and responding to risks from persons within the school, i.e., potentially dangerous students or personnel. Because some identified behavioral concerns may be manifestations of mental illnesses or other disabilities, it is essential that school officials strike an appropriate balance between respect for the rights of individuals under the IDEA, § 504, and the ADA, and protecting the safety of the community. In cases where the individual clearly poses a safety threat to the community, however, public safety must always be the highest priority.

The problem, however, is that it is often not clear whether identified behavioral concerns are relatively benign symptoms of mental illness; other disabilities; social maladjustment; or a red flag signaling an impending danger. Further, individuals may have pieces of information that do not indicate any imminent danger in isolation, but would indicate a serious danger if all the pieces of the puzzle were seen and understood together.

To address these problems schools establish a Behavioral Intervention Team (BIT) made up of persons with relevant multi-disciplinary expertise (e.g., a counselor; psychologist; special educator; social worker; health care professional; lawyer with relevant expertise; safety and law enforcement professional; etc.). The mission of the BIT is to:

1) Fairly and systematically review reports of behavioral concerns;
2) Help the identified individual whenever possible by proactively addressing recognized needs; and
3) Protect the individual and others in the institution by proactively preventing a potential crisis or imminent danger whenever possible.

The BIT can help school officials to make an informed decision concerning whether services are needed or intervention is warranted. Based on the findings of the BIT school officials may determine the individual poses no current threat; merits continued monitoring; needs educational or health services; needs a referral or mandate for counseling; should be reassigned; or should be removed from the school through the disciplinary process or a report to law enforcement officials.

Take action:

• Clearly establish emergency chains of command and command centers before a crisis so that everyone knows who and where to turn to for leadership in an emergency.
• Provide current maps of buildings and grounds to local emergency personnel. Have an electronic copy available for fast off-sight access if needed. Be certain that all rooms and areas are clearly and logically numbered (on-site and on the map), and that all strategic locations (e.g., helicopter landing sites; triage centers; emergency supplies; dangerous or flammable materials; utility shut-offs; etc.) are clearly identified on the maps.
• Establish strategically located triage and treatment centers for emergency care and adequately stock these areas with necessary emergency supplies.
• Identify safe helicopter landing areas in strategic locations (e.g., near school buildings; athletic fields; etc.). Keep the areas ready and free of parked vehicles, tree branches, and other obstructions.

• Locate and do an on-site visit of all utility shut-off areas (e.g., electricity, water, gas, etc.). Be certain these areas are accessible for emergency use and that the sites are recorded on maps of the buildings and grounds.

• Confirm that you have adequate and fully charged fire extinguishers ready for emergency use throughout buildings. Confirm that personnel know how to access and safely use the fire extinguishers.

• Develop a list of personnel with first-aid certification and experience. Support all personnel in learning additional emergency response skills as needed.

• Develop and practice a safe and fast emergency plan for getting children away from areas of danger, and for accounting for all children to assure that no one is left behind. Be certain to plan for children and personnel with special needs (e.g., mobility; vision; hearing impairments; etc.) in emergency planning.

• Develop systems for on-sight emergency communications to students and personnel (e.g., battery powered bullhorns, etc.), and off-sight communications to parents (e.g., e-mail; text messages; phone messages; mass media; etc.). Remember that inaccurate information can be worse than no information, and that people quickly stop paying attention to excessive information or noise. Emergency communications must be clear, accurate, concise, limited to high priority messages only, and transmitted without delay.

• Identify appropriate locations and develop procedures for parents to pick-up children out of the way of emergency personnel, vehicles, and operations, and safely away from a potentially dangerous disaster area or crime-scene.

• Work with local emergency personnel to conduct regular emergency drills to identify areas of needed improvement and to assure a rapid and effective emergency response.

• Establish or improve your Behavioral Intervention Team (BIT).

• Address potential problems before they become emergencies.

• Regularly review, update, and improve your school's emergency management plan. Additional resources and online training courses from the Department of Education's Readiness and Emergency Management for Schools (REMS) Technical Assistance (TA) Center can be found at: www.rems.ed.gov.

• Get everyone involved. Make safety and security discussions, preparations, and drills a regularly part of meetings with personnel, students, and the community.

- Brainstorm constructive ideas with colleagues and local safety personnel to assure that your school is well prepared for any emerging or foreseeable dangers.

State laws and local ordinances may address many of the above safety issues. The state department of education, local sheriff, fire chief, and other local officials may be helpful resources for information concerning compliance with state and local ordinances and safety protocols.

Essential Practice Tips

1) *Duty of care*: Tort law requires conduct consistent with what a reasonable person would do under the circumstances. When in doubt, err in favor of greater care. Tort law legal duties are only breached by falling below the ordinary standard of care. Extra care protects safety and prevents liability.

2) *Planning and prevention*: In the areas of safety and liability, an ounce of prevention can be worth many pounds of cure. Prevention is the key to protecting safety and avoiding liability. Time and resources spent now on wise planning and prevention efforts will ultimately save time and resources in the future. Look for potential dangers and correct them before they become emergencies. You may not only save time and resources in the future, you may also save lives.

3) *Professional, respectful, and fair treatment of all persons*: Accidents and errors are inevitable, but tort law suits are not. It is unnecessary and unwise to admit negligence prematurely. But it is humane and wise to express sincere concern regarding any accident or error, and to offer to provide needed help, e.g., "I am very sorry that happened; let me see what I can do to help" is professional, respectful, and fair without prematurely admitting negligence. Legal fault is a complex question that may be decided later in a court of law. A voluntary admission of negligence is not a necessary part of treating a mishap sufferer (and potential plaintiff) respectfully, humanely, and fairly after a regrettable occurrence. Kindness, genuine human concern, and an offer to help when possible are always appropriate under unfortunate circumstances. Persons treated professionally, respectfully, and fairly are generally less likely to become plaintiffs than persons further angered by unprofessional, disrespectful, and unfair treatment after an unfortunate incident.

Essential Points

- Tort law is civil law recognizing the plaintiff's legal right to just compensation for damages caused by the defendant.
- The main functions of tort law are to provide:
  - A lawful means of obtaining just compensation for damages; and
  - A deterrent against future injurious conduct.
- The law of torts and contracts are similar, but the tort "contract" is an implied social contract to act reasonably in interactions with others. Tort law is the means of enforcing the necessary social contract of mutually responsible conduct, with the compensatory role of tort law acting like the remedial function of contract law, and the deterrent role of tort law acting similar to the deterrent effect of criminal law.
- Without consequences for wrongful and negligent acts, there would be far more wrongful and negligent acts, and far less social and economic trust.
- Potential tort law causes of action include torts resulting from negligence; malpractice; defamation; assault and battery; false imprisonment; invasion of privacy; and intentional infliction of emotional distress.
- To establish a prima facie case of negligence the plaintiff must prove:
  - The defendant had a duty to the plaintiff;
  - The defendant breached that duty;
  - The breach was both the cause in fact and legal cause of damages; and
  - There are provable, compensable damages.
- Educators have a general duty to instruct, supervise, and protect children from known or reasonably foreseeable dangers. School officials have a general duty to reasonably supervise employees and students; to keep school property safe; and to protect against or warn of any known or reasonably foreseeable dangers to students, faculty, staff, or visitors.
- To prove a breach of duty the plaintiff must prove by a preponderance of the evidence that the defendant failed to use ordinary care and do what a reasonable person would have done under the circumstances. The conduct of the defendant is measured against the conduct expected from a reasonable person. If the defendant meets or exceeds the standard of the reasonable person, the plaintiff will fail in proving the case.

- Proof of two separate and distinct types of causation is required. The defendant's actions must have been:
  - The actual cause (cause in fact) of the plaintiff's injuries; and
  - The proximate (legal cause) of the plaintiff's injuries.
- These two different elements of causation require independent proof and both elements must be established to prove a claim of negligence.
- Negligence claims require proof of actual damages. These may include present and appropriately calculated future property loss, wage loss, medical expenses, compensation for pain and suffering, etc. Claims must be proven by a preponderance of the evidence, and must not be based on mere speculation about future possibilities.
- The defendant may attempt to rebut the plaintiff's case by attacking the plaintiff's arguments on duty, breach, causation, and damages. The defendant may also offer the following defenses or arguments for reductions in liability: Assumption of risk; plaintiff's negligence; or sovereign immunity (government defendants only).
- Under 42 U.S.C. § 1983 plaintiffs may also sue state officials for a "deprivation of any rights, privileges, or immunities" protected by the U.S. Constitution and federal laws. Plaintiffs may seek damages from both the school district and individual school officials. Individual school officials are only held personally liable for damages when they have personally disregarded well-established law.
- Successful educational malpractice suits are more likely in very specialized areas such as special education and counseling.
- Many states have codified the *Tarasoff* principle into state laws. These statutes require counselors and other professionals to warn of specific dangers to identified persons, whether these are warnings to parents if a minor child threatens to harm him or herself, or warnings of threats to targeted third parties.
- To establish a prima facie case of defamation, the plaintiff must show that the defendant's alleged defamatory declarations:
  - Contained untrue statements of fact concerning the plaintiff;
  - The statements were communicated to one or more persons other than the plaintiff;
  - The statements caused foreseeable prejudice towards the plaintiff; and
  - There are provable damages to the plaintiff.
- Intentional torts are distinguished from the tort of negligence in that the plaintiff must prove intent to cause harm, and not merely negligence in performing a duty. Because of the element of intent,

- many intentional torts are also crimes. Claims of intentional torts in educational institutions may include assault and battery; false imprisonment; invasion of privacy; and intentional infliction of emotional distress.
- Recognizing and reasonably addressing potential problems before they become emergencies is the key to safety and liability management.
- It is per se negligence to leave children unsupervised. A responsible adult must be in charge at all times, supervising children from the moment school officials take physical custody until physical custody is transferred back to the parent.
- School officials are responsible for reasonably supervising on-duty personnel and may be held liable for negligent supervision and the on-duty tortious acts of employees under the doctrine of respondeat superior.
- School officials have a legal duty to maintain and supervise public school buildings and grounds. To enhance safety and avoid liability buildings and grounds should be regularly inspected, identifying and correcting security risks and safety hazards.
- Safety equipment and procedures must comply with current standards of practice accepted in the field. School officials must comply with federal and state laws concerning hazardous materials; storage and use of chemicals; and any other significant environmental, biological, or other known hazards. Consistent with federal and state laws and local ordinances, school officials must have an emergency management plan ready to respond to the dangers most likely in their areas.
- School officials have a duty to keep confidential information protected. School computer systems must be adequately protected to secure information, and school Internet systems must be operated with a filtering system in compliance with the Children's Internet Protection Act (CIPA).
- Copyrighted works that are within fair use may be lawfully copied and used for educational and other purposes permitted by the U.S. copyright statute. Otherwise copyrighted works require lawful purchase or permission to avoid copyright violation liability.

Essential Terms

Causation: Requirement that the plaintiff prove that the defendant caused the damages and that the injury was foreseeable.

Constitutional tort: A lawsuit against government agencies and agents for monetary damages under 42 U.S.C. § 1983 for the deprivation of rights protected by the U.S. Constitution and federal laws.

Deep pocket: Substantial monetary resources for paying out damage awards.

Defamation: Legal cause of action allowing damages for unlawful harm to a plaintiff's public reputation.

Duty of care: The standard of care owed under the circumstances to potential plaintiffs by potential defendants concerning foreseeable harms.

Foreseeability: Whether a reasonable person could have foreseen that the defendant's conduct presented an unreasonable risk of harm to others under the circumstances.

Good Samaritan laws: Provide legal protections to persons who voluntarily provide reasonable assistance to others in need of help.

Negligence: Failure to use ordinary care.

Reasonable person standard: The legal standard by which negligence is determined, i.e., whether the conduct of the defendant fell below what a hypothetical reasonable person would have done under the circumstances.

Self-insurance: Allows institutions with substantial resources to save the added costs of commercial insurance premiums by setting aside funds sufficient to cover predictable and manageable risks directly.

Sovereign immunity: May provide some legal immunity to government agencies to protect limited government resources for the purposes for which they were allocated.

Essential Cases

Ex parte Young, 209 U.S. 123 (1908): Lawsuits in federal court may proceed regardless of immunity when state officials act unconstitutionally.

Hutchinson v. Proxmire, 443 U.S. 111 (1979): For defamation purposes the "public figure" designation does not extend to all public employees. Those not meeting the *Rosenblatt* standard are private figures.

New York Times v. Sullivan, 376 U.S. 254 (1964): To prove defamation as a public figure the plaintiff must prove "that the statement was made with actual malice . . . that is with knowledge that it was false or with reckless disregard of whether it was false or not." Private figures need only establish by a "preponderance of the evidence that the defendant failed to use ordinary care to determine the truth or falsity."

Rosenblatt v. Baer, 383 U.S. 75 (1966): For defamation purposes "public officials" are those government officials that reasonably appear to the public to have substantial control over governmental affairs.

Tarasoff v. Regents, 551 P.2d 334 (Cal. 1976): Duty to warn when there is clear evidence of an intent to harm so that targets of threats may take appropriate actions to protect themselves.

Wood v. Strickland, 420 U.S. 308 (1975): Ignorance of the law does not excuse government officials from the duty to comply with the law.

A Closer Look at the Law

An area of liability that is too often overlooked or intentionally ignored is copyright law and liability for infringement. Article I, Section 8, of the U.S. Constitution states: "The Congress shall have Power . . . To promote the Progress of Science and useful Arts, by securing for limited Times to Authors and Inventors the exclusive Right to their respective Writings and Discoveries." The purpose of this provision was to encourage the creation of useful intellectual properties by giving private owners public protection of those rights. Without these protections, there would be little financial incentive for the creation of intellectual property, and these works would not be available to contribute to the common good.

Congress has, however, extracted a fair price for the public protection of private property. As a condition of receiving copyright protection authors must allow the "Fair Use" of their works under the fair use test in § 107 of the U.S. Copyright statute:

§ 107. *Limitations on Exclusive Rights: Fair Use*

Notwithstanding [general copyright protections] the fair use of a copyrighted work, including such use by reproduction in copies . . . for purposes such as criticism, comment, news reporting, teaching (including multiple copies for classroom use), scholarship, or research, is not an infringement of copyright. In determining whether the use made of a work in any particular case is a fair use the factors to be considered shall include--

> (1) The purpose and character of the use, including whether such use is of a commercial nature or is for nonprofit educational purposes;
> (2) The nature of the copyrighted work;
> (3) The amount and substantiality of the portion used in relation to the copyrighted work as a whole; and
> (4) The effect of the use upon the potential market for or value of the copyrighted work.

In a case of alleged copyright infringement a reviewing court weighs the copyright entitlement against any claim of fair use based on the above four factors. Copyrighted works that are within fair use may be lawfully copied and used for educational and other purposes permitted by the statute. Otherwise copyrighted works require lawful purchase or permission which may be obtained directly from the copyright holder or through a copyright clearance agency. Educational institutions can mitigate their potential liability for copyright violations by showing a lawful published institutional policy governing fair use of copyrighted materials; evidence that faculty and students were instructed concerning fair use; and by promptly addressing and correcting any valid complaints of copyright infringement.

Copyright violations are serious. Under federal law they are criminal theft punishable by imprisonment and fines. People violate copyright laws because they either don't understand the law or they don't believe they will be caught violating the law. Under 18 U.S.C. § 2319 violations could result in up to 10 years of imprisonment, a $250,000 fine, or both. Given the potential legal consequences, and the ethical duty to respect the law and property rights, this leaves only one rational and ethical choice: Don't violate copyright laws. Avoid potential liability by lawfully purchasing copyrighted materials; only engaging in fair use; or getting valid permission for the use of copyrighted materials.

Law & Professional Ethics in Practice:

Among the more challenging ethical dilemmas are situations where persons with institutional power and status are violating the law or professional ethics with the approval of others in the school and community. For example, the locally famous football coach who in violation of NFHS safety rules endangers the health and safety of students exhibiting clear symptoms of concussion because he needs them playing to win the big game.

Or ignoring the locally revered coach's inappropriate conduct or even "dating" of students because a winning sport team is the real priority in the community. What is likely to happen to the untenured teacher who dares to take on the famously winning coach over this misconduct?

And in a fundamentalist southern Bible Belt community, who will dare to challenge the teachers, coaches, and administrators unlawfully and unethically using their unique positions of trust and access to other people's children, while they are away from their own parents, to aggressively recruit children to their church, coercing participation in their prayers, and socially punishing and excluding any who refuse, when this is the church attended by school board members and most of the people in the small rural community?

Will anyone be willing to expose school board members who are profiteering on school land deals and contracts, or engaging in nepotism and favoritism of their own family members? Or reveal that the expensive environmental remediation necessary to remove dangerous asbestos, lead, etc., wasn't properly done and was instead just superficially covered up?

It takes great personal courage to stand up to power and speak the truth. But unless people are willing to do this, corruption and the damage it causes continues. Laws and principles of professional ethics were created to address these problems. But laws and ethical codes are not self-administering. Someone must be willing to communicate the truth in a way that brings external authority to bear on people who are abusing their power.

The Whistleblower Protection Act, 108 STAT. 16, protects federal employees who disclose corruption, fraud, abuse, and waste. Many states have similar statutes. Vulnerable individuals may also disclose abuses to reputable reporters, off the record, so that the reporter may independently investigate and report on the abuses. As Justice Brandeis famously said: "Sunlight is the best disinfectant." Those engaged in corruption count on either hiding their corruption or on intimidation and fear to discourage people from reporting. Would you have the courage to stand up and expose corruption? What happens if you don't expose the corruption?

Stopping corruption requires courageously speaking the truth to people and agencies with the power to hold perpetrators accountable. Without the courage to act and the resulting "sunlight" exposing corruption our laws and ethical codes are just words on paper to be ignored by the most corrupt among us. All professionals need to know the law, so they understand what is lawful and what is not, and know the standards of professional ethics governing their profession, so they can comply and assure that others also comply for the common good. Are school officials in your community respecting applicable laws and standards of professional ethics? If not, what is the best means of addressing violations and assuring future compliance in order to protect vulnerable people and resources from abuse?

Questions for Further Exploration:

1) *Judging the tort law system*: Good laws establish a just and efficient system of problem resolution. In what ways does the U.S. system of tort law function well as a just and efficient system of problem resolution? In what ways does the system need to be reformed?

2) *Safety first*: What can you do to better protect safety in your school?

3) *Guarding against liability risks*: What can you do to better protect yourself and your school from liability risks?

4) *Open forum*: What other related issues or current events would you like to discuss?

Suggested Activities for Further Learning:

1) Conduct a safety and security inspection of your school, attempting to identify and address potential risks.

2) Conduct a safety and security inspection of the grounds and parking area of your school, attempting to identify and address potential risks.

3) Conduct a safety and security inspection of your play area. Check online for current standards for play area safety and do a field inspection of the play area to assure that the play area and equipment meets current safety standards. *See*: www.cpsc.gov/safety-education/safety-guides/playgrounds /public-playground-safety-checklist.

4) Conduct an environmental review of your school. For more information on improving environmental health in schools, *see*: www.epa.gov/schools.

5) Review your school's emergency management plan. Additional resources and online training courses from the Department of Education's Readiness and Emergency Management for Schools (REMS) Technical Assistance (TA) Center can be found at: www.rems.ed.gov.

Epilogue

Congratulations on completing your voyage through the law, a journey that is certain to both enrich your life and make you a more capable and confident professional. The law impacts every aspect of our lives, so acquiring a strong working knowledge of essential legal principles and their application in practice is a valuable and noteworthy achievement. The intellectual ground you have covered is vast, and what you learned is extensive. Nonetheless, it is certain that you will learn even more in the future, as your understanding of the law is further expanded and enriched through your personal experiences related to law and professional ethics.

Once a strong working knowledge of the law is acquired, over time this knowledge will continue to expand and you will see new facets, connections, and applications of the law grow in clarity with experience. It is recommended that you periodically review relevant sections of this book, as doing so will reveal new aspects of the law in the light of your new experiences. Also, to continue your learning *see*: JOHN DAYTON, EDUCATION LAW; JOHN DAYTON, HIGHER EDUCATION LAW; and JOHN DAYTON, LEGAL RESEARCH, ANALYSIS, AND WRITING.

I hope that you will find what you have learned life-enriching and highly beneficial both personally and professionally. Further, I hope that this is just the beginning of your journey to greater understanding and mastery of the law and professional ethics in practice.

With very best wishes for continued success.

John Dayton

Appendix

U.S. Constitution (1787)
(Abridged)

We the People of the United States, in Order to form a more perfect Union, establish Justice, insure domestic Tranquility, provide for the common defence, promote the general Welfare, and secure the Blessings of Liberty to ourselves and our Posterity, do ordain and establish this Constitution for the United States of America.

Article I

Section 1

All legislative Powers herein granted shall be vested in a Congress of the United States, which shall consist of a Senate and House of Representatives.

Section 2

The House of Representatives shall be composed of Members chosen every second Year by the People of the several States . . .

Section 3

The Senate of the United States shall be composed of two Senators from each State, chosen . . . for six Years . . .

Section 8

The Congress shall have Power To lay and collect Taxes, Duties, Imposts and Excises, to pay the Debts and provide for the common Defence and general Welfare of the United States; but all Duties, Imposts and Excises shall be uniform throughout the United States;

To borrow Money on the credit of the United States;

To regulate Commerce with foreign Nations, and among the several States, and with the Indian Tribes;

To establish an uniform Rule of Naturalization . . .

To promote the Progress of Science and useful Arts, by securing for limited Times to Authors and Inventors the exclusive Right to their respective Writings and Discoveries;

To constitute Tribunals inferior to the supreme Court . . .

To declare War . . .

To make all Laws which shall be necessary and proper for carrying into Execution the foregoing Powers, and all other Powers vested by this Constitution in the Government of the United States, or in any Department or Officer thereof . . .

Article II

Section 1

The executive Power shall be vested in a President of the United States of America. He shall hold his Office during the Term of four Years, and, together with the Vice President, chosen for the same Term, be elected . . .

Section 2

The President shall be Commander in Chief of the Army and Navy of the United States, and of the Militia of the several States, when called into the actual Service of the United States . . .

Section 3

He shall from time to time give to the Congress Information of the State of the Union, and recommend to their Consideration such Measures as he shall judge necessary and expedient; he may, on extraordinary Occasions, convene both Houses, or either of them, and in Case of Disagreement between them, with Respect to the Time of Adjournment, he may adjourn them to such Time as he shall think proper; he shall receive Ambassadors and other public Ministers; he shall take Care that the Laws be faithfully executed, and shall Commission all the Officers of the United States.

Section 4

The President, Vice President and all civil Officers of the United States, shall be removed from Office on Impeachment for, and Conviction of, Treason, Bribery, or other high Crimes and Misdemeanors.

Article III

Section 1

The judicial Power of the United States shall be vested in one supreme Court, and in such inferior Courts as the Congress may from time to time ordain and establish. The Judges, both of the supreme and inferior Courts, shall hold their Offices during good Behaviour, and shall, at stated Times, receive for their Services a Compensation, which shall not be diminished during their Continuance in Office.

Section 2

The judicial Power shall extend to all Cases, in Law and Equity, arising under this Constitution, the Laws of the United States, and Treaties made, or which shall be made, under their Authority . . .

Article IV

Section 1

Full Faith and Credit shall be given in each State to the public Acts, Records, and judicial Proceedings of every other State . . .

Section 2

The Citizens of each State shall be entitled to all Privileges and Immunities of Citizens in the several States . . .

Article V

The Congress, whenever two thirds of both Houses shall deem it necessary, shall propose Amendments to this Constitution, or, on the Application of the Legislatures of two thirds of the several States, shall call a Convention for proposing Amendments, which, in either Case, shall be valid to all Intents and Purposes, as Part of this Constitution, when ratified by the Legislatures of three fourths of the several States, or by Conventions in three fourths thereof, as the one or the other Mode of Ratification may be proposed by the Congress . . .

Article VI

. . . This Constitution, and the Laws of the United States which shall be made in Pursuance thereof; and all Treaties made, or which shall be made, under the Authority of the United States, shall be the supreme Law of the Land; and the Judges in every State shall be bound thereby, any Thing in the Constitution or Laws of any State to the Contrary notwithstanding.

The Senators and Representatives before mentioned, and the Members of the several State Legislatures, and all executive and judicial Officers, both of the United States and of the several States, shall be bound by Oath or Affirmation, to support this Constitution; but no religious Test shall ever be required as a Qualification to any Office or public Trust under the United States . . .

Amendment I (1791)

Congress shall make no law respecting an establishment of religion, or prohibiting the free exercise thereof; or abridging the freedom of speech, or of the press; or the right of the people peaceably to assemble, and to petition the Government for a redress of grievances.

Amendment II (1791)

A well regulated Militia, being necessary to the security of a free State, the right of the people to keep and bear Arms, shall not be infringed.

Amendment III (1791)

No Soldier shall, in time of peace be quartered in any house, without the consent of the Owner, nor in time of war, but in a manner to be prescribed by law.

Amendment IV (1791)

The right of the people to be secure in their persons, houses, papers, and effects, against unreasonable searches and seizures, shall not be violated, and no Warrants shall issue, but upon probable cause, supported by Oath or affirmation, and particularly describing the place to be searched, and the persons or things to be seized.

Amendment V (1791)

No person shall be held to answer for a capital, or otherwise infamous crime, unless on a presentment or indictment of a Grand Jury, except in cases arising in the land or naval forces, or in the Militia, when in actual service in time of War or public danger; nor shall any person be subject for the same offence to be twice put in jeopardy of life or limb; nor shall be compelled in any criminal case to be a witness against himself, nor be deprived of life, liberty, or property, without due process of law; nor shall private property be taken for public use, without just compensation.

Amendment VI (1791)

In all criminal prosecutions, the accused shall enjoy the right to a speedy and public trial, by an impartial jury of the State and district wherein the crime shall have been committed, which district shall have been previously ascertained by law, and to be informed of the nature and cause of the accusation; to be confronted with the witnesses against him; to have compulsory process for obtaining witnesses in his favor, and to have the Assistance of Counsel for his defence.

Amendment VII (1791)

In Suits at common law, where the value in controversy shall exceed twenty dollars, the right of trial by jury shall be preserved, and no fact tried by a jury, shall be otherwise re-examined in any Court of the United States, than according to the rules of the common law.

Amendment VIII (1791)

Excessive bail shall not be required, nor excessive fines imposed, nor cruel and unusual punishments inflicted.

Amendment IX (1791)

The enumeration in the Constitution, of certain rights, shall not be construed to deny or disparage others retained by the people.

Amendment X (1791)

The powers not delegated to the United States by the Constitution, nor prohibited by it to the States, are reserved to the States respectively, or to the people

Amendment XI (1795)

The Judicial power of the United States shall not be construed to extend to any suit in law or equity, commenced or prosecuted against one of the United States by Citizens of another State, or by Citizens or Subjects of any Foreign State . . .

Amendment XIII (1865)

Section 1

Neither slavery nor involuntary servitude, except as a punishment for crime whereof the party shall have been duly convicted, shall exist within the United States, or any place subject to their jurisdiction.

Section 2

Congress shall have power to enforce this article by appropriate legislation.

Amendment XIV (1868)

Section 1

All persons born or naturalized in the United States, and subject to the jurisdiction thereof, are citizens of the United States and of the State wherein they reside. No State shall make or enforce any law which shall abridge the privileges or immunities of citizens of the United States; nor shall any State deprive any person of life, liberty, or property, without due process of law; nor deny to any person within its jurisdiction the equal protection of the laws . . .

Section 5

The Congress shall have the power to enforce, by appropriate legislation, the provisions of this article.

Amendment XV (1870)

Section 1

The right of citizens of the United States to vote shall not be denied or abridged by the United States or by any State on account of race, color, or previous condition of servitude.

Section 2

The Congress shall have power to enforce this article by appropriate legislation . . .

Amendment XIX (1920)

The right of citizens of the United States to vote shall not be denied or abridged by the United States or by any State on account of sex.

Congress shall have power to enforce this article by appropriate legislation . . .

Amendment XXVI (1971)

Section 1

The right of citizens of the United States, who are eighteen years of age or older, to vote shall not be denied or abridged by the United States of by any State on account of age.

Section 2

The Congress shall have power to enforce this article by appropriate legislation . . .

Table of Cases

Index

306

Made in United States
Orlando, FL
18 January 2023